AF655058

PEOPLE'S REVOLT IN ORISSA

PEOPLE'S REVOLT IN ORISSA
(A STUDY OF TALCHER)

D.P. MISHRA

ATLANTIC PUBLISHERS AND DISTRIBUTORS

Published by
ATLANTIC PUBLISHERS AND DISTRIBUTORS
B-2, Vishal Enclave, New Delhi-110 027
Phones 5413460, 5429987

Sales Office
4346/4C, Ansari Road, Darya Ganj,
New Delhi-110 002
Phones 3273880, 3285873, 3280451
Fax 91-11-3285873
e-mail gupta.atlantc@axcess.net.in

Copyright © The Author, 1998

ISBN 81-7156-739-8

No part of this book may be reproduced in any form without permission from the publisher except for the quotation of brief passages in criticism

Typeset at
APD Computer Graphics, Delhi

Printed in India at
Mehra Offset Press, Delhi

DEDICATED TO
THE LOVING MEMORY OF
MY LATE FATHER

Foreword

The Indian National Movement is a curious conglomeration of several streams in which the State People's Movement finds a prominent place. Gradually, more and more researchers are plying their attention at a micro-level to the problems, conditions and developments in individual princely states. Dr. Mishra's work is an able attempt to study the people's movement in the state of Talcher in Orissa. From sporadic, unorganised local uprisings towards the end of 19th century to the more broad-based in the thirties and forties of the present century speaks enough about the maturity of the movement that culminated ultimately in the merger of the State of Talcher with the province of Orissa.

The chief merit of this work is comprehensiveness and proper documentation. Starting from the National scenario of the state people's movement, the author smoothly travels to the state situation and ultimately makes a vast canvass of the state of Talcher, in which he puts the people, their grievances, uprisings and ultimate popular triumph in proper perspective. The British were not only interested to protest the ruler of Talcher from popular anger as a general part of their 'break water policy', but also the lucrative coal-mines prompted them to be more protective towards the ruler. The determined people of Talcher, in a unique Gandhian style of protest, went on hizrat (mass exodus) to the neighbouring British territory and remained there for nearly eight months to protest against royal oppression. Even the British authorities did not hesitate to fire from air on the ground to the *Prajamandal* Workers during the 1942 upsurge. This firing was one of the five such incidents of aerial firing done during the 1942 days, which is the highest watermark of the movement. The supreme sacrifice of the people of Talcher forms a glorious chapter in the annals of Indian National Liberation Struggle.

The publication of this work is well timed as India is celebrating the fiftieth year of her Independence and reminds the country men of the individual service done by the state people's movement in general and Talcher in particular in waging a relentless struggle against the feudal lord and its overload, the paramount power, which culminated in the merger of the princely state with the province of Orissa after National Independence in January, 1948 and brought the people to the National mainstream.

I am sure the work of Dr. Mishra will be found useful by all the serious scholars and students of Indian National Movement.

Dr. Ashok Kumar Patnaik,
Head
P.G. Department of History
Utkal University, Vani Vihar,
Bhubaneswar-4 (Orissa)

Preface

The spirit of nationalism and the urge for freedom found the shape of resistance and people's revolt in different States of India as well as in Orissa in the beginning of the twentieth century. There were risings and revolts often in massive form against the authority to put forth the common cause and to unfurl subsequently the banner of independence. Along with the *Prajamandal* Movements in different States of Orissa in the beginning of twentieth century, that of Talcher was in the form of sporadic outbursts of resistance, and later crystallised to aim for complete independence from feudal rule and its protector, the British. It caused uneasiness in the rank and file of the Raja's administration. But till now no sincere work has been done on this particular aspect of the history of Talcher. The attempts made by Ghanashyam Mishra (*Talcher Itihas*, 1934), Anant Mishra (*Talcher Andolan,* 1948), Sashibhusan Roy (*Adhunik Talcher*, 1940) and Pabitra Mohan Pradhan (*Muktipathe Sainik* in 3 Volumes) have not placed in proper perspective the *Prajamandal* movement in Talcher. Even distinguished publication of *Freedom Movement in Orissa* (Five Volumes) edited by H.K. Mahtab and *Who's Who of Freedom Workers*, edited by N.K. Sahu and S.C. De do not deal exhaustively with this aspect of the history of Talcher and a vast plethora of documents remained unused at various places in and outside Orissa.

Therefore, an attempt has been made to bring to light the history of People's Revolt in Talcher with the help of mostly the original and unpublished records available in National Archives of India, New Delhi; Nehru Memorial Museum and Library, New Delhi; West Bengal Archives, Calcutta; Orissa State Archives, Bhubaneswar; Orissa State Museum, Bhubaneswar; Record Room of Board of Revenue, Cuttack; Dhenkanal Collectorate Record Room; Sub-divisional Record Room, Talcher; Talcher Palace Record Room; Sambalpur University Archives, Burla; Talcher Jail Record Room; Office of the Sub-Collector, Talcher; Office of the Tahsildar, Talcher; Office of the G.M., M.C.L., Talcher; etc. Besides, personal interviews were made with some prominent figures in their last of the life who participated in the people's movement. In addition to this printed books, journals and periodicals have been consulted in the National Library, Calcutta; Orissa State Museum Library, Bhubaneswar; H.K. Mahtab State Library, Bhubaneswar; Parija Library, Utkal University, Vani Vihar; Utkal Sahitya Samaj Library, Cuttack; Prajatantra Prachar Samiti Library, Cuttack; Orissa State Secretariat Library, Bhubaneswar; Orissa State Assembly Library, Bhubaneswar; G.M. College Library, Sambalpur; Sambalpur University Library, Burla; and the private libraries of the ex-Rajas of Orissa. Above all, many original documents, books and records have also been collected from the people of different feudatory States of Orissa. The thesis has been enriched mostly by first-hand information for which extensive field study was undertaken during last ten years.

The present work begins with a general introduction on the People's Revolt in various princely States in India and its place in national movement. It also includes a brief analysis of the movement in Orissan States to show the link with national scene and the birth and growth of it in the original setting.

The historical background of the State of Talcher forms the contents of the second chapter. It highlights the dynastic history and the importance of the State. It also deals with the relationship of the British with this feudatory State.

The third chapter contains the administrative structure of the State, the tale of Raja's excess and officials exploitations, people's hostility against the Raja's rule, their grievances, oppression, and economic exploitation. It also takes note of various taxes, cesses and extractions collected by the ruler at various times. It contains the conditions of local administration, welfare measures like education, health, sanitation, transportation etc. along with the budgetary allocations on different heads by the *Durbar* which speaks of the deep rooted socio-economic malice that brought the movement later.

In the fourth chapter, effort has been made to trace the movement from its earliest genesis towards the closing years of the nineteenth century till the beginning of the Second World War. It briefly deals with various short-lived unorganised, sporadic uprisings till the early thirties, as well as the organised ones in the later part of thirties leading to mass exodus in thousands from Talcher.

In the fifth chapter, the most militant phase of the movement is shown under the war conditions and under the influence of Quit India Movement. The nexus between Congress leaders and their programme with the *Prajamandal* leaders and their programmatic action during that period are discussed in details. It deals exhaustively on the Quit India Movement in the State of Talcher.

The sixth chapter portrays the last phase of the struggle during the years of march towards victory or what is called by the historians as 'Towards Freedom Years'. It deals with the complexities that disturbed the *Prajamandal* leaders on the question of merger with the Orissa Province. The anti-merger movement took shape during those years. The King's efforts to inject confusion by forming a so-called non-elected people's body is taken note of in it. Ultimately, the popular will and collective sagacity dominated and the process of merger was completed without much difficulties.

The entire movement, its gains, shortcomings, lessons and importance are drawn out in the conclusion.

I am extremely thankful to Dr. A.K. Patnaik, M.A., M.Phil., Ph.D. (J.N.U.), Reader, P.G. Department of History, Utkal University for the supervision and care he has undertaken to guide my work. But for his encouraging words this work would not have been taken its present shape. I am thankful to him for his invaluable help.

I owe my sincere thanks to Dr. C.R. Mishra, Professor, Post-Graduate Department of History, Sambalpur University, Orissa and Dr. J.N. Patnaik, Reader in English, J.K.B.K. College, Cuttack for their help in various ways. I also record my indebtedness to the authorities of the State Archives, Orissa; National Archives, New Delhi; N.M.M.L., New Delhi; National Library, Calcutta; H.K. Mahtab State Library, Orissa; Sub-divisional Record Room, Talcher and others who had helped me in collection of materials from their sources. I also take this opportunity to express my thanks to the authorities of the University Grants Commission for awarding me the teacher fellowship to complete the work and the Utkal University to allow me to join and work as a Teacher Fellow in its History Department. My thanks are also due to Mr. Shatrughna Maharana who is the man behind my presentation of this work in the present form.

Above all, I cannot forget the support given to me by my parents, sisters, relatives and friends who constantly encouraged me during my whole period of work. My elder brother Sri B.P. Mishra, Deputy

Director of Geology, Government of Orissa and the younger brother Sri B.P. Mishra, Assistant Manager, IPITRON Times, Bhubaneswar helped and inspired me throughout the whole period of work. My wife, Mrs. Geeta Satpathy, Lecturer in Economics, Talcher College is above my formal thanks without whom I could not have completed my research unhindered and undisturbed and submitted it on schedule.

At last, I dedicate my work to those valiant fighters of Talcher, both living and dead, who had struggled and sacrificed in many ways to bring an end to the feudal autocracy in Talcher and usher a new era where men would live as men, without exploitation and inhuman oppression, that found its voice in the writings of Gurudev Rabindranath Tagore :

"Where the mind is without fear and the head is held high..."

DEBI PRASAD MISHRA

CONTENTS

ABBREVIATIONS

AICC	—	All India Congress Committee
AISPC	—	All India States' Peoples' Conference
BNR	—	Bengal Nagpur Railway
CP	—	Central Province
Col	—	Colonel
CMD	—	Chairman-*cum*-Managing Director
ESA	—	Eastern States Agency
Govt.	—	Government
Hon'ble	—	Honourable
INC	—	Indian National Congress
IPC	—	Indian Penal Code
Judl	—	Judicial
Lt	—	Lieutenant
MLA	—	Member of Legislative Assembly
M&SMRy	—	Madras and South Maratha Railway
NAI	—	National Archieves of India
NMML	—	Nehru Memorial Museum and Library, New Delhi
OSA	—	Orissa States Archieves
OSCT	—	Office of the Sub-Collector, Talcher
OSPC	—	Orissa States' Peoples' Conference
OGMMCL	—	Office of the General Manager, Mahanadi Coalfields Limited
Pol	—	Political
SECL	—	South Eastern Coalfields Limited
SUA	—	Sambalpur University Archives
SRT	—	Sub-Divisional Record Room, Talcher
TJRR	—	Talcher Jail Record Room
TPRR	—	Talcher Palace Record Room
WWCC	—	Who's Who Compilation Committee.

The States' Peoples' Movement in India : A Brief History

The East India Company, after establishing itself fully on the soil of India, decided to follow an aggressive policy towards Indian States. Under one pretext or the other it began to annex Indian States one after another and the process once started continued till 1857, when Indian administration was transferred from the Company to the Crown and the Queen of England at the time of take over made a firm commitment that henceforth there would be no annexation of Indian States and would allow them to enjoy autonomy and independence. Numbering over five hundred and exhibiting the most amazing dissimilarity among themselves, the States confirmed to no recognised law, international or municipal, in the matter of their status. As their critics often declared, they were neither fish nor fowl but a red-herring across the path of India's constitutional progress. They survived the tide of British conquest in the absence of a well-defined policy on the part of the pre-mutiny empire builders towards the country princes.[1]

The formidable uprising of 1857, which shook the British Raj to its very foundation, provided an unforgettable lesson to the foreign rulers. Most of the princes of the principal States rushed to the aid of their Suzerain by brushing aside affronts to which they were often exposed under the unnatural dispensation, and by conquering their fears about the future of their dynasties. The British generously rewarded their gesture by propounding the post-1857 dictum, 'Once a State always a State' and honoured their commitment as an enviable pledge. The British also guaranteed the princes against any threat to their autocratic power, internal or external.[2] There came into existence two

1. Hans Raj, *History of Modern India*, Delhi, 1987, p. 296.
2. V.B. Kulkarni, *Princely India and Lapse of British Paramountcy*, Bombay, 1985, p. 122.

'Indias, one princely and another British, though the country was essentially the area of the single government. While the eleven British Indian provinces and the centrally administered units moved in the direction of a modernised, bureaucratic government, the administration of most of the principalities was founded on their rulers' caprices. In consequence, there was a marked disparity in the progress of the two areas, thus posing a serious problem to the promotion of a uniform political system for the entire country. It was inconceivable that British India could hope to evolve its destiny in isolation by ignoring the existence of more than one-third of the country's territory.[3]

Till the advent of the British Raj, India was accustomed almost entirely to being governed by kings. The concept of Kingship as a divinely-ordained office had become an inseparable part of the political conviction of its people. The continued existence of the States till national independence, albeit as the dependencies of an alien authority, played its own part in sustaining this famous belief. Indians, no matter to which religion they belong, are political *idolaters*. The hoary practice of genuflecting before personified authority comes naturally to most of them. Political maturity, acquired through proper education and a higher level of living, alone could have cured the people of this debilitating malady.[4]

The variegated pattern of the British conquest of India, and the different stratagems through which the various parts of the country were brought under colonial rule, had resulted in two-fifths of the sub-continent being ruled by the Indian princes. These people, numbering over ninety-three millions, were treated as India's step children. The areas ruled by the princes included big Indian States like Baroda, Mysore, Hyderabad, Travancore, Gwalior, Kashmir and Bhopal, that were equal in size to many European countries, and numerous small States which counted their population in the thousands. While the British took no statutory cognisance of the unfortunate people's existence, in most States their rulers looked upon themselves as no better than a dependable and perennial source for financing their ostentatious living and costly eccentricities. The common feature was that all of them, big or small, recognised the paramountcy of the British Government.

In return, the British guaranteed the princes against any threat to their autocratic power, internal or external. Most of the princely States

3. V.B Kulkarni, *op. cit.*

4. *Ibid.*

were run as unmitigated autocracies, with absolute power concentrated in the hands of the rulers, or their favourites who acted in fascist manner.[5] The burden of the land tax was usually heavier than in British India, and there was usually much less of the rule of law and civil liberties. The rulers had unrestrained power over the State revenues for personal use and this often led to ostentatious living and waste. Some of the more enlightened rulers and their ministers did make attempts, from time to time, to introduce reforms in the administration and in the system of taxation and even granted powers to the people to participate in the government. But the vast majority of the States were bastions of economic, social, political and educational backwardness, for reasons not totally of their own making.

Condition of People in the Indian States

The condition of the people under princely States were very bad and deplorable. The rulers did not care for the welfare of the subjects. By and large they did not undertake any social welfare activity. In the large States like Baroda, Mysore and Hyderabad etc. the higher grade civil services were as a rule tolerably efficient. In the majority of the States, however, they are underpaid and proportionately unreliable. They neither bothered to open any educational or health institution. Schools and hospitals used to be very few and these too were available to the rich. The officers in the States used to be very corrupt and neither honour nor property of the people was safe. They all lived at the mercy of their rulers. Appointments were not made with due regard to merit and suitability; a higher trained electrical engineer, for example, may find himself posted to the palace Amusements Department; a chief engineer, responsible for great public works, may suddenly be transferred to a confidential appointment on a princess's staff.[6]

The administration in the States was personal and arbitrary in nature. There was, of course, separate departments like health, education, finance, industry, etc., but these were a pale, lifeless copy of the bureaucratic set-up in the provinces. A first-hand account of conditions obtaining in the States in the twenties has come down from Jawaharlal Nehru's experience of trial and detention in Jaito in Nabha State. In a contravention of the order of the State Government, he entered into the State territory whereupon he was arrested and tried for conspiracy. He was handcuffed and kept in the lock-up. About his two weeks' experience

5. Bipan Chandra, *India's Struggle for Independence*, Delhi, 1988, pp. 356-60.
6. Barton Sir, W. *The Princes of India*, Vol. 26, Delhi, 1987, pp. 65-79.

in the lock-up and Jail and his trial in a so-called court, Jawaharlal says:

> "Two or three days later, we were taken to court for our case, and the most extraordinary and Gilbertian proceedings went on there from day-to-day. The magistrate or judge seemed to be wholly uneducated. He knew no English, of course, but I doubt if he knew how to write the court language, Urdu. We watched him for over a week, and during all this time he never wrote a line..."[7]

The written petitions, which Nehru submitted to the court, were not looked into and Jawaharlal was not allowed to engage a lawyer from outside.[8] But he took all this in good humour and referring to the incident he says:

> "Most of the Indian States are well known for their backwardness and their semi-feudal condition, their personal autocracies, devoid even of competence of benevolence. Many a strange thing occurs there which never received publicity. And yet their very inefficiency lessens the evil in some ways and lightens the burden on their unhappy people. For, this is reflected in a weak executive, and it results in making even tyranny and injustice inefficient. That does not make tyranny more bearable, but it does not make it less far reaching and widespread. The assumption of direct British control over an Indian State has curious result in changing this equilibrium. The semi-feudal conditions are retained, autocracy is kept, the old laws and procedure are still supposed to function . . ."[9]

The ruler of a State on his part largely used to be a pleasure loving one. He cared more for his personal comforts rather than those of his subjects. He lived a life of comfort in his beautiful palace. The story of *Maharaja* of Indore who risked and lost his throne for a dancing girl is well known.[10] The Maharaja subsequently abdicated and his father, too, had abdicated during Lord Curzon's time. There was no distinction between personal and State income and as such the money collected by way of taxes was spent in the way the ruler liked. Lots of money was

---

7. Jawaharlal Nehru, *An Autobiography*, Delhi, 1986, p. 111.
8. *Ibid*., p. 112.
9. *Ibid*., pp. 113-14.
10. Barton Sir, W., *op. cit*.

spent on ceremonial occasions. The ruler very much depended on his hand picked officials, who always misguided him to have personal gains. The so called democracy, as known in British India was not alluring to them. Even where a form of representative government existed, as in Mysore, the peasantry was not enthusiastic in its support. It was too much in the hands of the urban intelligentsia.[11] In most cases, the development of representative institutions did not approximate to the growth of self-governing institutions in the provinces. For example, Hyderabad, the biggest and most important Indian State, never had a popularly elected Legislative Assembly till it was taken over by the Central Ministry in 1948. Till 1935 an overwhelmingly large number of States had no municipal committees. Thus the ruler and the ruled did not come nearer and closer to each other.

Sometimes even in the larger States a more conventional facade often concealed a medley of irregular practices, official delinquencies and oddities. There was a well-known *Maharaja* who used to keep his budget in his head. Here is the budget for 1929-30 of the Bikaner State, which was specially praised and favoured by the imperialism:

	In Rs.
Civil List	1,255,000
Wedding of the Prince	82,500
Building and Roads	618,384
Extension of Royal Palaces	426,614
Royal Family	222,864
Education	222,979
Medical Service	188,138
Public Utility	30,761
Sanitation	5,729[12]

Education, medical, public utilities and sanitations, thus, received less than one-fourth of what went to the Princes, his family and palace.

The privy purse of the rulers was usually not fixed and even where it was fixed this was not adhered to. On the one hand there was extravagance and luxury of the princes, on the other, there existed extreme poverty of the people. The king of England receives roughly

11. Barton Sir, W., *op. cit.*

12. R.P. Dutt, *India Today*, Calcutta, 1979, p. 445.

one in 1600 of the national revenue, the king of Belgium one in 1000, the king of Italy one in 500, the king of Denmark one in 300, the Emperor of Japan one in 400. No king receives one in 17 like the *Maharaja* of Travancore (which is the most progressive State in India), one in 13 as the Nizam of Hyderabad or the *Maharaja* of Baroda, one in 5 as the Maharaja of Kashmir and Bikaner. The world would be scandalised to know that a few princes appropriate one in 3 and one in 2 of the revenue of the States.[13]

In another State the Moslem ruler showed a sporting instinct in reprieving and taking into his *Zenana* a pretty young girl sentenced to death for poisoning her husband. In Hyderabad the old Quranic law of *gisas*, or retaliation, still prevailed, and no Moslem was sentenced to death for murder unless the relatives of the victim demanded the extreme penalty. According to the sacred law the sentence was to be carried out by the relatives, as was then done in Kabul. It was the custom in one Moslem State for nobles and high officials to take orphan girls into their households by a show of adoption. As the girls grew up they became house slaves.[14] The Indian States represented the most backward agrarian economy of a feudal type where slavery was rampant.

The British after the Muting of 1857 realised that they needed the cooperation of the Indian princes to maintain their hold over India. After the formation of INC and the growth of the national movement in the country, it became very clear to them that with base in the provinces and solid support of Indian princes against their subjects they could prolong their stay in India. British Residents in the States made the rulers clear that their interests were identical with the British interests and that the two did not clash. Accordingly, when the people of the States demanded some rights, the Britishers sided with the rulers rather than with the subjects, in spite of the fact that they claimed themselves champions of democracy and of human rights.

The British Government was responsible for the situation in which the Indian States found themselves in the twentieth century. The Butler Committee, which was commissioned to examine the constitutional position of the States in relation to the British Indian Government, flatly refused to the States' peoples' point of view on the unconvincing ground that its terms of reference precluded it from entertaining their plea. It reported, "The promise of the King-Emperor to maintain

13. J.S. Sharma, *India's Struggle for Freedom*, Vol. II, Delhi, 1965, p. 603.
14. Barton Sir, W., *op. cit.*

unimpaired the privileges, rights and dignities of the princes carries with it a duty to protect the prince against attempts to eliminate him and to substitute another form of government."[15] The problems of the States people could not be discussed in the three Indian Round Table Conferences in London with the argument that any discussion of the internal affairs of the States fell within the jurisdiction of the rulers concerned.[16]

As the national movement grew in strength, the princes were increasingly called upon to play the role of 'bulwarks of reaction'. They made every effort to ensure that the wave of national movement which was spreading in Indian provinces did not touch the princely States. They took all precautionary measures in this regard. Those leaders of the public opinion who tried to raise their voice in the States were discouraged and imprisoned. The entry of such newspapers which propagated national feeling was banned. All propaganda about having elected bodies etc. was completely crushed. Any sympathy with nationalism, such as that expressed by the *Maharaja* of Baroda, was looked upon with extreme disfavour.[17] Many a potential reformer among the rulers were gradually drained of initiative by the constant surveillance and interference exercised by the British residents.

For a long time, British Indian politicians turned a blind eye on the happenings in the States on the sentimental ground that they were governed by their own nationals. They did not want to antagonise the feudal chiefs as they still depended in some cases on their limited moral, financial support and physical protection from the hands of the British law enforcing authorities. The greatest folly of these leaders was their belief in a wrong hypothesis that in an unknown future these feudal lords would join them in a final struggle to oust the British. That was why the princes had no fear from the side of Indian nationalists and the assured support of the British Government made them pay a deaf ear to the genuine grievances of the subjects for quite a long time. But to every action there would be an equal and opposite reaction and this natural law was bound to bring slow but steady reaction from the princely subjects in due course of time.

15. Orissa Records, Sundergarh Papers, Acc. No. 1296, Viceroy's Speech, 22 November 1927 (OSA).

16. V.B. Kulkarni, *op. cit.*, pp. 149-50.

17. Bipan Chandra, *op. cit.*

People's Reaction

After the formation of the INC in 1885 political awakening started to consolidate in an organised form in British provinces. But the case of the most deprived and doubly exploited people of the States, exploited by the British indirectly and feudal lords directly, did not matter much for the Congress leadership. The repeated pleas of this suffering humanity for an impartial investigation into the quality of the princely rule fell on deaf ears. Petitions submitted to British residents, to the political agents, and, in the last resort, to the Viceroy were either pigeonholed or elicited only evasive replies, leaving grievances, however grave, unredressed and invited further vindictiveness. But the process of petition and prayer, traditional means of popular mobilisation and protest once started continued in these States. The rulers of the princely States with the help of their British residents made every effort to see that the wind of freedom movement which was blowing in Indian provinces should not touch the States.

The Patiala ruler, for example (Patiala was the biggest State in Punjab) would not allow any party to agitate for better administrative set-up or for grant of civil liberties to the people. The *Maharaja*, in the course of his talk with a group of people's delegates in August 1939 said:

> "My ancestors have won the State by the sword and I mean to keep it by the sword. I do not recognise any organisation to represent my people or to speak on their behalf. I am the sole and only representative . . . I can not tolerate any flag other than my own to be flown within my boundaries. You stop your *Prajamandal* activities otherwise I shall resort to such repression that your generation to come will not forget it . . ."[18]

But the growing tide of national movement in the provinces had certainly emboldened the princely subjects. Determined will to have a share in State administrations as was given in a limited way in British India through the various Acts like Indian Council Act of 1909 or that of Indian Council Act of 1919 only further enthused them with a new hope. The people in the States wanted to have a taste of freedom and rights. In many States, therefore, some local organisations were founded to achieve the purpose. These bodies were called *Prajamandals* or States peoples' conference. Each such *Mandal* concerned itself with

---

18. P.N. Chopra, *India's Struggle for Freedom* : *Role of Associated Movements.* Vol. I. Delhi, 1985, pp. 170-71.

the problems of its own State. Several factors significantly contributed to the growth of freedom struggle in the States and helped in the awakening of the people. These included:

(a) The freedom struggle in Indian provinces was becoming people's movement and it was impossible for the people of the States to have remained uninfluenced.

(b) Indian princely rulers did not change with the changing times. They continued to maintain their feudal character. They did not like to extend rights to their subjects.

(c) Indian soldiers who had gone abroad during the World War I had witnessed the fruit of freedom and democracy in various countries and were not prepared to tolerate feudal character of Indian States.

(d) Swadeshi and Non-Cooperation Movements had spread throughout India and caught the imagination of the people. The States were influenced by these national developments.

(e) The INC extended its moral support to *Prajamandals* to launch freedom struggle in the States and struggle for getting more and more rights from their rulers.[19]

The British Government and the State rulers were not at all sympathetic towards such movements. Their primary object was to crush these with a heavy hand, with the use of suppression. Both the Britishers and the princes combined in this regard. In order to provide a forum to Indian princes where they could come closer and nearer to each other to discuss their common problems, the British Government created a chamber of Indian princes in 1919. It was a British attempt to organise Indian princes against the States' people and their growing consciousness. It, however, provided an opportunity to State leaders to come closer and realise the nature of a common struggle against the united front of Indian feudal reaction supported by British imperialism. It is an irony of history that the British act to unite the princes became a catalyst to unite the State subjects and wage the struggle against the feudal reaction.

Some of the States in which the *Prajamandals* were organised were Mysore, Hyderabad, Baroda, the Kathiawad States, the Deccan States, Jamnager, Indore, and Nawanagar etc. This process came to a head on 17 December 1927 in Bombay, with the convening of All

19. *Indian Annual Register*, Vol. II, pp. 248-50.

India States' Peoples' Conference (AISPC) which was attended by 700 political workers from more than 70 States. The men chiefly responsible for this initiative were Balwantrai Mehta, Maniklal Kothari and G.R. Abhayankar. Dewan Bahadur Ram Chandra Rao presided over the conference and Gobindlal Shivalal Motilal was the Chairman of the reception committee. The Presidential address and the welcome speech of the Chairman of the reception committee explained the aims and objects of the conference and thereafter gave typical illustrations of the atrocities and corruption that prevailed in the States.[20] The Conference demanded that :

(a) Administrative reforms should be immediately introduced and administration should be purged of corruption.

(b) The people should be given representation in law making process.

(c) The grievances of the people should be redressed quickly and for the purpose necessary machinery should be created immediately.

(d) Distinction should be made between public and private funds. The ruler should use only private funds and the rest of the money should be earmarked for the welfare of the people.

(e) The ruler should not arbitrarily raise land revenue share of the State.

(f) Local self-government institution with elected representatives of the people should be developed.

(g) The executive and judiciary should be completely separated from each other.[21]

The first session of the AISPC had two major achievements to its credit. First, it set the tone of agitation for popular rule in the States. Second, it drew the Indian National Congress close to the States' people in so far as helping the latter and the need of coordinating the agitation for popular rule in the two parts of India were concerned. Not unexpectdly, did the AISPC, according to one of its resolutions, depute two of its leaders, Maniklal Kothari and B.S. Pathik to meet the Congress leaders and secure the active support of it for the States' peoples' demand. As a result in its Madras Session (December 1927)-

20. P.N. Chopra, *op. cit.*.

21. Hans Raj, *op. cit.*, pp. 298-99.

the Congress adopted a resolution endorsing the demand of the States' people for responsible government. Of course, the policy of the Indian National Congress towards the Indian States had been first enunciated in 1920 at Nagpur when a resolution calling upon the princes to grant full responsible government in their States had been passed.[22] But to hope any active Congress support in their struggle was yet a distant dream.

Partly as a result of the overt support, the Congress lent to the States peoples' conference, and partly the important nature of successive events occurring at the time, the activities of this newly born organisation received great momentum. Besides Mahatma Gandhi, Jawaharlal Nehru, Sardar Vallabbhai Patel, Jamnalal Bajaj, B. Pattabhi Sitaramayya, Satyamurti and many others in the Congress, the States' peoples' conference had the good luck of enjoying full sympathy and active support from non-Congress leaders like Srinivas Sastri, C.Y. Chintamani, Amritlal Thakkar of the Servants of India. Society, Sir Tej Bahadur Sapru, etc. On behalf of the States, alongwith the conference, the Congress demanded that the people of the States should be given civil liberties and due representation in administration. It pleaded for the growth and setting up of democratic institution,[23] When Congress decided that ultimate aim of freedom struggle in India would be complete independence, it made it clear that this freedom was both for the people of British India as well as for the native States. The Congress for the started taking more interest in the AISPC and coordinated its activities with it.

At the 49th Session held at Lucknow in 1936, the Indian National Congress while re-affirming the resolution regarding Indian States passed in the Calcutta Session of 1928 and expressing its approval of the policy laid down in the Statement issued by the AICC in Madras in October 1935, made it clear that the people of the States should have the same right of self-determination as those of the rest of India, and that the Congress stood for uniform political, civil and democratic liberties for every part of India. The Congress, however, clarified that the struggle for liberty within the States had to be carried on by the people of the States themselves.[24]

---

22. S.N. Bose, *Indian National Movement : An Outline*, Calcutta, 1982, p. 162.
23. *Indian Annual Register, op. cit.*
24. *Ibid.*, Vol. I, p. 25.

Within a short period the AISPC grew into a well-knit country-wide organisation. As a result of its policy and advice, *Prajamandals* were set up in individual States, which were affiliated to the AISPC. In Rajputana, Punjab and Central India most of the States established their own *Prajamandals*, which received the guidance from and were largely responsible to the parent organisation, the AISPC. *Prajamandals* grew up in many States that had not experienced the existence of any such body in their territories. Major struggles broke out in Bikaner, Jodhpur, Patiala, Nabha, Jaipur, Kashmir, Rajkot Hyderabad, Mysore, Travancore and the Orissan States.[25] Those who led the respective movements like Jai Narayan Vyas in Jodhpur, Balwantrai Mehta in Bhavnagar, Seva Singh in Patiala, Giani Zail Singh in Faridkot, Sant Ram in Nabha, Sheikh Abdullah in Jammu and Kashmir, Dassapa in Mysore, Swami Ram Tirath in Hyderabad had to undergo untold sufferings and all the repression that autocratic and irresponsible administration can let loose on the people.[26] The struggle and consequent repression was common phenomenon in all the princely States and Orissa was no exception to it.

People's Revolt in Orissan States

During the paramountcy of the Mughals, Todarmall, the Revenue Minister of Akbar, adopted the traditional policy of keeping the hilly region separated from the coastal plain and fertile region for efficient revenue administration. Accordingly, Orissa was divided into two revenue zones, *i.e.*, (i) *Mughalabandi* comprising the plain and fertile lands in coastal belt of Balasore, Cuttack and Puri districts under the direct administration of the Mughal emperor; and (ii) *Garajats*, comprising the hill tracts in the west under several Oriya chieftains who used to pay an annual tribute to the Emperor and in return were being recognised as feudatories exercising internal sovereignty.[27]

The Orissa States had a total area of about 29,000 square miles and a population of nearly fifty lakhs.[28] They were divided into 26 small States beginning with Tigiria with 47 square miles and a population of 24,000 ending with Mayurbhanj, the biggest States among

25. Sumit Sarkar, *Modern India*, 1885-1947, Madras, 1985, p. 367.
26. Bipan Chandra, *op. cit.*
27. A. Strilling, *An Account of Orrisa Proper or Cuttack*, London, 1846, pp. 32-33.
28. H.J. Todd, Resident, Eastern States Agency, Calcutta to Cornard Corfield, Political Advisor to Crown Representative, D.O. No. C3013/469, 6 May, 1946, File No. 17/7 (S)-46 (NAI).

the Orissan States with an area of 4,243 square miles and a population of about nine lakhs.[29] The Orissa States which were not homogeneous in their historical and political evolution, can be broadly classified into two groups. One group of the States was subjected to the operation of the British laws and regulations while the other group was originally known as Tributary Mahals and later Tributary States and finally were included under general description of Orissa.[30] Out of these twenty-six feudatory States in accordance with the nature of their relations with the British Government, seventeen States were included in Group I category known as Tributary Mahals. They were Athmallik, Athgarh, Baramba, Baud, Dasapalla, Dhenkanal, Hindol, Keonjhar, Khandapara, Mayurbhanj, Narsinghpur, Nayagarh, Nilgiri, Pallahara, Ranpur, Talcher and Tigiria. Two of these States Baud and Athmallik, however, for a time formed a part of the South-West frontier Agency and on 11 April, 1837 were handed over to Orissan Division. Group II category consisted of Bamra, Bonai, Gangpur, Kalahandi, Patna, Rairakhol and Sonepur. This group was known as Sambalpur *Garjat* States. In this group Bonai and Gangpur were attached to Chotanagpur Division where the rests five were attached to Chattishgarh Division until the partition of Bengal in 1905. The third group comprised of Sareikala and Kharasuan known as Singhbhum States which came under British sovereignty in 1826 and 1860 respectively.[31] But these two States were merged with Bihar in 1948.

The historical background of the feudatory States dates back to the ancient past. After the downfall of the *Gajapatis*, Orissa lost her independence in 1568 and it came to the hands of the Afghans, the Mughals, the Marathas, and the British for a long time of 379 years.[32] Before the British conquest of Orissa in 1803, twenty-four feudatory States, except Sareikala and Kharsuan were distributed among two *Subas* of the dominion of Bhonsla Raja of Nagpur, *viz.* the *Subha* of Cuttack and Chattishgarh.[33] In the same year, the Maratha ceded the

29. L.N. Ghose, *Modern History of Indian Chiefs, Rajas, Zamindars & Co.*, Part-I, Calcutta, 1879, pp. 200-203. And See Appendix A.

30. S.C. Padhi, *British Relation with the Chiefs and Rajas of Orissa* 1803-58, Calcutta, 1986, p. xv.

31. N.N. Singdeo, *Bengal District Gazetteers, Singhbhum, Sareikala and Kharasuan,* Calcutta, 1910, pp. 229-30.

32. M.N. Das, *Side Lights on History and Culture of Orissa,* Cuttack, 1977, p. 257.

33. Orissa Records, Sambalpur Papers, Acc. No. 1757, R.P. Chand to K.C. Neogy, 21 July, 1941. (OSA).

whole of Orissa along with the *Garjats* to the British.[34] The present State of Orissa is much larger than the nineteenth century Orissa, because the latter did not include all the Oriya speaking territories under its jurisdiction. Orissa in the nineteenth century mainly consisted of Cuttack, Puri and Balasore in the sea-coast and the native States in the hill region of the west. The present southern part consisting of Ganjam and Koraput Districts, was a part of Madras Presidency till 1936. The Sambalpur tract which constituted the western part of the State had remained with Central Province till 1905.

By the first decade of the nineteenth century, the feudatory States as a class had become sharply distinguished from the ordinary *Zamindaris* paying fixed or variable revenue to the British Government. The company continued its traditional policy of separating the *Mughalbandi* areas from the *Garjat* territories with an intention to keep the latter as buffer States around its frontiers. It would give them sufficient protection from any direct assault on its territories by any external enemy and thus would be beneficial to the company for many reasons. They would work as a shield for the company territory round the year with little investment. The States brought under this system through treaties, were assured of military assistance against external aggression and internal disturbances at their own expenses. They would not keep any relations with foreign powers without the knowledge of the East India Company. The chiefs would remain loyal to the British Government.[31] The States, thus, were brought under political control of the company and the British authority became paramount in effect.

The relationship between the British Government and the feudatory States with particular reference to the rights and obligation arose from treaties, engagements and *sanads*. The company in fact became *de facto* supreme power and could effectively impose its will on the States regardless of the terms of the treaties. It manifested the peculiar nature of complicated relation of the company with various shades of power.

Treaty engagements were exchanged with as many as eleven States immediately after British occupation. These States included Athgarh, Baramba, Dhenkanal, Hindol, Khandapara, Narsinghpur, Nayagarh, Nilgiri, Ranpur, Talcher, and Tigiria.[36] Next year in 1804, the rests

34. L.E.B. Cobden-Ramsay, *Feudatory States of Orissa*, Calcutta, 1982, p. 25.

35. S.A. Fraser, *Among Indian Rajas and Ryots,* London, 1912, p. 154.

36. C.U. Aitchison, *A Collection of Treaties, Engagements and Sanads, Relating to India and Neighbouring States*, Vol. I, Calcutta, 1862, pp. 180-91.

entered into with treaty engagement.[37] Engagements were entered into by all the chiefs binding themselves to maintain submission and loyalty to the East India Company's Government, and to pay an annual *peshkas* or tribute. All the chiefs, except Keonjhar, were also bound under these engagements to depute a contingent of force to assist the government against any opposition, the force to receive only rations from the government.[38] Treaty engagements were made with the tributary States and there was counter engagements by the British Governor. The third clause of the counter engagement stated, "The Government of East India Company was over gracious to those Rajas who were obedient to them and constant in the impartial administration of justice to all its subjects alike . . ."[39] The clauses of the treaty clearly explained the total moral, economic and military surrender on the part of the chiefs before the East India Company. No undertaking was given as to the nature of the internal administration by the chiefs in these treaties. This was the first phase of the British rule in India when the foreign masters were only interested in the commercial exploitation of the colony without any interference in administrative machinery then prevalent in the country. So the chiefs remained virtual master in their domain with little interference from above so long as their due to the company was paid in time and their obedience to it was beyond doubt.

The great event of 1857 marks a change in the attitude of the British towards the feudatory chiefs. The mutiny recognised the importance of the Indian States as "break waters in the storm". They were thought to be no source of danger to the British rather they needed to be preserved as a bulwork against the nascent nationalism.[40] Any rebellion against the British was nullified by the chiefs thereafter.

The feudatory chiefs were allowed to rule over their States more or less independently. Though there was separate authority, the chiefs were very powerful over their subjects in the field of law, and administration etc. The entire administration was unsystematic. There was restrictions in judicial powers of the chiefs. The British Government issued them '*Sanads*' which emphasised and directed the chiefs to administer fairly and impartially to all concerned respecting the

37. L.E.B. Cobden-Ramsay, *op. cit.*, pp. 24-25.

38. *Ibid.*

39. C.U. Aitchison, *op. cit.*

40. R.P. Dutta, *op. cit.*, p. 442.

legitimate rights of the people.[41] Indeed, the chiefs never honoured it and there was no rule of law. The judges were acting on the whims of the chiefs. There was absence of tenancy law. No effective rights in land were granted. Instead of general administration there was personal administration. Chiefs became very oppressive to their finger tips. They looked down upon their subjects as mere vassals. The States were ruled by inexperienced and uneducated officials. The police were generally untrained. Even in cases where a handful of trained police officers were employed, they were not properly supervised, and in cases, they were subjected to the constant interference of the rulers while discharging their duties. In judiciary there was also interference. The judges were far behind the knowledge of sufficient law to administer fair justice to the people. No qualification was required for any posts to be appointed in the States. It was the desire of the Chief to appoint anybody in any post. Most of the Chiefs in Orissa appointed their own relatives in different high posts in the State administration which virtually made it a family affairs in the State. Most of the times, these unqualified and under-qualified persons tried to keep the rulers in good humour and make out as much profit as possible for themselves. The political department appeared to have indirectly supported the internal administration of the States.[42]

Most of the States were quite backward in communication, education, health and sanitation. The last part of nineteenth century saw these States economically emasculated, educationally backward, physically emaciated and tortured. Though the British Indian territories were no better than these feudatory States, yet the growth of national consciousness and consequently emerging national movement brought some changes in various spheres of the life of the people of later category which was denied to the former. There was maladministration called '*Andharimulak*' or dark region where the victims were the poor, innocent and middle class people.[43] There was no reform or improvement made in the condition of the people of the States by the chiefs. So spontaneous, disorganised rebellion started among the people to redress their grievances which were easily suppressed.

Rebellion in the Last Part of 19th Century

The history of the rising of the people in Orissa States could be

41. C.U. Aitchison, *op. cit.*, Vol. II, p. 419.
42. *The Samaj*, 23 June 1937 and S. Patnaik, *Sambad Patraru Odisa Katha*, Vol. I, Oriya, Cuttack, 1972, p. 721.
43. *Deshakatha*, 9 December 1930.

traced back to the year 1866, the year of the great famine.[44] The Orissa famine may be considered as the epitome of her long tale of sufferings and forms of watershed in history. Perhaps one of the most severe and widespread famines that plagued India,[45] this famine was popularly known as *Naa-ank* as it fell in the ninth regnal year of the then *Gajapati* of Puri. Orissa fell victim to this calamity which took away one-third of her total population. The sufferings of the people knew no bounds for a long time. There were instances of taking human flesh by mentally derailed person.[46] The inhuman negligence and callous attitude of the administration was greatly responsible for it.

In the meanwhile the Government of India set up a Commission in December 1866 to enquire the catastrophe in Orissa. The Commission consisted of George Campbell, a judge of the High Court as President and Col. W.E. Morton and H.L. Dampter as members.[47] Sir Stafford Northcote, the Secretary of State for India, later admitted that the Orissan famine of 1866 was a monument of failure of the British policy.[48] Speaking on the Orissa famine in the British House of Commons on 2 August 1867, Sir Stafford remarked, "This catastrophe must always remain a monument of our failure, a humiliation to the people of this country, to the Government of this country, and to those of our Indian officials of whom we had been perhaps a little too proud".[49] The economic condition of the States had deteriorated. After this great famine there was a rebellion in Keonjhar State. This was a rebellion against the British administration by the *Adivasi* tribes called *Juanga*, *Bhuyans* and *Kols* during April 1868.[50] But the rising was suppressed with the help of British troops. Their leader Ratna Naik along with four of his followers were sentenced to death.[51]

The *adivasis* with the leadership of Dharanidhar Naik*, once again revolted in Keonjhar in 1891 against *Bethi* and other forced labour.[52] The king fled to Cuttack to seek help from the Commissioner of

44. S.C. Patra, *Formation of the Province of Orissa,* Calcutta, 1979, p. 74.
45. B.M. Bhatia, *Famine in India*, Bombay, 1963, p. 66.
46. *Utkal Dipika*, 11 August 1866.
47. *Report of the Famine Commission*, Vol. I, Calcutta, 1867, pp. 410-415.
48. C.E. Buckland, *Bengal under the Lt. Governor,* Calcutta, 1901, Vol. I, p. 386.
49. *Ibid.*
50. *Utkal Dipika*, 9 May, 1868.
51. R.N. Rath, *History of Freedom Movement in Orissa States*, Cuttack, 1964, p. 13.
* See Appendix B.
52. K.M. Mishra, *Keonjhar*, Oriya, Cuttack, 1939, pp. 45-46.

Cuttack. With the help of the police force the revolt was suppressed and Dharani Naik was imprisoned.[53]

In 1882 there was sporadic display of disaffection among the *Khonds* of Kalahandi against the *Kultas* backed by their *Raja* who economically exploited them. They demanded economic facilities, human rights and abolition of corruption. The *Sardars* of *Khonds* were captured and hanged. The *Khond* rising was short lived and suppressed.[54] There were also resistance movement in Nayagarh, Khandapara, Ranpur and Dasapalla during the last of nineteenth century which was violent but could not continue long.[55] In Dhenkanal, at the end of nineteenth century the manager of the State contemplated enhancement of rent under a new settlement. One thousand people came and protested, in consequence of which the idea was abandoned.[56]

These are all primary resistance movements by the subjects of the feudatory States. The growth of national consciousness in the country had its own limited impact on the feudatory State. Though late, the political consciousness was apparent by the beginning of the twentieth century. The national movement kindled, the flame of freedom in the hearts of the oppressed States' people. The States were unfortunately placed under their despotic rulers who because of British help were ruling their people in a high-handed way. The unholy alliance of the British rule with the most reactionary feudal elements brought the poor subjects to a condition of anything other than human beings. Imperialism combined the most archaic forms of feudal exploitation with the most advanced finance capitalist exploitation. Their tyranny and social oppressions caused indignation among the people who in the wake of movements in the British Indian territories could think in terms of defying their respective rulers. There were agitations, protests, demonstrations and rebellions in the States. The Indian National Congress encouraged and helped the formation of several democratic organisations in the States without any formal branch of it in those States to carry out the people's movement against the tyranny of the chiefs. Such organisations were formed in a number of States of Orissa during the thirties of the twentieth century as '*Prajamandals*'.[57]

---

53. K.M. Mishra, *op. cit.*
54. *Utkal Dipika*, 24 June, 1882 and S.A. Fraser, *op. cit.*, pp. 135-40.
55. M.N. Das, *op. cit.*
56. *R.N. Rath, op. cit.*
57. M.N. Das, *op. cit.*, p. 282.

PEOPLE'S MOVEMENT IN THE EARLY PART OF THE TWENTIETH CENTURY

Talcher Rising

In Talcher, when the miscellaneous cess was first levied in 1911, there was an agitation which was suppressed. The people were suffering a lot due to imposition of taxes like *magana*, *rasad* etc. Instead of looking after the benefits and socio-economic development of the people the chief, most of the time, was on tour outside the State. During 1921-22 he was on tour for 190 days and during 1922-23 he spent 175 days outside the State.[58] Such tours usually mixed with pleasure trips not only resulted in the drain of huge amount from State exchequer but also the long absence of the rulers affected the administration adversely. Their casual attitude to the people's grievances over the years caused the stir among the people. During 1922 and 1932 there were other movements in the State against forced labour and excessive rent and *abwabs* which were severely dealt with.[59]

Dhenkanal Movement

In 1922 the administration in Dhenkanal State wanted to enhance the rent. Forest rules were also revised and enforced just then. Agitation and resentment again started among the people against such acts.[60] Some redress was effected, but four of the leaders were charged with conspiracy and were sentenced to imprisonment for three years.[61] This gave a temporary set back to the movement.

Nilgiri Rising

In 1928, the people of Nilgiri vehemently opposed to pay heavy *abwabs* and do *bethi* in the celebration of the marriage ceremony of the princes of the *Raja*. By the advice of Harekrishna Mahtab* thousands of tenants migrated to a nearby British Indian territory, Balasore. With the intervention of Rev. C.F. Andrews a settlement could be arrived at. The *Raja* agreed to pay proper remuneration to the people for their labour. The tenants withdrew the agitation and returned home.[62]

---

58. General Review of the Administration of Feudatory States of Orissa and Chotnagpur for the year 1922-23, p. 39.
59. *Talcher Prajamandal Itihas Committee* (*Compl*), pp. 2-7.
60. *Orissa States Enquiry Committee Report*, p. 7.
61. M.N. Das, *op. cit.*, p. 285.
    * See Appendix B.
62. H.K. Mahtab, *History of Freedom Movement in Orissa*, Vol. III, Cuttack, 1957, pp. 94-100.

Mayurbhanj Ferment

During the First World War large number of coolies were required for the Labour Corps in Iraq and other war centres. Hence, the Government of India decided to recruit such coolies from different parts of India. Such recruitment was also going on in the Orissan States.[63] In Mayurbhanj, collection of tribal labourers** was made through the officers when the *Raja* was a minor and the State was under the court of wards. A rumour spread that the British Government was recruiting the tribals for making them *meriah* in a distant place.[64] This news aggravated the tribals and they rose into revolt against the administration in 1917.[65] The rising was so serious that the Commissioner of Orissa and the political Agent of the Feudatory States of Orissa reached Mayurbhanj to see the situation. Police from Balasore and military forces from Calcutta were recruited to suppress the risings. At last, this was checked with the use of armed forces and peace prevailed.[66]

Risings in Bamra State

There were five risings in Bamra State from 1908 to 1928 against unreasonable enhancement of rent and assessment of new *abwabs*. The first three risings were headed by Hari Pradhan, Bhagabat Pradhan and Jagannath Garnaik respectively. The last rising in 1928 became serious. Thousands of people met the Political Agent at Sambalpur for some redress but it was futile. The risings were suppressed forcibly and leaders were thrown behind the prison. Some *gountias* were deprived of their *gountia* rights.[67]

Daspalla Rising

There was a serious *Khond* rising in Daspalla in 1914. The old *Raja* had no male issue. One of his cousins Baisnab Deo was to succeed to the *Gadi*. But a minor (Raja's daughter's son) of Parikud was adopted which would be greater benefit to Dewan Bhabagrahi Biswal as the State would automatically come under the Court of Wards. After the death of the Raja there was discontentment among

63. H.K. Mahtab, *'Odisa Itihas'*, Oriya, Cuttack, 1958, p. 376.

** Santhals, Kols, Khonds, Gonds, Sudhs, Gandas etc.

64. *Utkal Dipika*, 26 May, 1917.

65. *Ibid*.

66. H.K. Mahtab, *History of Freedom Movement in Orissa*, Vol. III, p. 99.

67. *Orissa States Enquiry Committee Report*, p. 6.

the eccentric aboriginal *Khonds* who were not happy for an outsider to succeed to the *Gadi*. They supported the cause of Baisnab Deo and there was *Khond* rising. In order to check the so called rising, on the report of the Dewan, who had then already became the Superintendent of the State under the wards management, police force rushed into Dasapalla from various parts of Orissa and the rising was quelled mercilessly.[68] It was alleged that the Dewan went so far as to burn down village after village of these aboriginal *Khonds* to strike terror amongst them and thus to cow them down. A case to this effect was filed by the State authority against the *Khond* leaders for conspiring to wage war and collecting men, arms, ammunition and money for this purpose against the Dasapalla *Raj* and conspiring to murder Bhabagrahi Biswal, the Dewan of Daspalla State. Leaders like Narayan Kaur, Mahanatha Jani, Sadai Mallik etc, got death sentence and some others were sentenced to transportation for life.[69]

We, thus, see the feudatory States in Orissa were not always a bed of roses. In spite of the iron rule exercised by the chiefs there were occasions when we find sporadic attempts by the people for securing some sort of rights and privileges from the State authorities. These risings were neither organised nor political in their character but were a mere show of the deep resentment of the people against the oppressive acts or arbitrary impositions of the rulers. The risings were confined to individual States. Prior to 1938 there was no political organisation which could organise and prepare the people of the States to present a common front against the arbitrary, administration of the ruling chiefs in the *Garjats*. Consequently, agitation of the people of different feudatory States were confined within the limits of their own States only and could not spread to the neighbouring States.[70] So it was very easy for the State authorities to put down the risings with iron hand backed by the paramount power. Yet these movements had their own contribution to the growth of a future united struggle of all these people against feudalism as a whole. These movements, though failed to achieve its objectives, did check for a time being the atrocities of the rulers, drew the concern of the respective *Durbars* for a temporary adjustment of State demands *vis-a-vis* the subjects actual condition of

68. H.K. Mahtab, *op. cit.*, Vol. II, pp. 94-100.

69. Orissa Records, Dasapalla Papers, Acc No. *Misc/1OD 56/1.* In the Court of the Commissioner of Orissa, Meli Case No. 1, 5 July, 1915. (OSA)

70. M.N. Das, *op. cit.*, p. 280.

payment and drew the attention of the paramount power to the happenings inside the States, which ultimately be a headache to them if it were to make a common cause with the British Indian subjects. So the movements that failed invariably, had otherwise contributed to the growth of political consciousness among the native subjects to go for a wider, mass based and properly organised movement, not independently but as a part of a national or provincial organisation in a coordinated manner. This lesson went a long way in future days to make a determined struggle in the thirties and forties of the twentieth century.

Growth of National Consciousness in Feudatory States of Orissa : 1938-39

With the emergence of Gandhiji in the political scene, the country witnessed a massive change, both qualitatively and quantitatively in the field of political activities. His call for non-co-operation in 1920 and his visit to Orissa awakened the Oriya people in British Orissa and to some extent the feudatory States like Sonepur, Keonjhar and Kharsuan.[71] During Civil Disobedience Movement, (1930-34) the national conciousness was not confined only to British districts. It also spread to the princely States where the neglected subjects were in search of civil liberty and political rights. In such circumstances the Orissa States Peoples' Conference was first organised at Cuttack on 19 June 1931 with the active co-operation of the All India States Peoples' Conference (AISPC).[72] Notable leaders of the States like Radhanath Rath*, Balukeswar Acharya, Madhusudan Patnaik and Govind Chandra Mishra convened the first meeting on 20 June 1931 at Cuttack, presided over by Bhubanananda Das, member of the Central Legislative Council. A working committee was formed with Brajasundar Das as the President and Balukeswar Acharya as the Secretary-*cum*-Treasurer. The co-operation of the rulers in the States was sought in this conference. They were requested to look after the benefit of their subjects, development of education, health, agriculture, trade, industry etc. and to abolish forced labour like *bethi*, *begar* etc.[73] The Working Committee was requested to see that *Bethi* and *Begar* finally were abolished from the States. However, the rulers refused to recognise the committee.[74]

---

71. *Utkal Dipika*, 31 March, 1923.
72. *Ibid.*, 27 June, 1931.
* See Appendix B.
73. *Utkal Dipika*, *op. cit.*
74. R.N. Rath, *op. cit.*, p. 17.

These appeals were made with the unfounded faith on the Indian rulers to be co-operative to give some concessions to their subjects. Like the early moderates of the Indian National Congress, they believed more on these rulers' sense of love and affection for their subjects in a paternalistic way than in their own organised strength to wrest concessions from them. Such mistaken notion was bound to fail and could not stir the feudatory subjects in any anti-feudal struggle. So after the conference the activities of the organisation became dormant for some time.[75]

When the British Orissa was observing *Satyagrah* at the call of Gandhiji, its echo was heard in the neighbouring feudatory States. Its people felt that the time had come, when they should organise themselves to fight for their just and legitimate right and to replace the feudal form of government that had imposed on them. On 1 April 1936 Orissa became a separate province where the feudatory States were not included. Thereafter democratic organisations were framed in the States and the dormant States Peoples' Conference of Orissa became active. Signs of marked enthusiasm were noticeable among the leading workers of the States who wanted to do something real and substantial in the direction of freedom struggle.[76]

The second session of the Orissa States' Peoples' Conference was held on 23 and 24 June 1937 at Cuttack.[77] It was presided over by Dr. Pattavi Sittaramayya, President of All India States' Peoples' Conference. Sarangdhar Das* of Dhenkanal who was a man of great influence and organising capacity took up the charge of the organisation as its Secretary. Balukeswar Acharya of Hindol was the Chairman of the Reception Committee.[78] About one hundred people from eight States out of twenty-six attended the session. The less number of attendance was due to the preventive measures taken by the States' administration.

In his Presidential Address Dr. Sitaramayya observed:

"You may not represent the whole of Orissa, but as representatives of the States your concern for your culture and civilization, for your own university and province is not less acute than that of

75. Lal Mohan Patnaik, *Resurrected Orrissa*, Cuttack, 1939, p. 329.

76. S.N. Patnaik, *Odisare Swadhinata Andolana,* Oriya, Cuttack, 1972, p. 144.

77. *Tha Samaj*, 24 June 1937 and Orissa Records, Kalahandi Papers, Acc No. 4 Kal, Resident, Chhatisgarh States Agency to Maharaja of Kalahandi, D.O. No. 669-CR/37, 22 July 1937. (OSA).

* See Appendix B.

78. Orissa Records, *op. cit.*, D.O. No. 422-CR/37, 21 May 1937.

your fellow citizens inhabiting the British Indian area. After all, how do differ from them? Are you not the blood of their blood and the bone of their bone? We are all so many sub-nationalities that make up the Indian National with a common faith and form of worship, a common historical tradition and a common biological descent. Administrative boundaries are an accident and no such artificial boundaries can operate as barriers against the enjoyment of equal rights by people inhabiting the two sides of the boundary. Is it not then highly surprising why the British Government in India consider that the people of the States should not have the privileges of franchise which the people of the provinces enjoy?... Perhaps the British consider the princes, whose subjects these are, as unworthy for some reason or other of having enfrachised people under them. If so, it must be the fault of the princes or of the British, not of the people of the States who are as intelligent, patriot and self-sacrificing as the people of the provinces...Federation is attractive and inevitable in a country like India where a third of the area and a fourth of the population are under the princes. These have to be brought into the picture of a common government on the principles of Federation".

He further said, "It is no exaggeration to say that life and limb, property and honour are not all secure in those areas. The trouble comes in there not only from the unruly elements in society, but also from the unruly greed and lust of the rulers themselves... The administrative position is still more complicated by the evil practice of appointing the relatives of the Ruler to the highest position of the State. The main difficulty in all the *Garjats* is arbitrary personal rule. Most of them are petty-minded, selfish and inefficient. The business, agriculture etc. of the people are dependent on the whims of the *Rajas*, which are uncertain as the rains....The States have thus become the ulster of India, where progressive ideas can gain no popularity, where politicians and political movements choked off betimes. The States are to the people of British India worse than the foreign countries of the world".[79]

The Conference passed many resolutions. The first resolution deplored the absence of codified laws and acts in the States and demanded that the laws should be published by the rulers. It also urged

79. *The Observer*, 23 June, 1937.

upon the rulers to confer upon their subjects the right of occupancy on their holding and their fundamental rights of citizenship.[80] A strong plea was made to abolish evil practices like *Bethi*, *Rasad* and *Magan*.[81]

In other resolutions of the Conference it was demanded for better administration of the States, proper audit of the annual budget, independence of judiciary from executive, recruitment according to law and rules etc. A Working Committee of the Conference was formed with the following persons.

President	—	Dr. B. Pattabhi Sitaramayya
Secretary	—	Sarangadhar Das (Dhenkanal)
Treasurer	—	Dr. Biswambhar Rath (Nayagarh)
Members	—	Lal Mohan Pati (Mayurbhanj)
		Balukeswar Acharya (Hindol)
		Radhanath Rath (Athgarh)
		Madhusudan Mohanty (Athgarh)
		Harmohan Patnaik (Dhenkanal)
		Govind Chandra Mishra (Daspalla)
		Madhusudan Patnaik (Tigiria)
		Gangadhar Mishra (Ranpur)[82]

The conference decided in that meeting to set up an 'Enquiry Committee' for collecting detailed information about the circumstances prevailing in Orissa States and condition of the people in different States under the rule of their chiefs.[83]

States Enquiry Committee

The Orissa States Enquiry Committee with Sri H.K. Mahtab as President and Sri Balwantrai Mehta and Lal Mohan Patnaik conducted their enquiry from June to August 1938.[84] They visited various places in Cuttack, Sambalpur and Puri districts to hear the people who came forward in hundreds to lay their grievances before them. The Committee examined nearly two thousand of witnesses in several sittings and

80. *Indian Annual Register*, Vol. I, 1937, p. 357.
81. Orissa Record, Kalahandi Papers, *op. cit.*, D.O. No. 669-CR/37, 22 July 1937.
82. *The Samaj*, 25 June, 1937, and *The Observer*, 26 June 1937.
83. Orissa Records, Kalahandi Papers, *op. cit.*, and *The Observer*, 26 June 1937.
84. *The Samaj*, 28 June 1938.

published their report in two volumes in 1939.[85] This report deals exhaustively with the maladministration then prevailing in the States. The most important suggestions of the report were : the power of supervision over the administration of the States so long entrusted to the Resident should be handed over to the Provincial Government; full civil liberty should be granted to the people, and permanent and impartial judiciary should be installed in the States.[86] This report was the first publication detailing the defects and lacunas in the administration of the feudatory States. Even the States Peoples' Conference could well realised that the State *Garjats* of Orissa urgently needed two things. First the *Rajas* have to be prevented from interfering with daily administrative routine, and a separate provision should be made out of State funds for the upkeep of the *Raj* families in proper style. Secondly, regular administrative machinery has to be set up, and run by properly qualified persons whose tenure is secure and whose emoluments keep them above temptation.[87]

Congress Attitude towards States' Problem

The Indian National Congress also had shown sympathetic attitude towards the people of feudatory States of the country. It stood for the political, civil and democratic liberties of the people living in every part of India. But it wanted that the movement in the States must be carried on by the people themselves.[88] Pandit Jawaharlal Nehru in his Presidential Address told at the 49th Session of the Indian National Congress held at Lucknow from 12 to 14 April, 1936:

> "The Indian States have long survived their day, propped up by an alien power, and have become the strangest anomalies in a changing world. The future has no place for autocracy or feudalism, a free India cannot tolerate the subjection of many of her children and their deprivation of human rights, nor can it ever agree to a dissection of its body and cutting up of its limbs. If we stand for any human, political, social or economic rights for ourselves, we stand for those identical rights for the people of the States. I have referred to the terrible suppression of civil liberties by the British Government in India. But in the States

85. N.K. Sahu and S.C. De, *Who's Who of Freedom Workers in Orissa, Dhenkanal District*, Cuttack, 1970, p. vi (OSA)
86. *The Samaj*, 2 August 1939.
87. *The Observer*, 23 June 1937, and *Indian Annual Register*, Vol. I, pp. 356-58.
88. *Indian Annual Register*, Vol. I, p. 25.

matters are even worse, and though we know that the real power behind those States is that of British imperialism, this tragic suppression of our brothers by their own countrymen is of painful significance. Indian rulers and their ministers have spoken and acted increasingly in the approved fascist manner, and their record during the past few years especially has been one of aggressive opposition to our national demands. States which are considered advanced ban the Congress organisation and offer insult to our national flag and decree new laws to suppress the press. What shall we say of the more backward and primitive States".[89]

The years 1938-39 witnessed new awakening in the Indian States and the intensification of the demand for the responsible governments and other reforms. These new developments brought about a significant change in Congress policy as well. Whereas, in the Haripura session in 1938, the Congress had reiterated its policy that movements in the States should not be launched in the name of the Congress but should rely on its own independent strength and fight through local organisations, a few months later, on seeing the new spirit among the people and their capacity to struggle, Gandhiji and the Congress changed their attitude on this issue.[90]

In an interview to *The Times of India* on 24 January 1939 Gandhiji said:

"The policy of non-intervention by the Congress was, in my opinion, a perfect piece of Statesmanship when the people of the States were not awakened. That policy would be cowardice when there is allround awakening among the people of the States and determination to go through a long course of suffering for vindication of their just rights . . . The moment we became ready the legal, constitutional and artificial boundary was destroyed."[91]

In March 1939 the Tripuri Session of the Congress partially revised its position and in a resolution to this effect stated :

"The great awakening that is taking place among the people of the States may lead to a relaxation, or to a complete removal of the

89. Proceedings of the INC, 49th Session, 12 April 1936, (NMML).

90. Tara Chand, *History of the Freedom Movement in India*, Vol. IV, New Delhi, 1983, p. 259.

91. Bipan Chandra, *op. cit.*, p. 359.

restraint which the Congress imposed upon itself, thus resulting in an ever increasing identification of the Congress with the States' people".[92] Also in February 1939, the All India States' Peoples' Conference elected Jawaharlal Nehru as its President and Pattabhi Sitaramayya as Vice-President for the Ludhiana Session, thus setting the seal on the fusion of the movements in princely India and British India.[93] Mahatma Gandhi became the political adviser of the movements carried out in the native States of the country, particularly the States of Orissa including Talcher which have been described in the following chapters.

BIRTH OF PRAJAMANDALS AND ITS MOVEMENTS IN ORISSAN STATES, 1938-39

Nilgiri

During May 1938 the ruler of Nilgiri created a serious situation in his State by imposing heavy fines on the people for the offence of inter-dining on a social occasion which badly hurt the people as a direct encroachment on their civic rights. In such circumstances a new democratic association named 'Nilagiri *Prajamandal*' was first established in this State in June 1938. Kailash Chandra Mohanty and Banamali Das became its President and Secretary respectively. A party of volunteers for propaganda in Nilgiri was organised by Sarangadhar Das. They demanded social, economic and political justice and condemned inhuman practices prevailing in the States.[94] Balawantrai Mehta, Secretary of AISPC came to Cuttack on 19 June 1938 and joined the States Peoples' Enquiry Committee along with H.K. Mahtab, Lal Mohan Patnaik and Sarangdhar Das. In a sitting of the Committee on 22 June 1938 the following allegations were brought forward against the ruler of Nilgiri.[95]

1. Forced labour was extracted by the State officials.
2. Labour was employed without wages.
3. Heavy taxes were imposed on the forest produce.
4. *Salamis* were taken from the people during marriage ceremony.[96]

92. Bipan Chandra, *op. cit.*
93. P.N. Chopra, *op. cit.*, Vol. I, p. 186.
94. Orissa Records, W.W.C.C., Acc. No. 38, p. 25.
95. *The Samaj*, 28 June 1938.
96. Orissa Records, W.W.C.C., Acc. No. 38, pp. 27-28 and H.K. Mahtab, *op. cit.*, Vol. IV, p. 16.

The ruler took repressive measures. In July 1938, 116 persons were arrested. Banamali Das, the Secretary of Nilgiri *Prajamandal* was arrested on 4 August, 1938. On 10 August the State Police resorted to firing on a procession of agitators. On 11 August there was *lathi* charge by the police causing injuries to a lot.[97]

As the situation deteriorated a settlement was made between H.K. Mahtab, the ruling chief and the political agent. The discussion ended in the proposal for setting up an Enquiry Committee with the chief as its President which was, however, objected by Mahtab. The attempt at settlement proved to be a failure as the chief refused to subscribe to some of the demands of the *Prajamandal.* At last the chief agreed to concede certain demands of the people and peace was restored for sometime. He released the people who were arrested, evil practices were abolished and some concessions were given to the people.[98] But the agreement was short lived. The proclamation issued on 20 August, 1938 by the *Durbar* containing concessions granted to the subjects had actually avoided the real demands of the people. It lacked the abolition of forced labour like *Bethi, Begar* etc. Imposition of heavy taxes were not abolished.[99] So this was not unanimously accepted by the people. The movement continued for years. On 5 February 1938 *Prajamandal* was declared illegal.[100]

After the *Prajamandal* movement at Nilgiri other States of Orissa like Dhenkanal, Talcher, Athgarh, Pallahara, Nayagarh, Ranpur, Keonjhar, Hindol etc. formed *Prajamandals* in their respective States and put forth their demands before the chiefs through that body.

Dhenkanal

The people's movement was seething with discontent in Dhenkanal State in the first quarter of 1938 against the oppressive and tyrannical rule of the chief. Meetings were held in different places by the leaders to organise the people in a planned way. But the chief was very shrewed and organised parallel meetings by his followers to counteract the meetings of the people. Motanga was one of such places where he organised a meeting on 7 August 1938 styled himself as the father of

97. Confidential D.O. No. 2245-C, 17 August, 1938, File No. 18/8/38, Home Pol. (N.A.I.).
98. H.K. Mahtab, *Sadhanar Pathe*, Oriya, Cuttack, 1972, pp. 185-88. And Confidential D.O. No. 275/C, 17 August 1938, File No. 18/10/38 Home Pol. (N.A.I.).
99. Orissa Records, Talcher Papers, Confidential Letter by Raja, Nilgiri to Raja of Talcher, D.O. No. 27/Con/26 September 1938 with a copy of the Proclamation (SRT).
100. Orissa Records, W.W.C.C., Acc. No. 38, p. 45.

the subjects and claimed to be with the people.[101] Accordingly, a bulletin was published and circulated among the people of Dhenkanal which contained that the people should not move with the voice of the leaders who were against his administration.[102] But the people rejected such royal proclamations. They stood unitedly to bring reforms in the State administration in general and village panchayat administration in particular which was far behind any semblance of democracy.[103] The movement went on gaining strength gradually.

On 29 August 1938 the State authority declared some concessions in favour of the people but it did not touch on the abolition of taxes, forced labour or reforms of village administration.[104] An 'Economic Board' named as *Prajamandal Samittee* was constituted with members drawn from among the royalists without any popular representation.[105] It was rejected by the people. The movement continued.

In the first week of September 1938 *Prajamandal* was formed at Dhenkanal with the following leaders:

Harmohan Patnaik	— President
Maheswar Subahu Singh*	— Vice-President
Laxmidhar Sahu	— General Secretary
Baishnab Patnaik	— Joint Secretary[106]

Some leaders who gave their blessings and moral support to this *Prajamandal* of Dhenkanal were Nabakrishna Choudhury, Malati Devi, Braj Kishore Dhal, Sarangdhar Das, Musa Mallik and several others.[107] The *Prajamandal* placed a charter of demands before the chief. It included demands like civil liberties, responsible government with people's representatives, abolition of forced labour like *bethi* and *magan*, abolition of monopoly system and amendment of forest laws.[108] On

101. Orissa Records, Talcher Papers, Bulletin, Dhenkanal State Publishing Department, 8 August 1938 (SRT).
102. *Ibid.*
103. *Krushak*, 8 August, 1938.
104. Dhenkanal State Gazette, Extraordinary, Published by State Authority, Dhenkanal, 29 August 1938. (SRT)
105. *Ibid.*
* See Appendix B.
106. H.M. Patnaik, *Dhenkanal Andolan*, Oriya, Dhenkanal, 1983, p. 17.
107. S .N. Patnaik, *op. cit.*, pp. 144-45.
108. *Ibid.* And Interview with Harmohan Patnaik on 14 August 1980 by the author at Dhenkanal.

9 September 1938, the chief declared some concessions regarding forest law.[109] But it failed to pacify the people. Meetings were organised where the demands were discussed before the people and leaflets were circulated. Apprehending a mass movement, the State authority declared a state of emergency prohibiting meetings, forming association, interference with administration etc.[110] But the agitators defied the *Durbar's* order. Carrying weapons with them they assembled in large numbers and started demonstration in the State on 12 September 1938.[111] To disperse the crowd the police opened fire causing injuries to many people. There was large scale arrest of people including the office bearers of Dhenkanal *Prajamandal*.[112] The next day more than 25,000 people gathered at Dhenkanal and demanded the release of arrested people. Armed Police from other States of the Eastern States Agency reached Dhenkanal in order to meet the situation and pursue repression in full swing. Repressive measures were taken and a reign of terror was let loose in Dhenkanal. *Prajamandal* was declared unlawful on 21 September, 1938.[113] Most of the workers escaped to Cuttack. Many of them including Harmohan Patnaik were arrested on 23 September 1938.[114] Discussion for a compromise between the chief, the political agent, H.K. Mahtab, Sarangdhar Das and Malati Choudhury was followed which was unsuccessful.[115]

Inhuman repression and tyranny continued in Dhenkanal. Most of the villages around the State were looted by the police. Firing and *lathi* charge were common on the people. On 10 October fire was opened on the village Bhuban resulting in the death of a person and injury to several persons who were admitted to the Cuttack Hospital.[116] On 11 October 1938 the same incident occurred at Nilakanthpur. Six persons died and eight were seriously injured due to police firing. Baji Rout*, a boy of eleven years who took the courage of facing the bullet of armed forces was shot dead on the spot and his name had become a legend in

109. Dhenkanal State Gazette, Extraordinary, published by Dhenkanal authority, 9 September 1938 (SRT).

110. *Ibid.*, 12 September 1938 and See Appendix C.

111. *Krushak*, 24 September 1938.

112. *Ibid.*

113. Confidential D.O. No. 2641-C, 3 October, 1938, File No. 18/9/38 Home Pol (NAI).

114. *Krushak*, 24 September 1938.

115. Orissa Records, W.W.C.C., Acc. No. 38, pp. 29-30.

116. Confidential D.O. No. 2751, 17 October 1938, File No. 17/10/38, Home Pol. (NAI).

* See Appendix B.

Orissa.[117] The dead bodies of Laxmana Mallik, Nata Mallik, Raghu Naik, Guri Naik and Hrushi Pradhan along with Baji Rout were taken on a large procession to the burial ground of Khannagar at Cuttack city for cremation.[118]

Out of fear thousands of villagers left the State of Dhenkanal and went to take shelter under the open air at Jenapur, Sukinda, Balarampur etc. in the nearby British territories.[119]

Lathi charge, firing were resorted to in many villages of Dhenkanal State by the police and armed forces. On 17 October at Hindol Road station fire was opened where the villagers of Balram Prasad, Murdanagpalli and Godidihi had taken shelter. Police also fired on 21 October in the village of Tumusingha and Sirimula. Both the incidents left many people dead and much more severely injured.[120] Firing was again resorted to by the State Police of Dhenkanal on 2 November, 1938 because the people armed with bows, arrows, axes and *lathis* had attacked the police station. Several police officers as well as some people assembled there sustained severe injuries.[121]

Another incident of firing took place on 11 November resulting in the death of a number of persons.[122]

During the 1st week of December 1938 *Satyagraha* was launched against the Dhenkanal State from Cuttack. Sri Nabakrishna Choudhury resigned his seat in the Orissa Legislative Assembly in order to lead the volunteers to offer *Satyagraha*, in Dhenkanal.[123] The socialist group of N.K. Choudhury had come forward to actively participate in the Dhenkanal agitation against the oppression of the chief and was arrested on 3 December 1938.[124] Feeling the pressure of the agitation in his State, the ruling chief of Dhenkanal during third week of December decided to allow the people's representatives to associate themselves in the administration of the State. But it was in vain.[125]

---

117. *The Samaj*, 14 October 1938.
118. *Krushak*, 15 October 1938 and *The Samaj*, 11 October 1985.
119. *Krushak*, 1 October 1938.
120. H.M. Patnaik, *op. cit.*, p. 36.
121. Orissa Records, W.W.C.C. Acc. No. 38, pp. 32-33.
122. *Ibid.*
123. *Ibid.*
124. Confidential D.O. No. 3211-C, 17 December 1938, File No. 18/12/38 Home, Pol (NAI).
125. Orissa Records, W.W.C.C., Acc. No. 38, p. 33.

The *Prajamandal* movement in Dhenkanal took more vigorous turn in 1939. The number of refugees from the State assumed such proportion that new camps were opened at Budhapanka of Angul to provide shelter to the displaced agitators.[126] A vernacular pamphlet named '*Hoshiar*' was published at Budhapanka camp serving as the organ of the agitators in Dhenkanal.[127] The ruler of Dhenkanal felt the impact of the agitators and adopted a conciliatory attitude towards his people. He announced in a *Durbar* held on 26 June 1939 a number of measures regarding constitutional reforms for improving administration of his State.[128] The declaration included remission of six months in sentences of persons undergoing imprisonment, withdrawal of proceedings against all persons awaiting trial, revival of old Panchayat which in the long run would be the foundation of *Praja Parishad*, introduction of elective elements in the administration of civil welfare of the people, improvement of High Court and establishment of a town municipality in Dhenkanal.[129] But these concessions were rejected by the *Prajamandal* as there was absence in it the question of civil liberty, non-withdrawal of warrants on the leaders etc. No improvement was seen in the State till September 1939.[130]

Nayagarh

The Nayagarh *Prajamandal* was established on 6 June 1938 under the Presidentship of Narayan Nanda.[131] The peasants demanded their right over the land, curtailment of excessive rents, and modification of forest laws. The oppression and misrule in the State was condemned through public meetings which were prohibited by the chief. Meetings were organised in different places against the State administration. On 22 September 1938 a meeting were organised by Kuber Sahu, the Joint Secretary of *Prajamandal* at Manik Patna *Hat*. About 7000 people attended the meeting.[132] On 25 and 28 of the same month more meetings were organised at Godipada and Sarankul.[133] Hundreds were arrested and sent to jail for attending the meetings. On 6 October 1938 thousands

126. *The Samaj*, 30 July 1973.
127. Orissa Records, W.W.C.C., Acc. No. 38, p. 47.
128. *Ibid.*, p. 54.
129. H.K. Mahtab, *History of Freedom Movement in Orissa*, Vol. IV, p. 267.
130. Orissa Records, W.W.C.C., *op. cit.*, p. 60.
131. S.N. Patnaik, *op. cit.*, p. 147.
132. *Krushak*, 15 October 1938.
133. *Ibid.*

of people had gathered at Sarankul to welcome the arrested leaders who were to be released on that day.[134] The Ordinance was disobeyed by the leaders of *Prajamandal* and it held meeting on 27 December 1938. The leaders of *Prajamandal* were arrested. The chief tried to suppress the movement by taking recourse to repressive measures and through diplomacy such as dissuading the people from joining the agitation with promise of concessions to them.[135] Despite the Ordinance, the people's movement was intensified. The *Prajamandal* offered *Satyagraha* during the last part of December 1938 and apprehending trouble from the agitators the chief of Nayagarh sought assistance of the political Agent, Orissa for crushing the agitation.[136]

The State authority issued an Ordinance prohibiting meetings and processions by the *Prajamandal* in the State. But people enmass gathered before the *Raja's* palace demanding the release of the *Prajamandal* leaders. On 9 January 1939 the Raja was forced to release the leaders and workers of the *Prajamandal*.[137] A temporary peace prevailed in the State due to the declaration of the Second World War.

Khandapara

During the first week of March 1939, about thirty thousand people of Khandapara State assembled on the sand bed of the Chitroptala river near Kantilo. There they decided to protest the repressive measures taken by the chief like forced labour (*bethi*, *begari* etc.), excessive taxation and deterioration of socio-economic condition.[138] Leaders like Daitari Parida and Somanath Mohanty were arrested and sentenced to rigorous imprisonment. Criminal cases were instituted against the leaders and out of fear they left for the neighbouring British territories.[139] The local police threatened the people not to appear before the States Enquiry Committee to give witness against the State's administration. But Raghunath Singh Samant, the grandson of astrologer Chandra Sekhar Samant was prosecuted on a bogus charge and imprisoned for it.[140] Gradually the agitation became violent which threatened the

134. Krushak, *op. cit.*

135. Orissa Records, W.W.C.C., Acc. No. 38, pp. 33-35.

136. *Ibid.*

137. S.N. Patnaik, *op. cit.*, p. 148.

138. R.N. Singhsamant, *Khandapada Prajamandalara Sankhipta Itihas*, Oriya, Cuttack, 1950, pp. 41-45.

139. *Ibid.*

140. *Orissa States Enquiry Committee Report*, pp. 21-22.

authority's position inside the State. By this time Khandapara *Prajamandal* was formed which vehemently opposed the illegal taxes imposed on the people. In July 1939 the *Prajamandal* of the State demanded before the chief the recognition of the association of elected representatives of tenants. But the chief did not agree to this point, as a result of which the agitation became more vigorous.[141] The refugee problem became formidable and after the intervention of H.K. Mahtab, their repatriation could be made possible. The chief gave the people some concessions.[142]

Athgarh

The people of Athgarh State were overburdened with heavy illegal taxes and doing forced labour or *bethi* for the *Durbar* during the first half of twentieth century.[143] A disorganised no tax campaign was made by the people in February 1938 which brought consciousness among the people.[144] Under the leadership of Radhanath Rath, Anant Mohapatra and Achyutananda Das a meeting was organised at Athgarh during September 1938 and after that the *Prajamandal* of Athgarh took its birth. This organisation demanded redressal of their grievances. But the *Durbar* took recourse to repressive measures like arrest, *lathi*-charge and firing.[145] *Prajamandal* was declared unlawful on 8 October 1938.[146] Many people were sent to prison and many left the State out of fear to neighbouring areas. The ruler at last, on 10 November 1938 granted some concessions like lifting monopoly licence on *bidi*, *betel, tamakhu, kerosene* etc., remitting the forest cess, freeing the political prisoners on production of bail certificate etc.[147]

Pallahara

The Pallahara *Prajamandal* was formed in September of 1938 with Fakir Pradhan as its President. The other active members of this organisation were Nabaghana Sahoo, Dayanidhi Sahoo, Maguni Charan Pradhan, Bhubaneswar Pradhan, Nepa Garnaik, Bansidhar Nayak and Udayanath Sahoo.[148] Though the people were the admirers of the *Raja*

141. Orissa Records, W.W.C.C., Acc. No. 38, p. 57.
142. R.N. Singhsamant, *op. cit.*
143. *Deshakatha*, 21 August 1938.
144. Orissa Records, W.W.C.C., Acc. No. 38, p. 12.
145. *Deshakatha*, 29 October, 1938.
146. *Orissa Review*, August 1989, pp. 130-31.
147. *Ibid.* and *Deshakatha*, 13 November 1938.
148. Interview with Udayanath Sahoo of Pallahara at his Bhubaneswar residence by the author on 31 October 1992.

Sarat Chandra Munipal, yet they were not in favour of the then existing administrative system. During October 1938 a meeting of the *Prajamandal* was held at the premises of Triribi Mahadev Temple where resolutions were passed unanimously to fight against the existing *bethi, bheti, magan*, excessive illegal tax and above all the British administration.[149] Revolt went on and hundreds of people were arrested. Many were beaten by the police in the custody and false cases were instituted against the organisers. Out of fear, leaders like Madhusudan Sahoo absconded. During the first half of 1939 another meeting was held by the *Prajamandal* at Kunjam which was attended by about 2000 people where decision was taken to carry on the movement till their demands were fulfilled. At last some concessions were made by the *Durbar*. A '*Praja Parishad*' was formed with some of the people's representatives like Udayanath Sahoo, Bhubaneswar Pradhan, Budhia Pradhan etc. as the members of it.[150]

Gangpur

Likewise the Gangpur *Prajamandal* had organised no rent campaign against what they considered highly arbitrary assessment. The Gangpur administration wanted to suppress the movement as they apprehended violence from the people. On 25 April 1939 a police force was sent to arrest Nirmal Munda, the main organiser of the movement. But they were confronted by five hundred armed *mundas*.[151] Armed Police went there and firing was resorted causing the death of about 32 *mundas* and 21 injuries.[152]

Mayurbhanj

In Mayurbhanj the foundation of *Prajamandal* laid in 1939 under the leadership of Sarat Chandra Das. The people took keen interest in the new movement and came in large numbers to enlist themselves as its members. The villagers gradually became politically conscious and united themselves in challenging the despotic administration, to save farmers from the clutches of money-lenders, to enjoy civil and political rights etc.[153]

149. Interview with Udayanath Sahoo, *op. cit.*

150. *Ibid.*

151. H.K. Mahtab, *Odisa Itihas,* p. 519, and Orissa Records, W.W.C.C., Acc. No. 13, p. 79.

152. Orissa Records, W.W.C.C., Acc. No. 11, p. 62.

153. *Orissa Review,* January 1989, pp. 13-14.

Ranpur

The *Prajamandal* of Ranpur fought seriously for the cause of the people in June 1938. The organisation with Banamali Ram as President, Kripasindhu Mishra as Vice-President, Raghunath Mohanty* as General Secretary and Dibakar Parida as Organising Secretary brought to the notice of the chief the enforcement of illegal taxes, forced labour and many others through a charter of demand.[154] Banamali Ram, the President of Ranpur *Prajamandal* handed over a list of demands to the ruling chief of Ranpur on 11 October 1938.[155] On 2 January 1939 Ranpur *Prajamandal* was declared unlawful and some leaders were arrested.[156] On 5 January huge crowds gathered before the palace of the chief and demanded the immediate release of the *Prajamandal* leaders.[157] The ruler instead of pacifying the people called for the assistance of military help from the Political Agent. Major Bazelgette, the Political Agent of Sambalpur who was present in the neighbouring State of Nayagarh rushed to Ranpur with a small force from Nayagarh. There was obstruction on the way by putting bullock carts and large branches of trees on the road. After a discussion with the ruler of Ranpur the Political Agent came out of the palace to meet the people who immediately attacked him. He then shot a man dead. Soon after, he was surrounded by the mob, beaten and stoned to death.[158] The death of the Political Agent was followed by a reign of terror. There was martial law and the civil life was completely paralaysed. Thousands of people fled away from the State and took refuge outside the State. Many were arrested and in a decision of the sessions court Raghunath Mohanty and Dibakar Parida were sentenced to death.[159] The killing of the Political Agent was condemned by Congress leaders like Gandhiji, Subash Bose, J.N. Nehru, Biswanath Das and many others. The Congress Working Committee passed the following resolution : "The Working Committee record their deep regret at the killing of Major Bezelegette by a crowd of Ranpur in Orissa and are of opinion that such acts of violence do great injury to the cause of freedom in the States . . . The Committee, therefore, earnestly trust that the people of

* See Appendix B.

154. J.N. Patnaik, *Odisa Itihasare Ketoti Romanchakar Kahani,* Oriya, Cuttack, 1990, p. 161.
155. For details see Appendix D.
156. Orissa Records, W.W.C.C., Acc. no. 38, pp. 36-37.
157. *Ibid.*
158. File No. 6(2) P. 15/39, Foreign Politicals, p. 6(NAI).
159. N. Routray, *Smruti O Anubhuti*, Oriya, Cuttack, 1986, pp. 113-14.

the States as well as those in other parts of India strictly adhere to peace methods in the struggle for freedom".[160] But Sri Sarangadhar Das and the radical nationalists, socialists and communists blamed the State authorities and the Political Agent to have provoked the common people to counter State-violence by popular violence.[161] The ghastly murder of Bazelgette was the culmination of the agitation in Ranpur and the unforeseen outcome of the heated feelings that ran high among the people of the State.

Sonepur

The Sonepur *Prajamandal* was formed on 12 December 1938 and the office bearers were :

Bhimsen Bhoi — President
Chaturbhuja Mishra — Joint Secretaries
and
Ramchandra Satpathy
Dolamani Das Gountia — Treasurer and Organiser

Besides them Laxman Satpathy, Makardwaj Purohit and Pitambar Satpathy were elected as members.[162] On 22 March 1939 the *Prajamandal* handed over a list of demands to the chief like civic rights to the citizen, establishment of self-government, abolition of illegal taxes etc. Instead of giving concessions to the people the administration went on suppressing the movement through arrests, *lathi* charge, warrants, beating etc. On 30 April 1939, when the *Prajamandal* was having a meeting in the village Sindurpur against the maladministration of the State the armed police attacked on the gathering there and arrested a good number of people along with Laxman Satpathy, Mohan Mishra, Bhimsen Bhoi, Hari Sahu and Mohan Parida.[163] The arrest failed to suppress the movement and it continued later.

Talcher

The Talcher *Prajamandal*, which was formed on 6 September 1938, carried on the agitation with unabated vigour and drew up a list of demands including the right to form associations, hold meetings,

160. *Indian Annual Register*, Vol. I, 1939, pp. 308-09.
161. File No. 127, AISPC Papers, p. 245 (NMML).
162. *Utkal Prasanga*, January 1992, pp. 81-82.
163. *Ibid* and Orissa Records, W.W.C.C., Acc. No. 11, p. 62.

abolition of forced labour, modification of the tenancy and forest laws and better condition in the collieries. The people finding the repression of the chief too severe resorted to mass exodus (*Hizrat*) from Talcher under the leadership of Pabitra Mohan Pradhan* and on the advice of Mahatma Gandhi.[164] Thousands of people who left their homes and hearths as the only means of their protection against repression of the chief assembled in camps of Kosala and Kampsala in Angul near the border of Talcher. State on 16 September 1938.[165] They stayed in the camps for about eight months. On 21 and 22 September 1938 the police of Talcher opened fire on people at the village Chandrabil leading to the death of Bika Nayak, a worker of *Prajamandal* and serious injuries to a number of people.[166] Talcher *Prajamandal* was declared illegal thereafter.

Prajamandal activities were also carried on in Bamra, Boud, Hindol, Athmallik, Rairakhol etc. Everywhere the administration adopted repressive measures to suppress the mass movement. In spite of arrests, firings, loot and arson the people did not give up their struggle. Some chiefs were forced to give few concessions to their people. Hindol perhaps was the first State to announce to grant civil and political rights and some other benefits to the people on 15 January 1939.[167] Likewise the chiefs of Talcher and Dhenkanal also granted some concessions and temporary peace was restored in those States.[168]

By the middle of 1939 peace prevailed to some degree in the feudatory States of Orissa. The movements in the States shook off the fear of the ruler and their arbitrary rule from the minds of the people in the States. Confidence and consciousness made them strengthened. The thirties of the twentieth century marked a change in the people's struggle in the feudatory States along with the British Indian territories. The State subjects became more and more politically conscious and determined with their well-organised *Prajamandals* to go for massive movement for their socio-economic upliftment and civic, political and human rights. The crucial pre-World War II years prepared these State subjects for a future and bigger struggle during the war years.

---

* See Appendix B.

164. *Talcher Prajamandal Itihas Committee* (*Compl*) pp. 17-27.

165. *Ibid.*, and Orissa Records, W.W.C.C., Acc. No. 38, p. 30.

166. Orissa Records, *op. cit.*, p. 64, and S.C. De, *Diary of Political Events in Orissa*, Cuttack, 1964, p. 20.

167. *The Samaj*, 18 January 1939.

168. *Orissa Review*, August 1972, p. 62.

States During World War II and Quit India Movement

The Second World War broke out and the Congress Ministry in Orissa resigned from office. In spite of all the efforts the administration in the feudatory States could not be properly streamlined in the interest of the people. The hands of the chiefs were strengthened by the Defence of India Rules (DIR).[169] By this rule thousands of *Prajamandal* workers were arrested in the feudatory States of Orissa and put inside the prison even without trials. But during the Quit India Movement the people revolted openly against the authorities and the movement assumed a vigorous form in Talcher, Dhenkanal and few other States.

During the Second World War, the repressive measures of Talcher *Durbar* grew in its attempts to quell the popular agitation. Meetings and processions were forbidden. Leaders were arrested under D.I.R. Some of them absconded and guided the *Prajamandal* movement in disguise.[170] The head office of the *Prajamandal* was maintained at Angul and its branches were working at Talcher. Once again the *Prajamandal* became quite active in the State when the Quit India Resolution was passed by the Indian National Congress. Pabitra Mohan Pradhan, the leader of Talcher *Prajamandal* escaped from jail in August 1942 and went underground.[171]

The Talcher *Prajamandal* defied the *Durbar* Government and a parallel Government was established.[172] The people made heroic attempts to snatch away the control of Talcher administration from the hands of the chief. On 6 September 1942, about eight thousand people with their crude weapons assembled at Talcher while the State forces were reinformed by the British Army and the Air Force.[173] There was aerial bombing and machine-gunning to disperse the swelling crowd. Thousands were injured and a reign of terror prevailed in the State. But the *Prajamandal* continued its movement secretly and through underground activities. The situation remained unchanged till 1946.

Mayurbhanj

Early in 1940 the chief of Mayurbhanj played a diplomatic action by declaring to establish a *Prajasabha* to take the wind out of the

169. *Orissa Review*, January 1989, pp. 21-22.

170. *Ibid.*, August 1972, p. 63.

171. Interview with Pabitra Mohan Pradhan by the author on 18 December 1980 at Bhubaneswar.

172. *Ibid.*

173. *The Samaj*, 2 September 1990.

shells of the *Prajamandal.* But it misfired. On 18 December 1940 a conference of the *Prajamandal* was held at Ambajoda. The State administration promptly created a counter institution called State *Prajamandal* consisting of persons close to the authority.[174] False cases were filed against the leaders, causing them physical and financial harassment. The new weapon of the authorities for dealing a death-blow to the *Prajamandal* did not work at all. The annual session of the *Prajamandal* was held at Kuradhia from 9 to 11 May 1940.[175] In 1941 construction of a dam in the river Budhi at Naranga and in 1942 another construction of a dam at Sighati near Pargana Khunta were taken up by the *Prajamandal* workers which was disallowed by the authorities. The workers were arrested. Sarat Chandra Das, the prominent leader of Mayurbhanj *Prajamandal* attended the All-India States People' Conference at Bombay. During the Quit India Movement the *Prajamandal* organised several meetings against the autocracy of the chief. Picketting of excise shops and boycott of *Hats* were done. In 1944 the third. session of the *Prajamandal* was held at Madhunanda of Manitri Pargana.[176]

Dhenkanal

Repressive measures were taken by the chief during World War II. Most of the leaders of Dhenkanal *Prajamandal* were in jail. Leaders like Baishnab Patnaik and Maheswar Subahu Singh were arrested under DIR on 29 June 1940.[177] So the *Prajamandal* had to chalk out its programme during war period by remaining outside Dhenkanal. On 13 January 1941 the *Prajamandal* organised a public meeting at Budhapanka near Angul where a good number of resolutions were accepted. These included abolition of *bethi-cess*, proper representation of public in *Praja Sabha* and *Praja Parishad*, protection of civil liberties, immediate relief measures to drought affected areas etc. Several other meetings were held in different villages like Kanti, Kandarsingha, Mendhapada, Jaka and Kankadahad. Many leaders went underground. Baishnab Patnaik was released in May 1942 conditionally. False cases were instituted against him by Dhenkanal *Durbar.* But he escaped to Cuttack in August to continue his work from there. By this time

174. *Orissa Review*, January 1989, pp. 14-15.

175. *Ibid.*

176. *Ibid.*

177. Interview with Baishnab Charan Patnaik by the author at Dhenkanal on 10 August 1980.

Nabakrishna Choudhury was residing at Salipur of Cuttack as the Office of the Congress Party of Orissa was going on there for some time. So Baishnab Patnaik had to stay with him at Salipur for some days.[178]

When the 'Quit-India' resolution was adopted by the Congress, the Dhenkanal authority immediately promulgated a state of emergency on 11 August 1942.[179] Meetings and processions were banned. *Prajamandal* was declared unlawful on 16 August 1942 and most of its leaders were arrested.[180] On 26 August 1942 Baishnab Patnaik with a group of agitators armed with guns, axes, bows and arrows attacked the Sub-Divisional Headquarters of Murhi (presently Kamakhyanagar), burnt government houses, took away arms and ammunitions, looted the treasury and grannary worth of twenty thousand rupees and distributed it among the poors.[181] The workers had formed a suicide squad and took an oath to die for the cause of the people. The next attempt was made on 2 September 1942 when about five hundred agitators led by Baishnab Patnaik burnt the police station and Tahsil Office at Chandpur.[182] Then the mob proceeded towards Parjang armed with guns, bows and arrows. The mob encountered the State Police force on the way at Janhapara where firing was opened by the force on 4 September 1942 resulting in one death and twelve injured.[183] Baishnab Patnaik who sustained bullet injury went underground.[184] On 5 September the party of Debraj Patra, a close follower of Baishnab Patnaik burnt the police station and the beat-house of forest department of Gengutia near Talcher.[185] The situation became so serious that police forces along with magistrates were deployed in the villages of Murhi, Parjang, Garh Palasuni and Bhuban. To meet the challenge of Baishnab Patnaik the Dhenkanal authority requisitioned two more platoons of

178. Interview with Baishnab Charan Patnaik by *Samaj*, 15 August 1992 Issue.

179. Orissa Records, Talcher Papers, Dhenkanal State Gazette, 11 August 1942 (SRT).

180. Interview with Baishnab Charan Patnaik by author at Dhenkanal on 10 August 1980.

181. Orissa Records, Sambalpur Papers Acc. No. 1026S/P-1-26, Situation Report of Dhenkanal State to Political Agent, Orissa who was in tour to Murhi, Letter No. 1026/20 dated 28 August, 1942. (OSA) And, Interview with Baishnab Charan Patnaik by *Samaj*, 15 August 1992 issue.

182. *The Samaj*, 2 September 1990.

183. *Ibid.*, and H.M. Patnaik, *op. cit.*, p. 40.

184. Orissa Records, *op. cit.* Acc. No. 1026/87 Raja of Dhenkanal to Raibahadur, D.O. No. 454-P/42, 8 September 1942 and R.C. Ram, *Sangrami,* Oriya, Cuttack, 1986, p. 79.

185. *Amrit Bazar Patrika*, 11 October 1942.

joint police force.[186] Raids were conducted in different villages for arresting leaders. An amount of fifty thousand rupees was collected as collective fines by 20 September 1942.[187] Terrible repressive measures were adopted by the chief. The people, men or women, were indiscriminately assaulted and their properties were confiscated. Cash awards were announced for capturing the absconders.[188] Baishnab Patnaik, however, remained underground and continued his activities from his hideout.

Nilgiri

Besides Talcher and Dhenkanal there were signs of unrest in Nilgiri. In early 1940 Kailash Chandra Mohanty, President of Nilgiri *Prajamandal* was arrested for giving anti-war statements. Banamali Das, the Secretary of *Prajamandal* was expelled from Nilgiri State for his activities in the Communist Party.[189] *Satyagraha* and different activities against the chief's maladministration went on in the State. Harekrishna Mahtab had been to Nilgiri to see the situation and had a talk with the leaders.[190]

During the Quit India Movement the State again rose into revolt. The *Praja Sabha* convened by the chief became a farce as its elected members did not join it. The people with huge numbers made an attempt to capture the palace. A clash between the mob and the armed force occurred causing the death of Raghu Naik and Ganga Mallik and leaving many others wounded.[191] Ultimately, the chief was deprived of ruling power and sent to Ranchi in November 1942.[192] This was a great achievement for Nilgiri *Prajamandal*.

Nayagarh

The Nayagarh *Prajamandal* with the co-operation of the people vehemently opposed the British Government's action against Gandhiji. To meet the situation the chief of the State arrested leaders like Sridhar Das, Banchhanidhi Senapati, Laxman Moharana, Sukuru Behera, Udayanath Prusti and Bidyadhar Mantri on 17 July 1942 under D.I.R.[193]

---

186. Interview with Baishnab Charan Patnaik by the author on 10 August 1980 at Dhenkanal.
187. *Amrit Bazar Patrika*, 20 September 1942.
188. Orissa Records, Sambalpur Papers, *op. cit.*
189. Orissa Records, W.W.C.C., Acc. No. 60, p. 4.
190. *Ibid.*, p. 12.
191. The Nilgiri State Administration Report, 1943-44, pp. 35-36.
192. *Ibid.*
193. *The Samaj*, 2 September 1990.

Instead of calming down, it aggravated the situation. Each region of the State declared its independence. The mob attacked government offices and police station and burnt most of them. Repressive measures were adopted by the chief. Hundreds were arrested, and their properties were confiscated. There was clash between the armed police and the people at Nuagan. Police opened fire on 10 October 1942 causing the death of Kasti Dakua and many of them were wounded seriously.[194] Oppression also started inside the jail. An old man Kanduri Parida and his son Budhi Parida were beaten to death inside the jail of Nayagarh.[195] The movement in the State by *Prajamandal* did not subside, it rather continued with enhanced vigour towards its goal.

Besides these States there were risings in Bamra, Palalahara and Keonjhar. But there the unrest did not break out into agitational activities.

The unrest in 1942 was sudden in its approach and fizzled out very soon. This was so because of the superior force of the authorities and apparently of the violent nature of the movement. There was no effort on the part of State leadership of States Peoples' Conference or the respective *Prajamandals* to coordinate their movement into a single one and to make it a part of national struggle at that time. Whatever efforts in that direction was made remained insufficient due to the contradiction of fixing the primary enemy target of the people's wrath. While in British India, it was the foreign masters, in feudatory States, it was still, the local rulers. Though there was no development in the relationship between the subjects and the rulers, the risings proved that the people once backward and undeveloped had become conscious of their individual rights, liberties and existence and were not prepared to accept the autocratic rule any more. If necessary they could be equally violent to assert their rights.

Movement in Post-War Period

After the end of World War II the political prisoners were gradually released. Dissatisfaction among the people continued as there was still oppression, despotism and tyranny in the States. Free and forced labour was still there. Social condition of the people did not improve at all after the war. Once again the *Prajamandals* in the States got set for a fresh attempt for attaining their goal. With vigour and spirit, the

194. S.N. Patnaik, *op. cit.*, p. 179.

195. *The Samaj*, 2 September 1990.

people's movement in the States took a new turn. Help came from all corners for these movements in the States. The formation of *'Garjat Chhatra Samilani'* at Cuttack on 10 February 1946 extended its moral support to the States' movement. This Conference criticised the administration of the Orissa States and demanded the release of political prisoners, the restoration of civil liberties and the amalgamation of the smaller States with British India.[196] The student leaders helped the *Prajamandals* in their respective areas. Above all, the Congress Ministry headed by H.K. Mahatab in Orissa during this period gave full support to the people of the States to carry on the movement in their respective areas with a non-violent manner. Different parties like the Congress, the Communist, and the Socialists came forward to support the cause of the people of the feudatory States.[197] A Conference of the Orissa States' Workers was held at Sambalpur where resolutions were passed demanding the release of political prisoners, the cancellation of warrants against political absconders, the establishment of responsible governments in the States based on adult franchise and the abolition of forced labour.[198] The press also played a vital role in espousing the cause of the State people and their demands and drew attention against the State administration, its police and other departments.[199]

Dhenkanal

The people's movement in Dhenkanal became more active and demanded through its *Prajamandal* to return the collective fines. A public meeting was organised on 19 March 1946 at Parjang under the Presidentship of Pravakar Rout. Another meeting was held on 30 March 1946 at Rakula in Kamakhyanagar Sub-Division under the Presidentship of Ram Chandra Patnaik. In both the meetings it was resolved to restore peace in the State, adequate compensation for the people whose houses were demolished in 1942-43 by the State, abolition of forced labour, release of political prisoners etc.[200] The *Prajamandal* also organised another meeting on 20 December 1946 under the Presidentship of Braj Kishore Dhal where the amalgamation of the State with the province was demanded. This was supported by Baishnab

196. Orissa Records, W.W.C.C., Acc. No. 50, p. 68.
197. *Ibid.*, *op. cit.*, Acc. No. 35, p. 35.
198. *Ibid.*, pp. 70-71.
199. Orissa Records, W.W.C.C., Acc. No. 47, p. 5.
200. Orissa Records, Dhenkanal Papers, Acc. No. 1026S, Letter of Baishnab Charan Patnaik, 21 June 1946, (OSA).

Charan Patnaik, Maheswar Subahusingh and Norottam Das in different meetings at Parjang and Dholpur in the month of January 1947.

A newspaper, *The New Orissa*, described the administration of the chief of Dhenkanal as a veritable hell on earth where the most terrible atrocities had been committed.[201] The *Praja Parisad* which was an organ of the authority was denounced by the *Prajamandal* as most of its members were nominated by the chief. The Communist Party headed by Baishnab Patnaik, the Congress Party and many other organisations held different meetings in the State in support of the people. After India got her independence the *Prajamandal* of Dhenkanal with its headquarters at Jenapur near the border of Cuttack decided to form an independent Government in the State. Baishnab Charan Patnaik, with the help of the Communist Party trained about ten thousand volunteers with arms and weapons to capture power from the authority and establish a popular ministry. The *Prajamandal* Working Committee demanded it before the chief. The chief was having correspondence with Sardar Patel and V.P. Menon who were in charge of the Indian States. He also went to Delhi to meet them and wanted an amicable settlement.[202] Sardar Patel and the Orissa Ministry requested the *Prajamandal* of Dhenkanal to postpone the agitation till the end of the Rulers' Conference in 1947.

Talcher

After the World War II most of the political prisoners were set free. But the authority of Talcher did not release the political prisoners whose number was more than four hundred. The warrants were still in force for those who were absconding. After much pressure from all sides the prisoners were released towards the end of 1946. But Pabitra Mohan Pradhan was still in jail. The warrants against him were lifted on 29 August 1947 due to heavy pressure from all parts of the country. He entered Talcher on 6 September 1947 and organised the workers to carry on the movement once more till the finalisation of the merger of the State with Orissa province.[203]

Boudh

During the last part of 1946, the *Prajamandal* of Boudh demanded a responsible government in the State. But the chief did not listen to it

201. Orissa Records, W.W.C.C., Acc. No. 47, p. 12.

202. H.M. Patnaik, *op. cit.*, p. 51.

203. *Talcher Prajamandal Itihas Committee* (*Compl.*)., p. 62.

and started repression. The people's movement in the State was non-violent one. There were meetings and processions highlighting the demands of *Prajamandal*. At Baghibahal a large meeting was arranged on 14 November 1946 which was attended by 12,000 people.[204] Another meeting was held at Boudhgarh on 19 November. The resolution passed in this meeting was submitted to the chief and political department. But suppressive measures were taken by the authority. In the *lathi* charge many people including Durga Charan Panda, a *Prajamandal* worker were injured.[205] On 2 December 1946 an appeal to redress some grievances was made by Bhagaban Panda, Secretary, Boudh *Prajamandal* which fell in deaf ears.[206] About thirteen *Prajamandal* workers were arrested on 11 December 1946. The State administration kept a close watch on the activities of the *Prajamandal* workers. To counter the movement of the people in the State the authority started a parallel and counter organisation called *'Prajamandal'*.[207]

Patna

The *'Krushak Mandal* Party' of Patna raised its voice of high rates of customs duties on various articles including vegetables, high handedness of the authority, corruption and harassment of the customs authorities. On 10 December 1946 some people were arrested on the charge of smuggling on the border. The situation became tense. On 19 February 1947 large number of people attacked the Agalpur Police Station.[208] The *Krushak Mandal* Party held a big meeting at Bolangir on 23 February 1947 and it was decided to start non-cooperation with the administration, demanding civil rights to the people and responsible government.[209] To tackle the situation the State authority of Patna requisitioned the services of the Eastern States Joint Armed Police Forces.

Sonepur

The Sonepur *Prajamandal* organised a meeting on 19 April 1946 in the village Kalapathar against the chief of Sonepur which was

204. Orissa Records, W.W.C.C., Acc. No. 11, pp. 3-5.

205. *Ibid*.

206. *Ibid*.

207. *Ibid*.

208. Orissa Records, Sambalpur Papers, Acc. No. 1180S, Chief Minister, Patna State to Political Agent, Chhatisgarh States, D.O. No. 32/Confidential, 21 February 1947. (OSA).

209. *Ibid*., Proceedings of the Meeting of Krushak Mandal Party, 7 March 1947.

attended by thousands of people. They demanded to stop repression on the weavers of Binika and stoppage of collection of octroi tax from the people of Sonepur. The police attacked the people. More than twenty were injured and one named Gurubari Meher was killed on 30 January 1947 due to *lathi* charge by police.[210] People of different villages such as Mendha, Bolenpalli, Sagarpalli, Kumarkelli, Tarava, Govindpur, Bhabanipalli, Digsira etc. joined their hands against the suppression and tyranny of the chief.[211] It continued till its merger with the rest of India.

Mayurbhanj

The *Prajamandal* in Mayurbhanj State began to prepare itself for making the last phase of freedom struggle in the State. A *Paik Sammilani* was organised under the Presidentship of Baikuntha Sadul, a member of the Executive Committee of the *Prajamandal* to protest against the order of the State administration for confiscating *Paik Jagirs* lands when a *Paik* died having minor issues. Baikuntha Sadul was imprisoned as he defied the order of the authority to leave the State within twenty-four hours. The people including the *Paiks* and *Prajamandal* workers protested it. On 30 March 1947 thousands of people paraded on the main streets of Baripada condemning the arbitrary action of the State authorities.[212]

The *Prajamandal* in its Fourth Annual Session held at Pratapur in May 1947 adopted resolutions requesting the chief to introduce democratic form of Government, forming an interim Government of ministers duly elected by people and making election on adult franchise before the end of June 1947. But the chief denied to do so. So the executive committee of the *Prajamandal* met at Ambojoda on 30 July 1947.[213] A war council consisting of Sarat Chandra Das, Harihar Mohanty, Gour Mohan Pradhan, Ananta Rath and Prasanna Kumar Dash was formed. Agitation started and the *Praja Parisad* was boycotted. At last the Ruling Chief of Mayurbhanj accepted the proposal of the *Prajamandal* for an interim government. A ministry of three members was formed on 10 December 1947 with Sarat Chandra Das as the Chief Minister.[214]

---

210. *Utkal Prasanga*, January 1992, p. 81.

211. *Ibid.*

212. *Orissa Review*, January 1989, pp. 16-18.

213. *Ibid.*

214. *Ibid.*

Thus the qualitative leap of the type of demands made by the *Prajamandals* had shown the increasing influence of national movement on their organisation and struggle. Their demands were no more confined to some concessions of socio-economic nature or democratic and human rights; it now came of age to insist on the merger of these States with the rest of India, a realisation of wide ramification. This generalisation was not to deny the regional variations of movements of various States. Talcher, with no exception, speaks volumes on its specific character and ultimate integration with the States' peoples' movement of India and later with broader national movement of India.

◆

II

Talcher : Its Dynastic History

The feudatory State of Talcher lies between 20°52' and 21°18'N, and 84° 54' and 84°16'E with an area of 399 square miles.[1] It is the sub-divisional headquarters of Talcher Sub-division of Dhenkanal District of the modern Orissa. It is situated 64 kilometres away in the North-West of Dhenkanal.[2] It is bounded on the north by the Bamra and Pallahara States, on the east by Dhenkanal State and on the South and West by Angul. The Brahmani river traverses the State, and Talcher which contains the Chief's residence (*Raja's* palace), is picturesquely situated on the bend on its right bank.[3] The Lion's Gate of the Raja's palace overlooks the river. This small town is beautified with large and impressive gateways on many sides, plantation of trees along the road close to river Brahmani, and many good looking buildings and temples. The town proper is walled on all sides but for want of space inside, the built up area has been extended even outside the boundary walls. A branch of the Bengal-Nagpur Railway line was opened from Cuttack to Talcher in April 1926 which is now under the S.E. Railways.[4] The Talcher-Ranchi Road[5] goes by its side through Rourkela. Talcher was the headquarters of the ex-State of Talcher till the merger on 1 January 1948. According to 1991 Census the population of Talcher is 2,34,370[6].

The place commands potentials to become the very fast industrial areas of Orissa in the Rourkela-Talcher belt. The Talcher Thermal

---

1. L.E.B. Cobden-Ramsay, *op.cit.*, p. 329.
2. Department of Tourism, Government of Orissa, Tourism Directory, Orissa, Bhubaneswar, 1982, p. 174.
3. A. Mishra, *Radhanath Granthabali*, Oriya, Cuttack, 1951, pp. 451-52.
4. Orissa Records, Talcher Papers, File No. 18/45-46, Raja of Talcher to the Political Agent, Orissa States, Sambalpur, Talcher 17 November 1945 (SRT).
5. National Highway 23 which joins Cuttack-Sambalpur National Highway 42 at Banarpal, 12 kilometres away from Talcher Town.
6. Orissa Records, Talcher Papers, Census File 1991, General and Misc. No. X. 3 (OSCT) See Appendix E.

Power Station, a product of Indo-American collaboration; the Fertilizer Corporation of India, the largest coal based fertilizer plant in the world; the Heavy Water Project, a Government of India Undertaking; Rengali Dam site, a Hydro-Electric Project and the National Thermal Power Corporation, which is going to be completed soon enchance the importance of the sub-division at present. Besides, various other industries are going to be set up in this area. Above all, the Talcher Coal received attention from the very early times. Talcher has got a vital position in the world map for the existence of coal in a vast area. The *Raja* of Talcher executed a mining lease on 22 April 1921 with the former owners M/s Villiers Ltd., B.N. Railways and M.S.M. Railways mainly to meet the requirement of steam-coal of superior grade from underground mines for locomotive boilers.[7] Subsequently it was owned by National Coal Development Corporation, the first public sector coal company in India in 1956; then by Central Coalfields Ltd., then South Eastern Coalfields Ltd., and ultimately this coalfield is under the jurisdiction of Mahanadi Coalfields Ltd.[8] Now there are ten numbers of collieries named as Anant, Kalinga, Balanda, Jagannath, Bharatpur, Dera, Deulbera, Nandira, Handidhua and Lingaraj having the annual production capacity of more than twenty million tonnes. It has been estimated that coal reserve in the Talcher Coalfield is the second highest reserve amongst all Collieries in India.[9]

Dynastic History of Talcher

The history of Talcher can be traced back to 15th century A.D. The progenitor of the ruling family of Talcher was Narahari Singh who belonged to the solar dynasty.[10] He succeeded in making himself a ruler of the place in 1471 A.D. He was a scion of the family of the Suryavanshi Gajapati Kings of Orissa who ruled in the 15th-16th century A.D. According to tradition Narahari Singh was one of the five sons of Arjun Singh, the Chief of Jaipur in Rajasthan.[11] After the

7. Orissa Records, Talcher Papers, Correspondence File, 1947, State Officer in Charge of Development, Talcher to Administrator, 19 January 1948. (SRT)
8. Collected from the Memorandum given to Mr. P.A. Sangma, Minister of Coal, Government of India on his visit to Talcher on 4 February 1992 by SEC Ltd., Talcher. (OGMMCL)
9. Collected from the Memorandum given to CMD on his visit to Talcher on 8 October 1988 by SECL, Talcher. (OGMMCL)
10. G.S. Mishra, *Talcher Itihas,* Oriya, Talcher, 1934, p. 6 and Orissa Records, Sambalpur Papers, Acc. No. 970, Political Agent, Orissa Agency to Secretary to Resident, Eastern Agency, Sambalpur, D.O. No. P. 1-5, 14 February 1946. (OSA)
11. L.E.B. Cobden-Ramsay, *op.cit.*, p. 330.

death of Arjun Singh the eldest son Kural Singh succeeded to the throne. Due to fratricidal war, the other four sons Narahari Singh, Bijay Singh, Ajay Singh and Man Singh left Jaipur and came to Orissa on pilgrimage to see Lord Jagannath at Puri. In their pride of Suryavansa and Rana Thakur family to which they belonged, they failed to properly salute the then *Raja* of Puri. They were not therefore allowed to see the idol of Jagannath and were ordered by the *Raja* to be imprisoned. But Narahari with another brother could escape and fled to a place named Nadhara, near Dhenkanal State, and there established a fort under the name Bhimnagari* on the bank of river Brahmani.[12] During his arrival this *Dandapat* was very weak and was divided into many small divisions. The people were also suffering a lot under the rule of Bidyadhar Mohapatra who was the representative of the Gajapati King. The people were in search of a true and benevolent ruler when Narahari Singh succeeded in making himself the ruler of the place. He was quite brave and a great warrior too. He built there a temple and installed the idol of Ramchandi Devi which now belongs to Dhenkanal.[13] Narahari Singh is said to have ruled from 1471 to 1480.

Narahari Singh was succeeded by his son Udaynarayan Singh who ruled Bhimnagari from 1480 to 1520. He extended all possible help and assistance to the Gajapati King of Orissa against Muslim invasion for which he was bestowed the title of 'Birabar Harichandan' by the Gajapati King.[14]

Udayanarayan was succeeded by his eldest son Govind Charan who ruled Bhimnagari from 1520 to 1527. During his rule Chaitanya Deva had been to Puri to spread the cult of Vaishnavism in Orissa.[15]

The ninth ruler of this line was Padmanabha Birabar Harichandan who renamed the State as Talcher** after the name of the family Goddess

---

* Bhimnagari was one of the important places among the thirty six dandapats in Orissa at that time.

12. L.E.B. Cobden-Ramsay, *op.cit.*
13. R.C. Nanda, *Dhenkanal Itihas,* Oriya, Dhenkanal, 1929, pp. 111-12.
14. N. Senapati, *Orissa District Gazetteers,* Dhenkanal District, Cuttack, 1972, p. 59.
15. *Orissa Review,* April 1991, pp. 52-53.

** On the origin of the name of Talcher, a legend relates that in the remote past, *Raja* Padmanabha Harichandan crossed the river Brahmani on hunting expedition. Near Taleswari Devi, a hare killed the *Raja's* dog, and the *Raja* accordingly established a fort there. After sometime he was defeated by the *Khonds* of the place and fled to the forest. One day while asleep in the forest, Hingula Devi appeared to him in a dream and addressed him thus: "If you worship me and Taleswari, you will become victorious

Taleswari in 1578.[16] He had also worshipped Hingula Devi before establishing the new State.[17] He constructed many temples in the State. He ruled from 1575 to 1598 A.D. and is remembered as a pious ruler. He died at the age of 48.

Ramachandra Birabar Harichandan was the twelfth ruler of this dynasty who ruled from 1711 to 1729. Owing to his generosity and liberal administration he was being compared by his people with Ramchandra of the epic fame.[18]

The fourteenth ruler of this line was Lal Singh. His reign from 1740 to 1752 was full of problems caused by internal disturbances and by the Marathas, who were attacking on Talcher off and on to collect *peshcas* which was imposed by force. But this was denied by Lal Singh as a result of which the Marathas made plunder and burnt many villages of Talcher. Lal Singh was able to protect the State from the Marathas with the help of the *Paiks* of the nearby villages.[19]

Raja Lal Singh was succeeded by his son Krishna Chandra who came to the *Gadi* in 1752. By this time Orissa had been occupied by the Marathas in 1751 and Krishna Chandra signed a treaty acknowledging their overlordship and agreeing to pay an annual tribute of Rs. 1,000.[20] He is said to have had a fair complexion and so he was nicknamed "Nimakoli" meaning that his complexion was as fair as the Neem fruit.

The seventeenth ruler of this line was Ramachandra Mansingh Harichandan who ruled from 1766 to 1774 A.D. During his reign Orissa witnessed two great famines in 1770 and 1774 which took a heavy toll of human life.[21] Due to lack of organised measures, a large number of people suffered a lot. He died at the age of 32 without an issue.

---

over your enemies, and in that case you should name the place Talcher". The *Raja* followed this advice and took the field. During an action Hingula Devi appeared in the shape of a tiger and destroyed the opponents of the chief. After that when the *Raja* was asleep, the Devi again appeared to him in a dream, and said that it was she and not the tiger that had destroyed his opponents. She advised the *Raja* to sign his name of on a tiger's head. The *Raja* named the place Talcher and bestowed a village named Padmanavpur (Kakudi) on *Brahmans*. The emblem of the State was tiger.

16. G.S. Mishra, op. cit., p. 37 and S.B. Roy, *Adhunik Talcher*, Oriya, Talcher, 1940, pp. 11-12.
17. See Appendix F.
18. N. Senapati, *op. cit.*
19. *Orissa Review, op.cit.*
20. G.S. Mishra, *op. cit.*, p. 73.
21. *Ibid.*, p. 79.

Bhagirathi Birabar Harichandan, the nineteenth ruler of the dynasty ascended the *Gadi* in 1778 A.D. At the time of accession he was a minor. Being adopted by the ex-ruler, Bhagirathi, faced oppositions from many sides and left the State for sometime. He ruled the State under the guidance of his minister Vigneswar Raiguru for a long period till 1846.[22] Among his popular works the most important one was the Jagannath temple at Talcher which he built with huge stones. Besides, he also constructed a temple of Lord Ram Chandra at Bijigol and many more temples in different villages. Bhagirathi was very brave but arrogant for which the people were quite afraid to talk to him. He had got three queens and many kept wives.[23] For offences like theft, murder or rebellion heavy punishment like cutting of limbs, beheading and ousting from the country was given.[24] During his tenure, Lieutenant Kittoe of Geological Survey of India visited the Tributary Mahals in 1837 and accordingly a report was given on the existence of extensive bed of good quality and glistening coal at Gopal Prasad of Talcher.[25]

Bhagirathi was succeeded by Dayanidhi who devoted most of his time to the study of scriptures and religious books. The British Government had conferred on him the title 'Mahindra Bahadur' for his help to the British Government in subduing the Angul rebellion in 1847.[26] In 1854 he had performed a *Soma Jajnaya* which continued for twenty-one days and for that he was honoured with the title *Rajarshi*.[27] It was during his rule that the famine of *Na-anka* occurred in 1866, but this pious ruler took all possible measures to save the people from starvation. He ruled upto 1873 and was succeeded by Rama Chandra Birabar Harichandan.

Ram Chandra went to the *Gadi* on 9 November 1873 at the age of fourteen. He was very fond of Sanskrit literature and his court was adorned by many Sanskrit scholars. He set up a Sanskrit TOI at Talcher. He had compiled a book on the history of India in Oriya entitled

22. N. Senapati, *op.cit.*
23. G.S. Mishra, *op.cit.*, pp. 97-99.
24. *Ibid.*
25. Orissa Records, Talcher Papers, Development Scheme, File No. 1-DI-5/48, p. 26 (SRT).
26. Orissa Records, Sambalpur Papers, Acc. No. 970, Political Agent, Orissa State Agency to Resident, Eastern State Agency, Sambalpur, D.O. No. p. 1-5, 14 February 1946. (OSA)
27. G.S. Mishra, *op. cit.*, pp. 116-18.

'*Bharatara Sankhipta Itihas*' which was prescribed as a text-book in the middle vernacular classes of Orissa.[28] He was also a very religious man.

Ramachandra started his work on land settlement for the benefit of the people. In 1879 he established courts of Judicature, Accounts Section, *Tauzi, Nizarat* and insisted on regular maintenance of official rules. *Sadar* Police Station was established at Talcher and separate police stations were set up in the village areas of Srirampore, Kansamunda, Bajrakot and Gaham. A jail was constructed for the prisoners. He established the departments of Public Works, Education, Health, Excise and Forests. Besides, a hospital, a middle vernacular school and a Middle Girls' School were established through his effort. He encouraged local self-government and set up a municipality to look after the health and sanitation of Talcher Town.[29] This town was beautified by construction of *pucca* roads and road side plantation. The magnificent Lion's Gate (wheel shape) having artistic work is the symbol of his love for art and painting.[30] In 1877 he constructed the Victoria Hall, Circuit House in commemoration of the Diamond Jubilee Celebration of Queen Victoria. This ruler also took some measures for the needy people of the society. Before writing the famous Oriya poem 'Usha', Kabibar Radhanath Rai, the renowned poet of Orissa, in his dedication letter to *Raja* Ramchandra Dev Birabar Harichandan of Talcher wrote on 20 July 1888 : "I have never seen such a pious ruler elsewhere who regularly feeds a good number of beggars and destitutes from his own grannary".[31] Ramachandra died in 1891 and was succeeded by his adopted son Kishore Chandra.

Kishore Chandra was born on 9 June 1880 at Talcher. He succeeded to *Gadi* as a minor on 18 December 1891. He assumed the ruling powers on 9 June 1901.[32] He married the fourth daughter of Basudev Sudhol Dev, the *Raja* of Bamra on 27 February 1899. He was proficient in the art of music both vocal and instrumental. Besides a good player in football and circket, he was an expert horse rider.[33] He was very fond of hunting and on every Sunday he went for it. He became

28. S.B. Roy, *op.cit.*, p. 29.
29. N. Senapati, *op.cit.*, p. 60.
30. S.B. Roy, *op.cit.*
31. A. Mishra, *op. cit.*, p. 80.
32. Orissa Records, Sambalpur Paper, Acc. No.970S, Political Agent Orissa States to Secretary to Resident Eastern State, Cal.No.p.1-60, 25 November 1945. (OSA)
33. A. Mishra, *op.cit.*, pp. 487-88.

famous in hunting inside as well as outside the State. Kishore Chandra was also a writer in Oriya. Every Sunday he joined a discussion forum of poets and writers. He established a printing press known as 'Kishore Press' in Talcher and published a weekly named '*Gadajat Basini*'.[34] He himself had presided over the session of *Utkal Sammilani* in its Balasore session in 1906.[35] Kishore Chadra was nominated as a representative of Orissa States in the chamber of princes from 1923 to 1934. Again in 1942 he became a member of Chamber of Princes. He was also elected President to the Governing Body of Raj Kumar College, Raipur and continued as a member till his death.[36] During the Jubilee celebration, the chief established the George Hospital at Talcher in 1912 in commemoration of the *Durbar* of the King Emperor George V held at Delhi.[37] He established a High English School in 1913,[38] one Girls' Middle School, one Elementary Training School, a Sanskrit TOI many U.P. Schools etc. He introduced a legislative body called *Byabastha Parishad* where more than half of its members were nominated by him.[39] He set up an Executive Council and nominated three Councillors to run the administration of the State. The Chief himself was the President with his youngest son, who was the Dewan, as the Vice-President of the Council.[40] His eldest son was the sessions judge of Talcher Court. A *Dharmaadalat* was established to dispose of the cases relating to religious matters.

Kishore Chandra had beautified the town by erecting many gateways in different places. He gave a finishing touch to his residential palace building which is appreciated by many visitors. A natural Zoo called 'Rani Park' was an important pleasure garden covering an area of about 64 square kilometres which attracted many outsiders to the State.[41] Due to his efforts only, this garden was filled up with both

34. G.S. Mishra, *op.cit.*, p. 169.
35. Orissa Records, Sambalpur Papers, Acc.No. 1164S, Dewan to Secretary, E.S. Agency, Sambalpur, 9 November 1945 (OSA).
36. *Ibid.*
37. *Deshakatha,* 9 June 1931.
38. Orissa Records, Talcher Papers, File No. 13, Letter No. 543. Raja to Director, Public Instruction, Bihar and Orissa dated, The Talcher State, the 5th/15th January 1916. (SRT).
39. *Ibid.*, File No.18/45-46, Reply of Raja Hruday Chandra to Political Agent, Orissa, Sambalpur, Talcher Durbar, 17 November 1945. (SRT).
40. Orissa Records, Sambalpur Papers, Acc. No. 1164S, Talcher State Gazette, No. 6, Vol. 9 (OSA).
41. Department of Tourism, Government of Orissa, *op. cit.*

fruits and flower bearing trees. This huge park was surrounded by walls on all sides and the jungles created inside preserved different varieties of wild animals and birds from all parts of the country. Some of them had also been imported from outside the country. Inside the park, roads were laid to facilitate observation of the wild life from close quarters.[42] About 2.5 lakhs of rupees was being spent for this construction.

Kishore Chandra constructed many roads and bridges and established a post and telegraph office in his capital. In his period the collieries came into existence. He gave leases to Villiers Ltd., Madras and Southern Maratha Railways and Bengal Nagpur Railways to extract coal from the mines at Handidhua, Dera and Deulbera respectively.[43] In 1911, he appointed P.N. Bose, a Geologist and Harish Chandra Rao, a Mining Surveyor to give a detailed study of the coalfield to explore coal mines and succeeded in obtaining first class coal.[44] A railway line was constructed and in April 1926 a branch of the Bengal-Nagpur Railway was opened from Cuttack to Talcher to serve the coalfields of the State.[45] He had electricity from thermal power at Talcher Power House Field and supplied electricity to his own residential Palace and Talcher Town in 1924. After a long tenure of 54 years of reign, he died on 7 November 1945.[46]

Hrudaya Chandra, the eldested son of Kishore Chandra succeeded the *Gadi* on 7 November 1945 and assumed the charge of administration.[47] He was born on 27 February 1902. He was educated in Ravenshaw College, Cuttack. During the tenure of his father he acted as District and Sessions Judge in the State for many years.[48] Hruday Chandra was a member of Chamber of Princes. He was a good tennis player and a good shooter. He was a good horse rider and was owner of some excellent trophies for the games.[49]

The succession *Durbar* of Hruday Chandra took place on 20 March

42. A Mishra, *op.cit.*
43. S.B. Roy, *op.cit.*, p. 38.
44. Orissa Records, Talcher Papers, File No. 8, Raja, Talcher to Political Agent, Sambalpur, Letter No. 70, dated Talcher 11 May 1915. (SRT)
45. Orissa Records, Talcher Papers, File No. 18/45-46, *op. cit.* (SRT).
46. Orissa Records, Sambalpur Papers, Acc. No. 1164S, Dewan Bahadur P.C. Dev to Secretry, Eastern States Agency, Sambalpur, No. P1-60/45, 9 November 1945. (OSA).
47. Administrative Report of Talcher, 1945-46, pp. 2-3.
48. Orissa Records, Sambalpur Papers, Acc. No. 970S, *op. cit.*
49. Administrative Report of Talcher, 1945-46, *op.cit.*

1946 in which the Hon'ble Resident Mr. H.J. Todd, C.I.E. presented the *Kharita** from his excellency, the Viceroy on behalf of His Majesty the King Emperor.[50] In presenting the *Kharita* the resident, Eastern States, Orissa made a brief address to which the chief also gave a reply assuring staunch loyalty to the person and throne of His Majesty.[51] The resident on his congratulating speech said:

> "Changes are everywhere in the air but they are changes of our own seeking and it is for us to fashion them to a new and better purpose. Mankind seeks to discard the unworthy and the unsuccessful and to set up new and healthier standards of life. It is time for dedication to greater effort, to greater understanding, to greater service and above all to greater tolerance and peaceful collaboration. You have been called to play a greater part than many but you have succeed to the ancestral *Gadi* at a mature age and have had time to see and gauge for yourself the trend of affairs both within and out of the State. You are now entrusted with the destiny of the State, the welfare and entertainment of its people. I recommend to you to try and make the task a happy partnership between the Ruler and Ruled. Consult the best interests of your people and seek to command their loyal collaboration and goodwill. They are your own people, your own partners make their best interest, your first and foremost concern when I am sure they will respond in full measures for they have their citizen duties and responsibilities.
>
> I now hand over this sword in accordance with custom as a symbol of your investiture. May it rest firmly in your hand the symbol of peace as well as of justice and strength".[52]

In his reply the chief stated:

> "I fully realise that the heritage to which I have succeeded after my late father is not an easy one. If on one hand it gives power and dignity on the other it loads me with responsibility and with the care of my people. It will be my endeavour Sir, to fulfil the

---

* *Kharita* was printed in white and golden border with golden letters.

50. Orissa Records, Sambalpur Papers, Acc. No. 970S, Secretary to Political Agent of Orissa, Letter No. R 13-10/45, 26 December 1945 (OSA).

51. Administrative Report of Talcher, *op.cit.*

52. Orissa Records, Talcher Papers, Durbar for resident's visit, File No. 18/1945-46, "A short congratulatory speech delivered by the Hon'ble Resident in the occasion of the Durbar of the Ruler Talcher and Ruler's reply" (SRT).

task entrusted to me with care and consideration. I pledge myself on this solemn occasion to regard the interest, happiness and well being of people on my own and to do all in my power for their economic and moral upliftment. I want people to be proud of their State and I will be looking forward to the day when I can have their close and active association with the administration of Talcher. I have my schemes in mind but this is not the occasion to propound them.

I will be failing in my duty if I do not on this occasion request you Sir, to convey to His Majesty the King Emperor through his excellency the Crown representative that I am fully determined to maintain the tradition of the loyalty of my House and State to the Ruling House of Windsor".[53] During the rule of Hrudaya Chandra the State merged with Orissa on 1 January 1948. He died on 11 September 1970.

Until 1803 the Tributary Chiefs of Orissa were feudatories of the *Raja* of Nagpur. By that time, the British had already kept in their mind the question of the occupation of Orissa because of its strategic importance. As Orissa was situated between two British provinces of Bengal and Madras, the British authorities planned to connect both these by Orissa through occupying it. Wellesley, the Governor-General had informed to the Secret Committee of the Court of Directors on 1 August 1803 that he had already engineered a plan for the conquest of Orissa. In his report, he explained that "by the reduction of Cuttack in Orissa an affectual blow would be struck against the *Raja* of Berar's resources, the maritime territory of the Marathas in the eastern side of Peninsula of India would be secured from all intercourse with the French, a valuable addition would be made to our revenue and a strong barrier added the frontier of Bengal and the territories of Fort St. George would also be protected from interruption".[54] Consequently, Wellesley declared war against the Maratha confederacy and instructed Arthur Wellesley to destroy completely the Maratha strength without coming to any pacific settlement.[55] The war that now started between the English and Marathas is known as the Second Maratha War. The British conquest of Orissa was a part of the Second Anglo-Maratha war which commenced on 3 August 1803.[56] The objective of the

53. Orissa Records, *op.cit.*
54. *Bengal and Madras Papers* (1757-95) Vol.III, Acc. No.75(0)/PI-1/3, p.235 (OSA).
55. W.K. Thronr, *Memoir of the War in India*, London, 1818, pp. 252-55.
56. *Bengal and Madras Papers, op. cit.*

Company Government was to occupy Orissa with a little bloodshed as possible. Either by the policy of diplomacy or blackmailing, the British wanted to secure the loyalty of the feudatory chiefs of Orissa who had then the key role in Orissan politics. Meanwhile, secret survey of the area had been made and Maratha Officers had also been seduced by bribe.[57]

British military operation started from Ganjam on 8 September 1803 to occupy Orissa.[58] Without much difficulty the British with Commander Colonel Harcourt could occupy Puri on 18 September 1803, and the Maratha troops immediately evacuated Puri. After occupying Puri the British won over the *Pandas* of Jagannath Temple and promised not to interfere in the religious affairs of the Hindus.[59] Meanwhile English Captain Margaon reached Balasore from Calcutta on 21 September 1803 with his troops. At the entrance to the town the English forces were vehemently challenged by a Maratha detachment. But the British forces defeated them and the Maratha *Faujdar* of Balasore fled away towards Cuttack. During the night of 21 September 1803 the Marathas evacuated the Fort of Balasore and Captain Morgaon succeeded in occupying Balasore the next day morning after a token resistance.[60]

After making necessary arrangements for keeping the line of communication open between Ganjam and Puri, Harcourt began his military expedition towards Cuttack. The English troops reached Cuttack on 10 October 1803 after frequent engagements with the Maratha army on the way. Thus, Harcourt ordered for necessary charge and attack on the fort of Barabati which was the Headquarters of the Maratha Government.[61]

The fort of Barabati was strongly built of stone and surrounded by a wet ditch, varying from 35 to 135 feet in breadth, had only one entrance with a very narrow bridge leading over the ditch to it.[62] The batteries were placed by the night of 13 October, five hundred yards from the south face of the fort and the British troops commenced firing in the next morning. By 11 A.M. all the defences had been knocked to

57. B.C. Roy, *The Foundations of British Orissa*, Cuttack, 1960, pp. 18-20.

58. Martin, *Despatches and Minutes*, Vol. III, pp. 167-69.

59. B.C. Roy, *op. cit.*, p. 27.

60. S.C. De, *Guide to Orissan Records,* Vol.I, Cuttack, 1961, p. xxii.

61. A.K. Samal, *The Political Turmoil in Orissa : An Attempt for the Revival of Hindu Rule in the 18th Century,* unpublished Ph.D. Thesis, B.H.U., 1989, pp. 314-15.

62. L.S.S.O'Malley, *District Gazetteers of Cuttack,* Patna, 1933, p. 264.

pieces and the guns of the fort silenced. The storming party advanced to attack the fort. The bridge was quickly passed under a heavy fire from the fort but it was nearly forty minutes before the wicket was blown sufficiently open to admit one man. The English passed singly but such rapidly that notwithstanding the resistance at the inner gates, they entered with the garrison, who after a very severe loss abandoned the fort.[63] On 14 October 1803 the British troops entered the fort and took possession of it and the town. Meanwhile, there had been military action from the northern and eastern sides of the province and Orissa passed to the hands of British.[64]

Soon after the occupation of Orissa British troops were stationed at strategic places to establish law, order and discipline. Special security measures were adopted in the regions of the feudatory States. At last, the second Anglo-Maratha War came to an end by the Peace Treaty of Deogan, concluded on 17 December 1803. By this peace treaty Raghuji Bhonsla, the *Raja* of Nagpur ceded to the East India Company in perpetual sovereignty, the province of Cuttack, Puri and Balasore along with the feudatory States. He also agreed to confirm certain treaties which had been concluded in course of the war with his feudatories by the British Government. The chiefs of the Orissan States submitted to the British with the occupation of Orissa.[65] This treaty was ratified by the Governor General in Council on 9 January 1804 although the official intelligence was received in Cuttack on 14 January 1804.[66]

Thus, Orissa was conquered by the English without much resistance by the Marathas. During the course of the occupation of Orissa by the British, several of the feudatory chiefs threw off the Maratha yoke. In fact, the people of Orissa were happy to get rid of the Maratha administration.[67] The British thought that it would not be possible for them to rule the province without the feudatory chiefs. The East India Company agreed with the existing arrangement of Tributary Mahals.[68]

Treaty Engagements and Counter Engagements with the Feudatory Chiefs

Immediately after the occupation of Barabati Fort of Orissa the

63. B.C. Roy, *op.cit.*, p. 29 and R.C. Nanda, *op.cit.*, pp. 290-91.
64. *Journal of Kalinga Historical Research Society,* Vol. I, No. 4 March 1947, p. 382.
65. C.U. Aitchison, *op.cit.*, Vol.I, pp. 415-17.
66. *Ibid.*, Vol. III, Calcutta, 1863, pp. 97-99.
67. H.K. Mahtab, *History of Orissa*, Vol. II, p. 385.
68. W.W. Hunter, *History of Orissa,* Vol. II, London, 1872, p. 277.

Governor General appointed a Board of Commissioners for the affairs of Cuttack consisting of Colonel George Harcourt, John Melville and Ernest, the Magistrate of Midnapur.[69] The Board was to open negotiation with the feudatory chiefs and inducing them to acknowledge the British authority. As such, in the first instance, on 22 November 1803, treaty engagements were executed with as many as eleven States of the Tributary Mahals namely Athgarh, Baramba, Narsinghpur, Dhenkanal, Talcher, Tigiria, Hindol, Khandapara, Ranpur, Nayagarh and Nilgiri.[70] Within a little more than a year the chiefs of Angul, Banki, Daspalla and Keonjhar came forward to accept the British sovereignty and engagements were executed with these States.[71] The provision of those engagements were:

(a) The chiefs professed perpetual friendship with and loyalty to the East India Company.

(b) They were to pay to the Company's Government fixed annual tributes in specified instalments.

(c) They were to supply to the troops of the Company passing through his territories all *ressums* at fair prices.

(d) They were to depute immediate on applications, a contingent of forces of their own to assist the forces of the Government for bringing an unruly or rebellious *Raja* or any other person to subjection and such troops were to receive from the Company's Government all *ressums* and supplies at fair prices.

(e) They were not to stop or cause any hindrance to, any subject or personnel, police or revenue, of the Company's Government proceeding through their *Zamindaries* by land or water with goods or orders of the Government.

(f) They were to seize and send by undesirable *ryot* of the Comapny's Government who might take shelter within their territories.

(g) They were to deliver up any *ryot* of their territory committing depredations or crimes within the *Mughalbandi*-Government's land.

(h) They were never to exact any duty on passengers or goods passing through their territories".[72]

---

69. C.U. Aithcison, *op. cit.*, Vol. I, pp. 186-92.

70. *Ibid.*

71. *Ibid.*

72. *Ibid.*

On behalf of the East India Company, Colonel Harcourt and John Melville exchanged counter-engagements or *Qubulnama* with those chiefs, by which they acknowledged the tribute fixed in perpetuity and also assured that no further demand, however small, should be made or received from the said chief as *Nuzzur* or otherwise, promised to meet any just representation and complaints made to the Government by the *Rajas* who were loyal and obedient to them and who too were impartial in the administration of justice to all his subjects.[73]

As such engagement was made with the State of Talcher and *Qubulnama* was given to its chief Bhagirathi Birabar Harichandan. The main provisions of the engagement executed to the chief of Talcher by the East India Company's Commissioners for the Soobah of Cuttack, November 22, 1803 were:

Clause I — The annual *Peshkus* payable by the *Raja* for his *Rajgee* of the said *killah* (Talcher) is fixed in perpetuity to 6,715 *Kahuns* and *Cowrees*.

Clause II — No further demand, however, small, shall be made on the said *Raja* or received from him, as *Nuzzur* supplies or otherwise.

Clause III — The Government of the Honourable East India Company, it is well-known, is ever gracious to those *Rajahs* who are always loyal and obedient to them and constant in the impartial administration of justice to all its subjects alike and therefore in like manner extends the same impartially to the *Rajas* such as have been indicated above and seeks always their prosperity and peace. Therefore, any just representation or complaints made to the Government by the said *Rajah* of Talcher will meet with a decision in accordance with justice.

Dated 22 November, 1803

Sabun 6th, 1211

Sd/- G. Harcourt, Lt. Colonel

Sd/-J. Melville.[74]

---

73. C.U. Aithison, *op. cit.*

74. Orissa Records, Talcher Papers, Qubulnama, East India Company to Raja Bhagirathi Birabar Harichandan, Talcher, 22 November 1803. (TPRR)

After the engagement was signed there was, however, counter engagement made by the chief of Talcher, Bhagirathi Birabar Harichandan with the Honourable East India Company on the same day, 22 November 1803 where the chief acknowledged the perpetual friendship with loyalty to the East India Company and agreed to pay the stipulated tributes.[75] The counter engagement stated:

> I, Bhagirathi Birabar Harichandan of *killah* Talcher in the *Soobah* of Orissa, engage faithfully and correctly to abide by this engagement entered into by me with Honourable East India Company, as contained in the following clauses to wit:
>
> Clause I — I will always hold myself in submission and loyal obedience to the Honourable East India Company aforesaid.
>
> Clause II — I will continue to pay without demur to the said Government, as my annual *peshkush* or tribute, 6,715 *Kahuns* of *cowrees,* in three instalments as specified here below.
>
> Clause III — I will, on demand to that effect, cause any person who is an inhabitant of the *Soobah* appertaining to the Honourable Company aforesaid, and who may have fled and come into my territory, to be forthwith arrested and delivered over to the Government.
>
> Clause IV — Should any person, who is a resident in my territories, commit a crime within the limits of the *Mughalbandi,* I hereby engage, on demand to that effect, to cause such person to be arrested and delivered over to the Government authority. Moreover, I further bind myself, in case when I may possess any claim or demand on one who is an inhabitant of the *Mughalbandi*, not of my own authority to enforce such claim; but I will notify the same to the constituted authority, and will act in accordance with such orders as may issue from him.
>
> Clause V — I engage that whenever the troops of the Honourable Company's Government shall pass

75. C.U. Aitchison, *op.cit.*, Vol. II, p. 346.

through my territories, I will direct the people of my *Killah* to supply to the extent of their capability, all *russud* and supplies, which shall be sold at fair prices. Further, I will on no manner of pretext whatever, everstop or detain, or offer any let or hindrance to, any subject of the Honourable Company's Government or to any other persons whatever, who may be proceeding by land or water, with goods or orders, or with any *perwannah* on the part of the Government, through my boundaries, and with rather take care that no loss or inconvenience shall be full such parties in life or goods.

Clause VI — In case any neighbouring *Raja* or any other person whatever shall offer opposition to the said Government, I engage, on demand any without demur, to depute a contingent force of my own troops with the forces of Government for the purpose of rebuking and chasting such rebel and bringing him under the subjection of the aforesaid Government. Such contingent to receive only rations agreeably to the previously current practices, so long they shall be present.

The *Peschkus* were collected in three instalments in the month of *Cheyt, Jeyt* and *Asar*.

Dated the 22nd November, 1803

Sabun 6th, 1211 Umlee.[76]

The statistics regarding income and tributes (paid to British Government) of the State of Talcher for the year 1803 was:

"1. Name of the Killah - Talcher

2. *Peshkus* or Tribute to Government (in rupees) - 974-10-16-3

3. Income of the State (in rupees) - 12,000

4. Area in Sq. miles - 250"[77]

76. C.U. Aitchison, *op.cit.*

77. G.S. Mishra, *op.cit.*, p. 112.

Though the fixation of tribute was not arbitrary, yet the area of the States was not taken into consideration. While a small State like Athgarh with an area of 168 square miles paid 28,111 *Kahan* (Rupees 2,800), a big State like Mayurbhanj with an area of 4,263 square miles paid only 23,125 *Kahans*.[78] The tributes were much less than their real earning. W.W. Hunter observed, "When we became possessors of the country, we found that if we were to live in peace with the hill chiefs, we must tax them very lightly".[79]

By the regulation 12 of 1805, passed on September 5, 1805, these feudatory States including the State of Talcher were exempted from the operation of the British laws and regulations. The regulation also exempted the territory of Mayurbhanj from the operation of the British laws and regulations like other States. It was left to the Collector of Cuttack to conclude a settlement with the chief of Mayurbhanj on the principle accepted by other chiefs.[80] All these *Garjats* or *Tributary Mahals* were kept under direct supervision of British authority at Cuttack. The chiefs of these Tributary Mahals[81] enjoyed full freedom in their internal administration. They had to act as subordinate allies under the supreme authority of the British. According to the treaties they were not to allow any troops of the enemy to pass through their territories and would behave them as their own enemies. By the regulation of 14 of 1805 the Judge-*cum*-Magistrate of Cuttack remained in formal charge of these Tributary Mahals.[82]

Administrative Relations of the British with the Tributary Mahals

The administrative relations between the British and the Tributary chiefs including Talcher was liberal. The British authority realised that it would be difficult to execute law and order in the feudatory States due to its geographical obstacles of inaccessible jungles and hilly regions whose people were considered as rude, rustic and uncivilised race. The chiefs were left free to rule according to their own administrative system. The British Government avoided to interfere

78. C.U. Aitchison, *op.cit.*, Vol. I., p. 108.
79. W.W. Hunter, *op.cit.*, Vol. II, p. 413.
80. Bengal Judicial (Civil) Proceedings, No. 32 of September 5, 1805, Regulation 12 of 1805. (OSA)
81. (1) Angul, (2) Athgarh, (3) Banki, (4) Baramba, (5) Dhenkanal, (6) Daspalla, (7) Hindol, (8) Khandapara, (9) Keonjhar, (10) Mayurbhanj, (11) Nilgiri, (12) Narsinghpur, (13) Nayagarh, (14) Ranpur, (15) Talcher and (16) Tigiria.
82. Bengal Judicial (Civil) Proceedings, No. 34 of September 5, 1805, Regulation 14 of 1805. (OSA)

in the internal affairs of the States as the Government was busy in consolidating their possessions in other parts of the country. So they desired to leave the administration of the States in the hands of their respective chiefs. They also defended the British from the attacks of the Maratha in the frontiers.[83]

In 1805 Regulations regarding the administration of revenue, criminal and civil justice passed for the Tributary Mahals (including Talcher) were specially exempted from the operation of these British Laws. By the above regulation the Judge-*cum*-Magistrate of Cuttack remained in formal supervision of the Tributary Mahals. The feudatory chiefs of the Tributary Mahals enjoyed full freedom and the British Government avoided intervention in their internal administration. Of course, this status they enjoyed not as sovereign with absolute rights but as subordinate allies under the supreme authority of the British Government.[84]

The British authorities had not taken any bold step against some feudatory chiefs who did not honour the engagements. The chiefs of Narsinghpur, Hindol and Tigiria were defaulters of payment of their tributes to British Government during the year 1804. But no action was taken against them and only *Parwanas* were issued to them.[85] In 1805 the chiefs of Talcher, Dhenkanal, Athgarh and Hindol imposed heavy duties on the merchants of Cuttack town who were passing through their States. But this system was not there in the engagements and as such the merchants submitted a petition to the Judge-*cum*-Magistrate of Cuttack. But he only issued the chiefs mere *Parwanas* where they were asked not to levy such heavy duties on the merchants of Cuttack.[86]

Though the policy of the British was non-intervention in the internal affairs of the Tributary Mahals, yet it could not become silent observer regarding any internal disturbances inside the States. In case of succession, the primary aim of the British authority was to preserve peace and tranquility in those territories by solving the succession problem.

In 1812 troubles arose over the question of succession in Angul.

83. J.N. Patnaik, *Feudatory States of Orissa,* Vol. I, Allahabad, 1985, pp. 122-25.

84. *Ibid.*

85. Orissa Records, Board's Proceedings, Acc. No. 3, C. Grome to Thomas Fortesque, 18 April 1805. (OSA)

86. *Ibid.*

Jaraor Singh's brother Jay Singh became the *Raja* of Angul after the death of the former in 1811. Only a few months after, he was murdered by one of his brothers, Pritvi Singh. The latter took possession of Angul. Subsequently his right of succession was challenged by Loknath Singh, an illegitimate son of Jaraor Singh. He appealed to the Government to consider his case and accused Pritvi Singh of the murder of his father.[87] The Government in reply appointed a Commission to investigate the matter with John Richardson, the Settlement Commissioner and W.C. Ward, the Judge and Magistrate of Cuttack as its members. The Commission asked Pritvi Singh to appear before them and clear himself of the charge of murder. But he did not appear before the Commission. The Governor-General in Council ordered that if Pritvi Singh did not attend their court within a specified period, all the rights, title and interests which he might possess in Angul should be confiscated by the Government.[88] Even then he did not appear before the Commission and the Estate was confiscated. To make the example impressive and instructive to others, *Parwanas* were circulated to all *Garjat* Chiefs. For full publicity a copy of the order was put up at the office of every police *darogah* throughout the British possession in Orissa.[89] However, by a subsequent decision, the confiscation order was withdrawn and Somanath Singh, a fourteen year old boy of the royal family, was put in possession of Angul.[90] Since he was a minor the Government appointed a guardian to collect revenue, manage the judicial matters and exercise the powers of the hand of police of the *Mahal* until the *Raja* came of age.[91]

There was a dispute over succession in Dhenkanal and the Government had to intervene to settle the matter in 1814. In that year the Government received information regarding atrocious crimes committed by its chief. The Magistrate of Cuttack was directed to take action. The Chief of Dhenkanal was acquitted but fined for inflicting injuries on some of his subjects.[92]

87. Orissa Records, Boards' Proceedings, Acc. No.8, Edward to W.B. Bayley, 9 October 1815. (OSA)
88. *Ibid, op.cit.*, Acc. No. 183, J. Richardson to G. Dowdeswell, 7 September 1814.
89. *Ibid.*
90. *Gadajat,* Commemoration Volume, 1986, pp. 59-60.
91. *Ibid.*
92. J.N. Patnaik, *op.cit.*, Vol. I, p. 129.

In such circumstances, the Governor-General Lord Moria made a special arrangement for the management of the Tributary Mahals of Orissa. He established the Office of the 'Superintendent of the Tributary Mahals of Orissa' which would check the misconduct of the rulers and would give correct information about the States to enable the British Government for introduction of good adminsitration there.[93] The Judge and Magistrate of Cuttack was entrusted with the duties of the Superintendent with a separate allowance of Rs.500.00 per month. George Oswald became the first incumbent of the new office on 10 February 1814.[94] This was the first effort on the part of the Government to check and supervise the affairs of the Tributary Chiefs. The main task of the Superintendent was to prevent any possible crime committed by the Tributary Chiefs. If any Tributary Chief failed to maintain law and order in his *Mahal,* the Superintendent could take over the administration of the concerned State and manage through an alternative.[95] In fact, this was the biggest threat to the power and position of the Tributary Chiefs and their estates were brought under close supervision.

The non-interference policy of the British Government continued upto 1839-40. With the assumption of A.J.M. Mills as the Commissioner and Superintendent of Tributary Mahals there began a period of vigorous action and interference in the affairs of the Tributary Mahals. In 1840 Rules were framed for the administration of civil and criminal justice in the States by A.J.M. Mills.[96] However, the Government desired that there should be certain norms and code of conduct fixed for the Tributary Chiefs so that they might be guided by them.

By these rules the Chiefs were, among other things, prohibited from exercising the powers of life and death, and from allowing the practice of *Sati* and human sacrifice. In 1842 all the States including Talcher accepted to suppress *Sati.*[97]

A.J.M. Mills who was the Commissioner and Superintendent of the Tributary Mahals was in favour of the policy of intervention in the affairs of Tributary Mahals. Intervention being the settled policy of the

93. K.M. Patra, *Orissa under the East India Company,* New Delhi, 1971, pp. 283-84.
94. Orissa Records, Board's Proceedings, Acc. No.183, G. Dowdeswell to O.G. Oswald, 10 February 1814. (OSA)
95. L.E.B. Cobden-Ramsay, op.cit., pp. 25-26.
96. See Appendix G.
97. C.U. Aitchison, *op.cit.*, Vol. II, p. 323.

Company's Government, A.J.M. Mills made its drastic application as a solution to the problem of misgovernment or disloyalty only in two cases. By this recommendation the State of Banki was confiscated in 1840 because of misgovernment and several atrocious murders committed by the Chief. Similarly, the State of Angul was annexed in 1848 on the grounds of misgovernment and disloyalty of its Chief.[98] We can discuss here on the annexation of Angul as it lies in the border of Talcher State.

Raja Somnath Singh, the son of Gopinath Singh of Angul, was considered by the British authorities as a very proud and obstinate ruler. He ascended the *Gadi* on 3 October 1814 and was found to have managed his estate peacefully till 1831 A.D. It was after 1831 he repeatedly disobeyed British instruction in handing over rebel leaders of the Ghumsar uprising. Besides he entered into serious hostilities with the neighbouring rulers of Dhenkanal, Athmallik, Hindol, Boud and Dasapalla. He defied the order of payment of compensation of Rs.1450.00 to the *Raja* of Dasapalla in the event of his attack on several villages of that State.[99] In January 1837 he also instigated the murder of six persons for which the British Government ordered him to hand over the culprits, but he did not pay any attention to it.[100] His active support to the rebels, Dora Bisoyee and Chokra Bisoyee, the heroes of Ghumsar rebellion, seriously annoyed the authorities. He was repeatedly asked to capture and make over the rebels to the British authorities. Under pressure he arranged the surrender of Dora Bisoyee only.[101] He was secretly helping Nabaghan Kahnar and Chakra Bisoyee in mobilising the *Khonds*.[102] When the suspicions of the British authorities mounted against him he was asked to report at Cuttack which was disobeyed by him. Repeated defiance of orders and insubordination compelled the authorities to depose Somanath Singh and order for the annexation of Angul in 1845.[103] Somnath Singh, who fled away from the palace on hearing the British march, was finally captured in February 1848 and kept in Hazaribagh prison on the ground

98. G. Rayguru, *Angul Itihas*, Oriya, Cuttack, 1986, pp. 76-77.

99. Orissa Records, Board's Proceedings, Acc. No. 134, A.J.M. Mills, Minute on Tributary Mahals, 23 January 1847, pp. 1-26.

100. *Ibid.*, Acc. No.53(Jud.) Henry Ricketts to Secretary to Government, 20 February 1837.

101. *Ibid.*, Acc. No. 134 *op.cit.* and Gadajat, *op.cit.*, p. 61.

102. L.E.B. Cobdon-Ramsay, *op.cit.*, p. 24.

103. R.P. Mohapatra, *Military History of Orissa*, Vol. 55, New Delhi, 1987, p. 169.

of several alleged cirminal charges. The State of Angul was finally confiscated.[104]

Thus the policy of intervention of A.J.M. Mills brought order and tranquility in the Tributary Mahals. After his departure in 1847 again the policy of non-intervention continued and the atmosphere in the States was calm and quiet. In 1855 the Superintendent of Tributary Mahals was empowered to refrain the chiefs from granting rent-free lands of their *Mahals* to their relations and dependants.[105]

The administrative policy of the Company Government continued with this range of vision till the Great Upsurge of 1857. The upsurge was destined to bring a good number of changes. The Chiefs of Mayurbhanj and Keonjhar rendered some good services to the British during the period and subsequently they were conferred with the titles of *'Maharaja'* by the Government.[106] The Government became more sensitive and realised that without the support of the Chiefs, a country so huge as India could not be governed. The Tributary Chiefs were guaranteed full protection from the British Government and the Government had to make some kind of compromise as it thought that the fate of the millions living under the feudatory Chiefs could not be left in the hands of the uneducated and irrational rulers.[107]

The Governor-General of India granted *Sanads* to the Chiefs of the Tributary Mahals in 1862 and guaranteed them the right of adoption. This year the chief of Talcher received a *Sanad* of adoption.[108] In 1874 the hereditary title of '*Raja*' was conferred on the Chiefs of the Tributary Mahals by a *new Sanad*.[109] On 21 May 1874, Ramachandra Birabar Harichandan, the Chief of Talcher got the title of *Raja* through a *Sanad* issued to him by Northbrook, the then Viceroy and Governor-General of India.[110]

---

104. Orissa Records, Board's Proceedings, Acc. No. 99, F. Gouldsbury to Government of Bengal, No. 270, 24 February 1848. (OSA)
105. K.M. Patra, *op.cit.*, pp. 314-15.
106. Orissa Records, Board of Revenue Proceedings (Pol.) Acc. No. 172, G.F. Cockburn to Secretary to Government of Bengal, 25 May 1858. (OSA)
107. K.C. Jena, *The Ascendancy of the British Raj in Orissa,* Calcutta, 1982, p. 142.
108. Orissa Records, Sambalpur Papers, Acc. No. 970S, Political Agent, Orissa States Agency to Secretary to Resident, Eastern State Agency, Sambalpur, D.O. No.P.1-5, 14 February 1946. (OSA)
109. C.U. Aitchison, *op. cit.*, Vol. II, p. 323.
110. Orissa Records, Talcher Papers, Sanad, Acc. No.439, 21 March 1975. OSA). See Appendix H.

On 25 November 1874 in a special gathering of the Tributary Chiefs of Orissa at Cuttack the Viceroy promised to give full co-operation with them if they would not put the British-Government in difficulty. He advised the Chiefs to educate their subjects, to collect reasonable rent, to make economic development, build roads, build boats, and keep their affairs in their control. They should regard the Commissioner as the friend, philosopher and guide and to follow his decisions.[111] But a change in their relation with the British took place when in 1882 the Secretary of States for India in Council decided in accordance with the decision of the Calcutta High Court that the feudatory States of Orissa did not form the British India.[112] A special Act, called the Tributary Mahals of Orissa Act, XI of 1893, was passed to indemnify certain persons and to validate acts done by them in the *Mahals*, and to admit of certain sentences passed there being carried into effect in British India.[113]

New *Sanads* were granted to the Chiefs on 27 October 1894 defining their status, powers and position relating to the British Government.[114] The same day the chief of Talcher *Raja* Kishore Chandra Dev also received the said *Sanad* from Elgin, the Viceroy and Governor-General of India. It stated:

(i) You *Raja* Kishore Chandra, son of *Raja* Ramachandra Birabar Harichandan, are hereby formally recognised as the feudatory Chief of Talcher State, and you are permitted, as heretofore, to generally administer the territory of the said Talcher State, subject to the condition hereinafter prescribed. In like manner your heirs and successors shall become entitled to your privileges and liable to your obligations, provided that no succession shall be valid until it has been recognised by His Excellency the Viceroy and Governor General in Council.

(ii) You shall continue to pay the tribute or *Peshkush* of Rupees one thousand and thirty-nine, *annas* ten and paise five per annum which you and your predecessors have heretofore paid.

(iii) You shall try in your courts all criminal cases occurring in your territory, except (a) those in which Europeans are concerned, and (b) Leions Offences such as murder, homicide,

111. K.C. Jena, *op. cit.*, p. 143.

112. C.U. Aitchison, *op. cit.*

113. L.E.B. Cobden-Ramsay, *op. cit.*, p. 27.

114. *Ibid.*

dakaiti, robbery, and torture. You shall refer the cases excepted above for the disposal to the Superintendent of the Tributary Mahals or to such of his assistants as he may indicate. Sentences passed by you on criminal offenders shall be regulated by the instructions issued from time to time for your guidance by his Honour the Lt. Governor of Bengal, and shall exceed, unless His Honour is pleased to entrust you with more extensive powers, in which case you shall be entitled to exercise such further powers in the manner, to the extent, and subject to the condition, if any, in the case of fines a sum of one thousand rupees and in the case of whipping, thity stripes. All orders passed by you in criminal cases shall be subject to revision by the Superintendent to whom you shall send the records of any case for which he may call.

(iv) You shall deliver up any offenders from British or other territory, who may take refuge in your State. You shall aid British officers who may pursue criminals into your territory, and in the event of offenders from your own State taking refuge in British or other territory, you shall make a representation on the matter to the authorities concerned.

(v) You shall administer justice fairly and impartially to all alike.

(vi) You shall recognise and maintain the rights of all your people, and you shall on no account oppress them or suffer them to be in any way oppressed.

(vii) You shall levy to transit duties on grain, merchandise on any article of commerce passing your State.

(viii) You shall consult the Superintendent of the Tributary Mahals in all important matters of administration, and comply with his wishes. The settlement and collection of the land-revenue, the imposition of taxes, the administration of justice, arrangements connected with excise, salt and opium, the concessions of mining, forest and other rights, disputes arising out of any such concessions and disputes in which other States are concerned, shall be regarded as special important matters, and in respect of them you shall at all times conform to such advice as the Superintendent of the Tributary Mahals may give you.

(ix) The right to catch elephants in your State is granted to you as personal concession and as a matter of favour, but this concession is liable to withdrawal whenever it may seem desirable either on account of abuse or for other reasons, and it will necessarily be granted to your successor.

(x) All questions as to boundaries between your State and the British territory will be dealt with by the Superintendent of the Tributary Mahals or such other officer as His Honour the Lt. Governor of Bengal may appoint either generally or specially, in that behalf, with two assessors, one to be appointed by yourself and the other by His Honour the Lt. Governors, unless in any such case you should prefer that the question should be decided by such Superintendent, or other officer alone, in which case the question shall be referred for his decision accordingly.

Elgin,
Simla — Viceroy and
The 27 October, 1894 — Governor-General of India.[115]

On 12 October 1908 revised *Sanads* were issued to the States. It widened the scope of the ruler's power by replacing the limitations in the criminal powers of the rulers. Even since that year the sole restriction on the powers in criminal justice consisted in an obligation to refer to the political authorities any sentence of death for confirmation. The Chief of Talcher Kishore Chandra received the same.[116] Some changes were made in this *Sanad.* The definite limitations of criminal powers laid down in the *Sanad* of 1894 was replaced by a clause requiring the chief to conform to the instruction issued from time to time by the Lt. Governor of Bengal, and the clause of that *Sanad* whereby the right to catch the elephants was granted as a personal concession was deleted; arrangements for catching elephants, being included in the matters on which the chiefs were required to conform to advice. The designation of the Officer whom the Chiefs were to consult was changed from "Superintendent of the Tributary Mahals" to "Commissioner of Orissa Division".[117]

On 15 May 1915 the Viceroy and Governor General of India issued new Sanads to the feudatory States and also to Talcher Chief

---

115. C.U. Aitchison, *op.cit.*, p. 392.

116. Orissa Records, Talcher Papers, Acc. No.437 of 27 March 1975, Sanad, granted to Raja Kishore Chandra by Viceroy and Governor General of India (OSA).

117. Orissa Records, Talchar Papers, *op. cit.*

Kishore Chandra.[118] This was issued after the separation of the province of Bihar and Orissa from the province of Bengal. This *Sanad* was similar to that granted in 1908 except that the name of Lt. Governor of Bihar and Orissa in Council took the place of that Lt. Governor of Bengal.[119]

On 26 February 1937 the Viceroy and Governor General of India issued a revised *Sanad* to the Chief of Talcher.[120] The *Sanad* recognised the Chief as autonomous ruler of his principality with defined criminal jurisdiction. The existing restriction as the judicial and administrative powers of the State of Talcher was modified in the new document. The Viceroy has assured the Chief that so long he remained loyal to the crown, the British Government would continue to support the State. In place of the Lt. Governor of Bihar and Orissa in Council the Agent to Governor-General would be in charge of consultation regarding law and justice in the State. The State Chief was also authorised to suppress crimes in the State.[121] Thus by 1937 the once tributary and feudatory chiefs, the feeble remnants of pre-British feudalism were raised to the status of princehood and became full-fledged autocrats in the internal matters of their States.[122] Thus Talcher enjoyed full criminal and civil powers. Perhaps the new *Sanads* were necessitated after the implementation of the Government of India Act, 1935, by which a limited popular government came into being on the borders of the princely States which along with the rising tempo of national movement in the country as a whole and the State people's movement in particular was a threat to the stability of the fedual order with which was linked the continuance of the British rule in India. These *Sanads* were issued to the Chiefs of the feudatory States regarding rules and regulations of the administration. But the Chiefs of Talcher never abided by the '*Sanad*'. It is said that Kishore Chandra the Chief of Talcher ruled on his own throughout his life in spite of the *Sanads* given to him in 1915 and 1937.[123] They only knew how to please the Superintendents or the

---

118. Orissa Records, Talchar papers, *op. cit*, Acc. No. 435, Dated 21 March 1975. (OSA)
119. *Ibid.*
120. Orissa Records, Sambalpur Papers, Acc. No. 970S, Political Agent Orissa State Agency to Secretary to resident East. St. Agency, Sambalpur, D.O. No. p. 1-5, Dated 14 February 1946. (OSA)
     See Appendix I
121. Orissa Records, Talcher Papers, Acc. No. 436, dated 19 March 1975. (OSA)
122. P.K. Jena, *Orissa, A New Province,* Calcutta, 1988, p. 206.
123. Orissa Records, Sambalpur Papers, Acc. No. 1164S, *op. cit.*, (OSA).

Political Agents who were in charge of the State affairs. People had nothing to say as they were mortally afraid of being imprisoned by the Chief.

Although, the chiefs like Bhagirathi Harichandan, Dayanidhi, Ramchandra and Kishore Chandra had accepted the modernisation measures introduced by the British Government after its occupation of Orissa in 1803, Kishore Chandra in particular, tacitly introduced some new ideas in the State during his tenure. An *Anathashrama* or Orphanage was opened during his time in 1936 in Talcher. Preference in admission was given to the young beautiful women and the chief took personal interest of the inmates. But the entire cost, including the marriage expenses of the girls, was raised from the people who paid nine paise per rupee of the annual rent for this purpose. An original receipt had been filed before the State Enquiry Committee to prove it.[124] The Chiefs supported new revenue settlement and as such imposed new land taxes on the peasantry already groaning under financial burdens and feudal obligations. In the name of benevolent work huge amount of money in the form of tax was collected from the people. In the second session of the Orissa States Peoples' Conference held at Cuttack, in his Presidental Address, Dr. Pattabhi Sitaramayya referring to the internal condition of the States said:

"You are the representatives of 26 Indian States in Orissa covering an area of about 30,000 square miles and ranging in size and importance from a State like Mayurbhanj covering an area of 4,243 square miles and with a population of 8,86,745 and an income of Rs.26,60,000 to a small State like Tigiria with an area of 47 square miles, a population of 24,680 and an annual income of Rs. 2,35,000.[125] It is a well known fact that a certain modified form of slavery still continues in the States. There is also the system of forced labour, trade monopolies and interference in day-to-day administration prevalent in States all over and those in Orissa are no exception to this practice".[126]

The Chiefs of the States supported westernization by introducing British educational policy in the State and liberally donated for educational developments outside the State. These rulers adopted new

124. *Orissa States Enquiry Committee Report*, p. 108.

125. The Talcher State Administrative Report of 1935-36 shows that with an area of 399 square miles and with a population of 69,702 the annual income of Talcher was Rs.6,57,114-5-4.

126. *The Observer*, 23 June 1937. Extracted from the Presidential Address.

economic measures like construction of roads and gateways and beautified the State of Talcher which were in noway radical to ameliorate the socio-economic condition of the peasantry. The outward reformative activities like organising the army, police, judicial system, jails and administrative system in a way helped the growth of semi-capitalist development, a policy of the British albeit incomplete and coupled with feudal order, because without agrarian prosperity these measures were hollow. Above all, in the name of reformation the people were exploited both physically and economically. The administrative apparatus of the State was used by the rulers to that end throughout the entire history of Talcher.

◆

III

Administrative Structure of the State

The Chief

The Chief of the feudatory State of Talcher was known as *Raja*. He was the fountain head of all sources of power like all the feudal chiefs all over the world. Power was centred on the crown. The post of *Raja* was hereditary and he was ruling under 'the Divine Theory of Kingship'. He was the head of the Government. The heir-apparent was his eldest son or the *Jubaraj* who used to succeed him. The *Raja* was accepted as the State itself, his will was law and his powers were absolute. He was, what Louis XIV of France said: "I am the State". It was known that the king committed no error and he was the moving God. The British Government issued '*Sanad*'[1] to the *Raja* regarding the States' administration but the Chiefs went on their own way. Raja Kishore Chandra ruled on his own throughout his life in spite of the subsequent *Sanads* in 1917 and 1937 issued to him.[2] Though the

---

1. Orissa Records, Talcher Papers, Acc. No. 436, dated 19 March 1975. (OSA)

   Here are the relevant clauses of the *Sanad* issued to *Raja* Kishore Chandra Dev Birabar Harichandan of Talcher by the Viceroy and Governor-General of India on 26 February 1937.

   "1. ....

   2. ....

   3. That you shall do your utmost to suppress crimes of all kinds in your State.

   4. That you shall administer justice fairly and impartially to all alike.

   5. That you shall recognise and maintain the rights of all your people and on no account oppress them or suffer them to be in anyway oppressed and that in particular, you shall charge yourself personally with the welfare of the aboriginal population of your State.

   6. That you shall act in accordance with such advice as may be given to you by the Agent to the Governor General, Eastern States, or such other Political Officer as may be vested with authority in this behalf by His Excellency the Viceroy".

2. Orissa Records, Sambalpur Papers, Acc. No.1164S, *op. cit.*

people were aware of the '*Sanad*' they could not raise their voice against the *Raja*. Because of the Princes Protection Act, the people were mortally afraid of being imprisoned if they would act against the *Raja*. Moreover, the rulers knew quite well that under the condition of growing anti-imperialist feeling and consequent nationalist movement, the British Indian Government would not antagonise them. It emboldened them to care a little for British guidelines or *Sanads*. Thus the *Raja* was the supreme authority in exercising powers to issue orders and provide administrative arrangements.

The Raja was the final authority of the State in all matters such as Judiciary, Executive and Social Affairs etc.[3] Any order issued from the office of the *Raja* of Talcher was considered as the order of the *Durbar*. The court presided over by him was the Supreme Court of Talcher. The decision of the *Raja* was considered as final.[4] In order to perpetuate his position he used to show favours either in the form of cash or otherwise influential persons in different professions such as laywers, poets, writers, artists and travellers who praised the *Raja* lavishly during their tour to the State.[5] They went on praising the *Raja's* administration ignoring his loopholes. The British Government never wanted to interfere in the *Raja's* affair because they were the patrons of the British regime in India. The Chiefs of the State generally kept themselves aloof from the common mass with whom they had hitherto mixed freely and not infrequently had even marriage relations. Thus, they thought themselves to be in the highest position in the State and looked down upon the subjects as their mere vassals.[6] Even, general vehicles of commoners could not run on the road where the same of royal household were running. Thus, there was gradual widening of gulf between the rulers of the State and their subjects. The people of this State could not meet the Chief directly for any of their grievances. On account of education that the rulers of Talcher received and the behaviour that was expected of them by the paramount power made them to lose any contact with the people. They only ran after winning the favour of the political department of the British Government and for that they mixed freely with the Europeans who, on the contrary never took Indian rulers as equal to them in any way. Even natives of the highest rank never came into the presence of officials but with an inward fear and trembling. These feudal lords posed themselves as the

3. Talcher State Manual, 1937, p.1.
4. *Ibid.*
5. P.M. Pradhan, *Muktipathe Sainik, Oriya,* Cuttack, 1979, Part-I, p. 37.
6. *Ibid.*, pp. 48-49.

most loyal friends of the British which would give them an exalted status to them before their subjects. Prince Hrudaya Chandra had visited England and almost all the countries of Europe in 1938.[7] *Raja* Kishore Chandra remained absent in the State and visited a good number of places in India and outside India on hunting purpose.[8] Hunting was his greatest pleasure. Visiting places of pilgrimages was their hobby.[9] To maintain a status and to show their equal status with the other *Maharajas* of Indian States, they used to be a member of Chamber of Princes at the cost of their own people. For this purpose a huge amount was spent, the burden ultimately was borne by the subjects.[10]

For their own interest and safety of the throne, the Chiefs of Talcher were prepared to go to any extent. Such a case arose during the rule of Dayanidhi Harichandan when the British occupied Angul in 1848. Dayanidhi gave both physical and monetary help to the British and went against the Chief of Angul which lies on the border of Talcher area. Because of the assistance he was rewarded with the title of '*Mahindra Bahadur*', a Khilat and an elephant.[11] Likewise, the title of '*Raja Bahadur*' was conferred on Kishore Chandra in 1942 by the British Government for his assistance to the British Government during August Revolution of 1942.[12] He had suppressed with strong hands the revolution which was taken over by the *Prajamandal* workers at Talcher. This State continued to give all possible help from all its sources to the British war efforts in the Second World War during the reign of Hrudaya Chandra. It goes without saying that the help rendered was at the cost of the people of Talcher.[13] *Pattayat* Pramod Chandra, on the other hand, was the *de facto* ruler during his father's tenure. Even, after the death of his father, he continued to render all possible help to the British at the cost of the people of Talcher. For this, in a function of Talcher *Durbar,* the Resident, Eastern States Agency awarded him the badge and title of '*Dewan Bahadur*' on 20 March 1946.[14]

---

7. Administrative Report of Talcher State, 1945-46, p. 2.
8. G.S. Mishra, *op. cit.*, pp. 159-65.
9. *Ibid.*
10. Orissa Records, Talcher Papers, Raja Talcher to Deputy Secretary Chamber of Princes, New Delhi, Contribution of Rs.1600 annual fee towards Chamber of Princes, letter No. 332/15 November 1947 File No. 2, 1942.
11. G.S. Mishra, *op. cit.*, p. 116 and L.E.B. Cobdon-Ramsay, *op. cit.*, p. 330.
12. Orissa Records, Sambalpur Papers, Acc. No. 970, Political Agent Orissa to Secretary to Resident, Est. States Agency, Sambalpur, D.O. No. p. 1-5, 14 February 1946.
13. Administrative Report of Talcher State, 1945-46, p. 4.
14. Orissa Records, Talcher Papers, Preparation of Talcher Durbar for Resident's Visit, File No. 18/45-46. (TPRR)

Officials

All the officials of Talcher State were appointed, dismissed, suspended, degraded, promoted or transferred according to the sweet will of the Chief, who was the head of the State.[15] Most of the posts of officers of higher ranks were reserved either for the royal family or the families who were very close to the Chief. There was no fixed cadre. The system of pension on retirement was not generally introduced. There was no written principle of recruitment of public servants. It resulted in rampant nepotism in recruitment. Many a time, people were able to hold high posts by bribery or considerations other than merit. Unqualified and ill-suited persons came to occupy positions due to which the State administration suffered. The employees were ill-paid, which indirectly induced them for corruption and bribery. The whole administrative machinery was sterile, lacked dynamism and backward looking.

The Enquiry Committee of Orissa States vividly described the composition of Talcher State *Durbar* as follows :

1.	The Ruler	-	The Head of the State
2.	*Jubaraj,* the Eldest Son.	-	The Sessions Judge
3.	*Pattayat*, the Youngest Son.	-	The State Magistrate, Controlling Officer of all Departments and Revenue Officer.
4.	One brother of the Ruler.	-	Assistant Revenue Officer
5.	Two cousin brothers of the Ruler.	-	Tahsildars
6.	One cousin brother of *Raja*.	-	Chief Police Officer
7.	Another cousin brother of *Raja*	-	Excise Officer
8.	Another cousin brother of *Raja*	-	Forest Officer
9.	Another cousin brother of *Raja*	-	Asst. Settlement Officer[16]

15. Talcher State Manual; Talcher 1916, Oriya, Part I, p. 5.

16. *Orissa States Enquiry Committee Report,* p. 101 and p. 113.

Besides the above officials, some of the other attractive posts were held by the people who were very close to the Chief. People from the rural areas could not avail of these chances though they had got higher qualification, in some cases, in comparison to many incumbents. The ruler himself was under-matric, *Jubaraj* was undergraduate, the *Pattayat* was undermatric, Chief Police Officer and others were having middle English Standard Education. Thus, the administration in this State was almost a family affair.[17] Keshab Chandra Samant, one of the cousins of the ruler, though was an undermatriculate, was appointed as Deputy Superintendent of Police in 1934-35 when Dasarathi Mishra, a matriculate was already in service as a Police Inspector on the State.[18]

Justice

There was no justice inside the State. In the name of justice there was frequent deviation. There was no rule of law. Separation of power which to some extent had been introduced in British India was not there. The *Raja* of Talcher was the final authority of the State in all matters such as judiciary, executive and social affairs.[19] The court he presided over was the Supreme Court of the State. He could enforce any law or Act and add, amend, alter and cancel any Act or law.[20] The Annual Administrative Report of Talcher State showed the administration of justice during the year 1928-29 in the following manner.

The *Raja* was the sessions judge. *Jubaraj* Hrudaya Chandra Dev was the State Magistrate and Assistant Session Judge dealing with civil suits. *Pattayat* Pramod Chandra, the Assistant Magistrate exercised the power of first class magistrate. He tried civil suits upto the value of Rs.500. He was the Revenue Officer as well as Registrar of the State dealing with executive matters. Damodar Mishra was the Secretary to the *Raja* who held the post of the First Class Magistrate (*ex-officio*). *Pandit* Kapileswar Patjoshi, the Chief Priest was also an *ex-officio* Third Class Magistrate who presided over the Court of *Dharmadhyakhya*. Mahesh Chandra Samant, an *ex-officio* Second Class Magistrate was deputed as an Assistant Settlement Officer. The Court of *Jubaraj* was the original Court of the State. All criminal, civil and important revenue cases were originally filed in his court. The Assistant

17. S.B. Roy, *op. cit.*, p. 108.
18. Administrative Report of Talcher State, 1934-35, p. 12.
19. Talcher State Manual, 1937, pp. 2-3.
20. *Ibid*.

Magistrate and the *ex-officio* Magistrate tried such criminal and civil cases as were transferred to the file of *Jubaraj*. But generally major portion of the work was executed by the *Jubaraj* and his assistant, the *Pattayat*. The *Jubaraj* also heard the appeals against the decision of the Third Class Magistrate, and the *Dharmadhyakhya*. Above all the Chief used to hear the appeals from the courts of the *Jubaraj*, the *Pattayat* and the Secretary of the Chief.[21] Sometimes in a case when a person was not convicted by the lower court and the Chief was in doubt whether he or she must be convicted, he could call for the case and pronounce conviction.[22] None of them were well conversant with the canons of modern legal system. Neither they knew nor had any inclination to understand the laws in British Indian territories. Their own ego went against any such learning. So the trials were whimsical and judgments delivered arbitrarily without any respect for justice and fairplay. Naturally, it led the people to lose faith on any of these courts presided over by the royal family or its cronies, which had got serious effect on the psyche of the subjects.

The entire administration solely depended upon the wish of the ruler. He could appoint and dismiss any employee, high or low whenever he liked. Transfer and promotion also rested in his hand. He could give punishment or fine which could not be challenged in the court of law.[23] If somebody wanted to go outside the State for a job he had to take prior permission from the chief. For the reception of any award by an employee from outside the State, prior permission had to be sought.[24] The subjects and the employees of the State had no freedom but always had to dance according to the tune of the *Raja*. People having higher qualification were not appointed to key posts. But the *Durbar* was adorned by people having much less qualification and very little knowledge in law. It is not difficult to imagine how laws must have been interpreted and administered by officials with very low qualification and understanding.

The *Dharma Adalat* or the ecclesiastical court was to deal with social and religious cases and mostly caste cases which had become obsolete in other parts of the country and which was disliked by the people of Talcher. This created difference in the families, castes and villages. It made confusion more confounded. In 1920-21 the decision

21. Talcher State Manual, 1916, p. 5.
22. *Ibid.*
23. *Ibid.*, p. 22
24. *Ibid.*, p. 8.

of this court was not accepted by the weavers of Talcher and out of protest Bharat, Kanthia Das including seven others left Talcher.[25] It was presided over by the chief priest called the *Dharmadhakhya*. It used to hear cases only when referred to by the Chief.[26] Since it remained under the guidance and control of the Chief, it had no original jurisdiction. The *Jubaraj* was empowered to hear the appeals of the court of *Dharmadhakya*.[27] The *Raja* or the *Jubaraj* never observed the rules for breach of which people were fined or harassed. The purpose of this interference in social matters was to provide large personal income for the Ruler. A serious off-shoot of his type of interference was the choking of the process of any social reform in the State in any form.

The Chiefs conducted tours inside the State as a part of discharging their administrative functions. They spent a considerable amount of time on tours of inspection and supervision in the State. About 100 days a year they spent on tour.[28] The primary aim as advocated was to check corruption and oppression of the officials. But it was far from achieving the professed goal. The Chief was surrounded by corrupt officials and evil advisers. The mismanagement of Talcher State was brought to the notice of the Government by the Superintendent, after his inspection of Talcher State in January 1880, when it was found that the *Raja* had not dismissed the evil advisers who had been directed to be discharged from service, and had neglected to apply a remedy to the abuses in his administration that had previously been brought to his notice.[29] The relationship between the Chief and the people were also unsatisfactory; and in order to prevent to any further fallout, sanction was given to the appointment of a *Dewan* by the Superintendent in order to assist the *Raja* in his management of the *Killah*.[30]

The rules and regulations were compiled in a book called *Talcher State Manual* published by the authority of the *Raja* from Talcher in 1916. Another authorised book of this kind was published in 1937. But these books had no relation to the practice. All the rules were formulated which suited the Chief and his *Durbar*. The 'Annual Administrative

25. Anant Mishra, *op. cit.*, p. 5.
26. Talcher State Manual, 1916, pp. 59-60.
27. *Ibid.*, p. 12.
28. Administrative Report of Talcher State, 1928-29, p. 274.
29. Report of the Administration of Bengal 1879-80, Calcutta, 1880, p. 18.
30. *Ibid.*

Reports' which were published by the authority were not the real code of law but mere a 'Show Book' for the benefit of the Political Department of the British Indian Government. Many things were omitted deliberately in its pages such as marriage fees, religious fees, unpaid forced labour like *bethi, beggari* etc. and many other obnoxious taxes.[31] These reports were published for a few years (last 20 years upto merger). But the general public were not aware of it. Rules, regulations and circulars which governed the normal relations of the Ruler with the people were not generally published and made available to the public.

The village administration was looked after by a group of followers of the Chief who were very cruel to their finger tips. They were called as *Pradhan, Behera Pradhan, Behera, Dala Behera, Nayak, Gada Nayak, Bisoi, Dandapat* and *Makaddam*. For any disturbances, they punished the people heavily. The punishment imposed on villagers by the headmen, apart from monetary fines, was social boycott in the form of getting debarred from the services of washermen, barbers and could not get fire and water from any outside source. They could not raise their voice against the *Raja's* rule due to fear of the headmen. The chief was also interfering in the individual's religious practices in the villages. The cases regarding religion were referred to the *Dharma Adalat* where poor people were either fined heavily or punished. These headmen in return got the privileges of enjoying gifted lands from the Chief called *Bhogara* lands.[32]

Punishments

There were no safeguards against arrests as there was no rule of law. People were arrested on suspicion without warrants and detained by the police for long time. Detention without trial, deportation and confiscation of property were frequent in the State. For petty offences the punishment was severe. Beating was the frequent practice to extort confession. Sometimes the rulers themselves derived sadistic pleasure out of such torture of the subjects. Bhagirathi Birabar Harichandan, the Chief of Talcher was reported to have branded the Brahmins on their forehead with hot irons as they were suspected to have incited his son to go against him on his return from the place of pilgrimage.[33]

31. *Orissa States Enquiry Committee Report,* p. 103.
32. Talcher State Manual 1937, p. 21.
33. Orissa Records, Boards' Proceedings (Revenue) Acc. No. 134, pp. 1-26 AJM Mills' Minute on Tributary Mahals, 23 January 1847. (OSA) and G.S. Mishra, *op. cit.*, p. 113.

During his rule between 1778 to 1864, he had given severe punishments even to his own queens. It was said that the King was informed of a Dasi's illicit relationship with a *Khansama*. So he buried alive two of his queens, cut off breasts and ears of some *Dasis* and tattooed. *Nimak haram* on the foreheads of some Brahmins by hot iron.[34] For theft cases, punishment was cutting of limbs which was prevalent in medieval times. Criminal culprits, *Docoits* and robbers were beheaded. Those who were involved in rebellion against the king were tattooed and ousted from the State.[35] Such type of cruel punishments, remnants of medieval dark age was still in vogue in the State at a time when the legal procedure had taken a modern shape in the nearby British Indian territories to some extent. Some of the Rulers had a band of *Doms* (a scheduled caste group) in their employment and their job was to 'beat up' people who are found to be difficult. Spitting on man's face was another common method of applying third degree humiliation.[36] The defaulters of tax payment were punished severely. They were driven out of their houses forcibly. They had to keep standing on one leg on the hot sand with a big and hot stone on the head and holding aloft two hot stones with the two hands. This was done under the hottest sun in May and June. In winter they were punished by drowning in cold water and fanning with winnow.[37] Political offenders were also similarly treated. People like Daini Pradhan of village Badagunduri, Chandra Sahoo of Jarada, Mona Pradhan of Jarada and 27 others were branded on their buttocks as 'Ni-ha or *Nimak Haram* meaning ungrateful as they took part in the people's movement in Talcher against the King's arbitrary rule.[38]

The police officials had ill intention during the search of houses of political offenders or the defaulters of tax. During these operations, stealing of ornaments and utensils, throwing spittle on the people, beating ruthlessly on any member of the family or molestation of female member was an usual habit of the police officials. In some cases they were beaten to death.[39] Out of fear, some people ran to the forest to hide themselves leaving behind their properties, children and

34. G.S. Mishra, *op. cit.*, pp. 90-98.
35. *Ibid*.
36. *Orissa States Enquiry Committee Report*, p. 101.
37. *Talcher Prajamandal Itihas Committee (Compl)*, Talcher 1950, p. 9.
38. *Orissa States Enquiry Committee Report*, p. 102.
39. P.M. Pradhan, *op. cit.*, pp. 41-42.

old parents. Talcher State was regarded as a 'B' Class *Sanad* State since 1908 whose ruler could enjoy power only next in scope to the 'A' Class *Sanad* State. The *Raja* Kishore Chandra was so power-loving that he wrote to the political department to enhance his power by declaring Talcher as an 'A' Class State.[40] More power was required by the Chief so that more heavy punishment would have been given to the subjects and more fines could be extracted. The severe punishments and rude behaviour of the officials of the State gradually demoralised the people and there was a lot of discontentment among them which burst out in the form of sporadic risings from time to time.

Civil Liberty

Civil liberty was non-existent in the State of Talcher. No fundamental rights of citizenship were recognised. Freedom of speech and formation of association was not granted. The representation of grievances was considered seditious. In 1912, Purandar Pani of Bijigol, Banamaliparam Guru and Sudarshan Dhar of Jagannathpur with some of their followers had made petition before the Political Agent against the taxation policy of the State authority of Talcher. For that they were fined.[41] Sadananda Pradhan and others had to furnish security for good conduct, their offence being that they had protested against *Bethi* and taxation. In 1931, Chhual Singh, Brundaban Pradhan, Anadi Sahu, Jhula Khutia and many others were ordered to furnish bonds of good behaviour for having protested against certain features of the administration. Punitive suspicion that the villagers were holding meetings against the chief.[42]

The peasants paid a high land rent and many other taxes, but they had absolutely no right over the land which had been reclaimed by their ancestors and tilled by their families for generations. There were many valuable lands which were in possession of the cultivators for years had been confiscated by the State on ground of non-payment. The enquiry committee during its tour to different States of Orissa had accepted such original cases of confiscation signed by the Ruler of Talcher.[43] So the right over land actually belonged to the ruler and the peasants tilled as long as the King allowed without any proprietary right.

40. Orissa Records, Talcher Papers, 1947-48, Raja K.C. Dev to Political Agent, Sambalpur, Orissa, Letter No. Con. M/45-46-16 Talcher 23 September 1945. (SRT)

41. *Orissa States Enquiry Committee Report*. p. 103.

42. *Ibid*., p. 107.

43. *Ibid*., p. 110.

In 1925 a group of *Chasas*, the cultivating caste, in Talcher formed an association, and called it "*Soubhagya Samiti*" after the name of the son of *Jubaraj*. The object of this organisation was to bring about certain social reforms in their community and spread of English education amongst them. But the association was banned. Those who were in services and took part in the Association were suspended. The funds of the association (about one thousand of rupees) were confiscated. The organisers of the association appealed to the Ruler who happened to be its President, but the association was not allowed to function.[44] It shows how the ruler was morally afraid of any association in his State, as he feared that it would spread new ideas and consciousness, detrimental to the royal interest.

When the People's Movement took an organised shape by forming *Prajamandal* it was declared illegal by the State authority of Talcher. People were not allowed to hold public meetings. People were daily oppressed with a feeling of insecurity to their life and property. To counter the *Prajamandal,* the ruler framed his own loyal body where half of its members were elected on the basis of the so-called adult franchise and the remaining half were nominated by the Chief. It met twice a year and its term was for three years. It was presided over by the Chief. Naturally all the decisions would go in favour of the Chief as the nominated members had to support him along with the elected elements, who were cowed down by possible repressive measures. Though the primary object was to do some benevolent work for the community yet its activities only suited the *Durbar*. This was intended to counteract the activities of the People's Movement in the State. Its working was quite superficial.[45]

The municipality of this State had also got a Board consisting of eight members out of whom four were elected representatives of tax payers and four were nominated by the *Durbar*. The Chairman was also nominated by the *Durbar*.[46] So this was not at all a representative body where all the resolutions had to go in favour of the *Durbar*. Such type of mockery of elected bodies or democratic institutions were done in State, which only led people to keep distance from this *Durbar*-sponsored so-called popular bodies and gradually to drift more and

44. Orissa States Enquiry Committee Report, *op. cit.*
45. Orissa Records, Sambalpur Papers, Acc. No. 967S, Resident for Eastern States to Secretary, Crown Representation No. R-9-36/45, 23 October 1945.
46. Administrative Report of Talcher, 1945-46, p. 11.

more towards the course of mass movement. Strict watch was kept on the activities of any organisation and its organisers. The question of free press naturally did not arise under the then condition. Newspapers published from outside the State were either not allowed or persons subscribing to them were kept under strict supervision. The circulation of newspapers like *The Samaj* and *The Krushak* were prohibited.[47]

A weekly in Oriya called '*Gadajat Basini*' was published from Talcher Kishore Press. Nobody could have the courage to write a single word either against the *Raja's* administration or his *Durbar*.[48] Only the news items covering and praising *Raja's* administration were published. It published poems euologising the personal life and qualities of the *Raja*. Poor people's demand, sorrows, exploitation etc. never got a place in its pages.[49] The effort was to have their own controlled press with censorship on outside publications and thus to insulate the people of Talcher from the great national movement going on outside their domain, all over the country.

Detention without trial, summary judgment, trespassing into private dwelling units without valid authority, deportation and confiscation of properties were fairly frequent. Physical torture of both men and women by petty officials of the State or the police were ususal practice in the State.[50] Without any just administration to look into any complaint, people had to accept it as divinely ordained.

There was no freedom even in social matters. No marriage or death rituals could be performed or a meeting could be conducted without the permission of the authorities of the State. This permission was not granted as a matter of formality. Sometimes permission was refused without assigning any reason thereof.[51]

The people of the State were not allowed to participate in the administration. The *Byabasta Parishad* in 1938, was a shadow representative body filled with the supporters of the King without proportional representation and served as a convenient instrument in his hand for furtherance of his interest. Three types of such organisations were established, one each at Talcher sub-division, Kaniha and Talcher Town.[52] This was meant to hoodwink the outside world and to show

47. File No. 32/7/38, Home Political (Internal) 1938. (NAI)
48. *Deshakatha,* 3 February 1931.
49. *Ibid*.
50. *Talcher Prajamandal Itihas Committee* (*Compl*), *op. cit*., pp. 9-11.
51. *Ibid*.
52. Administrative Report of Talcher State, 1945-46, p. 11.

that the rule was with popular consent and through representative body of elected people.

SOCIO-ECONOMIC CONDITION

The general condition of people was very miserable. Besides heavy taxation and denial of all elementary rights of citizenship, the people of this State were suffering under a heavy dead-weight of customs, usages and exactions. They were rack-rented which can be divided into a number of classes such as *Bethi, Beggari, Magana, Rasad, Kara Samagri, Rath Bethi, Dashera Bethi* and *Bheti, Suniya Bethi, Paik Bethi, Hathikheda Bethi, Sadak Tiari Bethi, Shikar Bethi, Motorthela Bethi* etc.[53]

Bethi

Free and forced labour for construction and repair of roads, royal palace, culverts, temples, bungalows, playgrounds, Rajkumar houses and that of his cousins.

Beggari

Free and forced carriage of luggages of the *Raja* or his officers from camp to camp.

Magana

Free and forced contribution, both cash and kind on the occasion of royal marriage,[54] thread, ear-piercing ceremonies. death etc. in the *Raj* family, purchase of motors by the *Raja* and the royal blood. One-fourth of the annual land rent of the tenants was paid for it.

Rasad

Free ration supply to *Raja*, his cousins and his officials while camping in *moffussil* area.

---

53. *Talcher Prajamandal Itihas Committee* (*Compl*), *op. cit.*, p. 9.

54. At the time of the marriage of the Princess of Talcher *Raja* (Rani of Kurpam) the followings were collected as *Magan* per one rupee tax.

(i) Re. 0.8 *annas* paise

(ii) 2 *manas* fine rice

(iii) 3 *manas* coarse rice

(iv) 2 *Biswa* dal

(v) 1 *Biswa* ghee

(vi) oil, salt, spice, vegetables etc.

Kara Samagri

Supply of provisions, such as paddy, rice, *mung, biri*, ghee etc. to the Raja's palace at half the market price.

Ratha Bethi

Different classes of tenants and artisans, such as coolies, carpenters, black smiths, washermen had to come to the *Garh*, halt there for certain period to construct the *Rath* (chariot) of Lord Jagannath annually, for which they were given some nominal *Jagir*. The timber for the purpose had also to be obtained by the tenants from their respective jungles upto the *Garh* at their own expense.

Dashera Bethi and Bheti

The *Paiks* and *Saharas* had to work compulsorily for about a month or so on the occasion of *Dashera* every year for making all arrangements for the ceremony and the *Sarbarakars* and other prominent tenants had also to make compulsory presents to the *Raja* during *Dashera*.

Suniya Bheti

This was a new year's gift to the *Raja*. People were to contribute Re. 0-0-6 in the rupee of the land revenue to *Sarbarakars* who presented the amount to the *Raja* on the Oriya New Year Day of every year.

Shikar Bethi

The subjects were forcibly taken to jungles and *bethi* was raised without payment whenever *Shikar* parties were organised for the Ruler, members of his family or official guests. The incidental works in this connection such as free carrying of luggages of these parties from camp to camp were forced upon them. They had also to supply free rations to the camps.

Hatikheda Bethi

Catching wild elephants was one of the greatest pleasures of the *Raja* of Talcher. He felt proud to catch the elephants in the *kheda*; an enclosure set up to catch wild elephants in the forest. This *Kheda* was constructed by hundreds of people at their own cost. The labourers were to bring their own food. Leaving behind the ripe cornfields, they spent three to four months for doing this type of forced labour out of which they got nothing. Inside the forest they suffered a lot and nobody was there to look after them. In the meantime the ripe paddy plant and sugarcanes were being eaten by the wild animals. They might die in the forest due to snake bite, falling prey to wild animals or to any disease for which no treatment was there.

In 1904 *Raja* Kishore Chandra went to Hindol for catching elephants. In 1914 he decided to catch elephants in east of Sukinda in British Orissa and to sell them at a profit.[55] Hundreds of people from Talcher were forcibly employed in this *Kheda* and many lost their lives there.[56]

Besides this, all sorts of hard work were done by the subjects by the order of the king. The great compound wall attached to the Palace of Talcher was surrounded by a three mile long wall, the height and thickness of which was eight to ten feet and thirty to thirty-five inches respectively. The construction work covered a period of five to seven years through *bethi*.[57] Likewise many roads, residential houses of the State Officials, houses for *Raj* family, State office buildings, inspection bungalows, barrages, compoundwall of Ranipark etc. were all built by *bethi*. It is said that the '*Arjunakata*', a vast tank covering several square miles and looking like a sea was the creation of *bethi*.[58] The *Samant* quarters meant for the cousins of the Raja was made under *bethi*. The wet-ditch or water reservoir around the palace was dug by *bethi* during *Raja* Bhagirathi Harichandan in between 1800 and 1810.[59]

The Jubilee festival was being celebrated in the *Durbar* in every ten years of the reign of Kishore Chandra. In 1931, it was celebrated with pomp and ceremony and to make it a grand success the *Durbar* employed *bethi*.[60] In this way, there were large number of such forced contributions by the tenants for which they hardly got anything in return.

Besides *Bethi* people were forced to contribute towards *Rasad* and also supply rice, ghee, etc. on several occasions to the *Durbar*.

The Orissa States Enquiry Committee in its report observed that *Magan* or Compulsory Contribution had been realised from the people

55. G.S. Mishra, *op. cit.*, p. 164.
56. *Orissa States Enquiry Committee Report,* p. 109.
57. S. Pradhan, *Agrarian and Political Movements in the States of Orissa : 1931-49*, Delhi, 1985, pp. 59-60.
58. *Ibid.*
59. G.S. Mishra, *op. cit.*, p. 99.
60. *Deshakatha*, 1 June 1931.

on the folllowing occasions and on the following rates during last 20 years:[61]

1.	Marriage of Ruler's Daughter	-	Re. 0-8-0 per rupee of rent
2.	Marriage of *Jubaraj*	-	Re. 0-8-0 per rupee of rent
3.	Thread ceremony of *Jubaraj*	-	Re. 0-4-0 per rupee of rent
4.	Prince of Wales' visit to India.	-	Re. 0-0-3 per rupee of rent
5.	Thread of *Pattayat*	-	Re. 0-4-0 per rupee of rent
6.	Marriage of *Pattayat*	-	Re. 0-4-0- per rupee of rent
7.	Death of Ruler's own father	-	Re. 0-2-0 per rupee of rent
8.	Death of Ruler's own mother	-	Rs. 0-2-0 per rupee of rent
	Total :	-	Rs. 2-0-3

In spite of the Geneva Convention of 1929 abolishing forced labour, to which the Government of India was a signatory, this system persisted in the States. Under the terms of the *Sanads* governing the relationship of the chiefs with the paramount powers the former were bound to accept the advice of the political officers, who had, it appeared, not exercised their undoubted influence and weight on the side of abolition of this system. So everything occurred under the very eye of the British Indian Government to which they did not object firmly. Some notes, here and there with mild tone on the subject, to the rulers could not have got any desired result. Thus, the violation on human rights in every form continued in the feudatory States, which only added fuel to the fire of anti-feudal agitation in the States.

Peasantry

The backbone of any feudal system is the peasantry, which constitutes the bulk of population, pays heavily to the State for its existence and in the process creates the ground for the protest and revolution to overthrow the feudal order. What was said by Amir Khusrau, a court poet in fourteenth century was only a poetic reflection of reality. He commented: "Every pearl in the royal crown is but the crystallised drop of blood fallen from the tearful eyes of the poor peasant".[62]

The peasantry had no full land rights in the State of Talcher. It was liable to ejection in spite of its long possessions and enjoyment for

61. *Orissa States Enquiry Committee Report,* p. 108.

62. Quoted from Hiren Mukherjee, *India's Struggle for Freedom,* Calcutta, 1962, p. 12.

generations. Nobody could reclaim his right after ejection.[63] The land rent was forcibly collected. There was no question of remission of the arrears. Defaulters were either penalised or the land was confiscated.[64] Lands could not be sold, nor mortgaged nor transferred without the permission of the authority and high mutation fees were collected during this work.[65] Right of adoption was not recognised. The *Durbar* had the sovereign and proprietary right over all lands in the State of Talcher.[66] The lands were classified as *Khas-Dakhal, Lakhraj, Debottar, Kharposh, Jagir Bhogara, Raiyati* and under *Raiyati*.

Khas-Dakhal lands were all the waste lands which were under direct possession of the *Durbar*. The *Lakhraj* lands were rent free land given to Brahmins who were duty bound and loyal to *Durbar*. *Lakharajdars* were bound to attend religious function, ceremonies when called upon by the *Durbar*. *Jagir* lands were given to those who served the *Durbar* on free wages, and in case of misconduct these lands could be forfeited.[67]

The *Debottar* lands were granted to Hindu Deities for religious purpose in the State. *Kharposh* lands were given to the families of royal blood without any rent. This type of land could be enjoyed by the heir after the death of the father but not transferable. *Bhogara* lands meant rent and cess paying lands granted to *Sarbarakars, Garnaiks* and *Makadams*, the headmen of village to look after the welfare of the villagers to collect and deposit the rents from the villagers.[68]

Raiyati lands were held by *Raiyats* for purpose of use or occupation of such lands, and to render service to the *Durbar* when required on receipt of due payment. The owners could not be ejected till he paid the rent. Under-*Raiyati* was who held lands under a *raiyat* or tenant.[69]

Thus the agrarian situation in the State was quite bad. Those who got the rent free land were the people who stood with the State administration and paid no tax and also used forced labour in their land with nominal charge or free of cost. The rented land holders were naturally burdened with higher amount of taxes to compensate for the

---

63. *Orissa States Enquiry Committee Report, op. cit.*
64. *Talcher State Manual*, 1916, pp. 41-44.
65. *Ibid.*
66. *Ibid.*, 1937, pp. 17-26.
67. *Ibid.*
68. *Ibid.*
69. *Ibid.*

loss of revenue in the rent free land-holdings. Without any concern for the development of agriculture, the rulers paid little attention to the development of irrigation, whether it was the reclamation of the old facilities or providing new ones. As a result, the peasant had to depend on monsoon totally. Many valuable fertile land remained uncultivated or used for one cultivation due to scarcity of water depending on weather. Even seeds of good quality were not available to the farmers. Most of the cultivators of Talcher lived from hand to mouth. Being uneducated they meekly submitted to any hardship in the name of fate, which would otherwise had been removed, had there been the provision of cottage industry by the State for these people. Any casual observer ever visiting an interior village of Talcher would understand how miserable the people were and to what extent they needed the care of the State.

The cultivators of this State were not acquainted with the cultivation of any seasonal crop except paddy and *Rabi*. The lands in their possession could easily yield good winter crops but they were not very particular about it. Modern system of cultivation was practically unknown to them. They did not know the utility of fertilizer and they seldom got good seeds from foreign places to produce vegetables and other seasonal fruits which would have augmented their meagre income. Whatever was produced could not be kept longer due to absence of storage system in the State. The State *Durbar* did not take any initiative to give them the incentive in this direction. The agriculture department that existed in the State was quite defunct. Its work was most perfunctory. People hardly knew its existence.[70] The centre of agricultural farm was confined to one place only and there should have at least three to four centres of it in the interior areas of Talcher.

During natural calamities their condition could not be described. Land revenue was increasing every year but the condition of the peasantry remained as such or deteriorated.[71] The question of the security of tenure and liability to arbitrary increase in rents were the two stumbling blocks which created serious difficulties in the way of increasing cultivation over vast rich land. This would have brought prosperity to the peasantry class in the State and created a class of new bourgeoisie as in Europe, who would have become the pioneers of democratic revolutions in the Indian States.

70. Orissa Records, Talcher Papers, Development Scheme, File No. 1-DI-5/48 — Five Year Reconstruction Plan, pp. 30-31. (SRT)

71. *Talcher Prajamandal Itihas Committee* (*Compl.*), pp. 5-7.

The tenants laboured hard in the fields. But they had no right over it. Even they had to pay tax to the State for cutting a tree in their own field. Sometimes, they were deprived of the land without any prior notice and the land was given to others by the king's order.[72] After the death of the father, the son or the heir had to bribe the king for the acquisition of that particular land. As it was difficult to call the land one's own, the tenants could not sell or hand over them at their own will. During buying or selling of the land, the peasants had to pay twenty-five per cent of the price as fee to the State authority.[73] Naturally, it bred insecurity among the peasantry, which alienated him from developing his own land for his own use .

Depressed Classes

There was a considerable number of depressed class people in Talcher. They included *Pan*, *Hadi*, *Dom*, *Konds*, *Sawars* etc. They were practically the ignorant classes without any status in the then society. Agriculture and trade had in no way benefited them. Most of them were day-labourers. Their standard of living was far below than that of other caste people of Talcher. The strigency of caste system had not, in spite of rapid social changes, been softened and they were not even touched by the so-called high castes' people. To bring these depressed classes to a standard of equality with other people, the State authority did not do any beneficial arrangements for their education and health, improvement of their society and other amenities of life.[74] There was no attempt from the State side to change their evil habits and their mode of living to suit the then circumstances.

Taxation System

The system of taxation prevailing in this State was quite high. Land was heavily taxed without any calculation of the capacity of the peasants to pay. People were highly burdened with land tax. The service holders were very low paid except a few. In 1920-21 a school peon or a sweeper usually received only one rupee per month as his salary.[75] One can easily imagine how could he pay back the dues including land tax, cess etc. to the State beside his family burden. Money was a great

72. *Talcher Prajamandal Itihas Committee* (*Compl*), pp. 5-7.
73. *Ibid*.
74. Orissa Records, Talcher Papers, Development Scheme, File No. 1-DI-5/48, Five Year Reconstruction Plan, p. 7. (SRT)
75. Orissa Records, *op. cit*., Annual Budget for 1920-21, File No. G-1, Diary No. 32, 26 April 1920. (SRT).

problem for the people. There was a crushing system of taxation with unusual high land rent, except in one or two cases, and numerous taxes and cesses leading to progressive deterioration of the economic condition of the peasantry. The State did not follow the rules of Manu nor any scientific principle of land revenue. The rate of rent per one acre of land at Talcher was Rs. 3-4-1.[76] There was heavy land tax in the British Orissa but the land revenue in the State was still higher. The enquiry committee of Orissa has compared land rent in Talcher with that in the British territory of Angul. The comparative figures are given below.[77]

Talcher

Name of land	1st Class Village	2nd Class Village	3rd Class Village	4th Class Village
Saradh Special	3-4-1	3-4-1	3-4-1	—
Saradh I	2-15-11	1-15-11	2-7-7	2-1-4
Saradh II	1-7-7	2-1-4	1-6-11	1-6-11
Saradh III	1-6-11	1-6-11	0-14-7	0-14-7
Inferior III	0-10-5	0-10-5	0-10-5	0-10-5
Sugarcane I	6-6-1	6-6-1	6-6-1	6-6-1
Sugarcane II	4-13-1	4-13-1	4-13-1	4-13-1
Homestead I	10-0-0	10-0-0	10-0-0	10-0-0
Homestead II	5-0-0	5-0-0	5-0-0	5-0-0
Homestead III	2-8-0	2-8-0	2-8-0	2-8-0
Toila	0-6-3	0-6-3	0-6-3	0-6-3
Bonda	0-6-3	0-6-3	0-6-3	0-6-3
Bhagayat	0-6-3	0-6-3	0-6-3	0-6-3
Laik Patit	0-2-1	0-2-1	0-2-1	0-2-1
Baje Fasali I	2-7-7-	2-7-7	1-11-1	1-0-8
Baje Fasali II	1-11-1	1-11-1	1-2-9	0-10-5
Baje Fasali III	0-14-7	0-14-7	0.10-5	0.6-3

76. *Orissa States Enquiry Committee Report*, pp. 8-9.

77. *Ibid.*, p. 105.

Angul

Class of Land	1st Class Village	2nd Class Village	3rd Class Village
Saradh I	2-11-9	2-9-8	2-6-5
Saradh II	1-13-2	1-11-1	1-9-0
Saradh III	0-14-7	0-12-6	0-12-6
Harafasal	1-13-2	1-11-1	1-9-0
Chandana	1-13-2	1-11-1	1-9-0
Bajefasal	0-12-6	0-12-6	0-12-6
Bagayat	0-6-3	0-6-3	0-6-3
Toila I	0-6-3	0-6-3	0-6-3
Toila II	0-2-1	0-2-1	0-2-1

Bazar and Town Area

	1st Clas Village	2nd Class Village	3rd Class Village
Area I	100-0-0	—	—
Area II	50-0-0	—	—
Area III	30-0-0	—	—
Area IV	20-0-0	—	—
Area V	10-0-0	—	—

Due to the cheaper rate of the agricultural products, the tenants could not get enough money to recover the heavy tax. Between 1925 to 1937 the rate of the following articles were as such:[78]

Rice	35 to 40 *Ser*[79] a rupee
Dal	20 to 22 *Ser* a rupee
Oil	5 to 6 *Ser* a rupee
Ghee	1.5 *Ser* a rupee
Molasses	30 to 32 *Ser* a rupee

Nobody was purchasing vegetables because these were plentily available in everybody's field.

78. P.M. Pradhan, *op. cit.*, p. 41.

79. One Ser is equivalent to 1.25 Kilogram.

The land tax imposed a heavy burden on the people. The people were not getting enough money from selling their produce. Automatically, this taxation system put them into much trouble. The income of the State from land tax was about one-fourth of the total income. The following figure shows to this effect:[80]

Year	Total Income from all sources	Income from Land Revenue
1927-28	Rs. 3,16,512-11-7	Rs. 1,00,538-6-6
1934-35	Rs. 3,05,411-13-8	Rs. 94,304-1-10
1935-36	Rs. 3,25,079-14-0	Rs. 74,056-5-6
1940-41	Rs. 3,40,225-13-8	Rs. 1,08,284-8-6

The collection of and revenue had improved seven times within a span of forty-five years *i.e.* Rs. 82,353 in 1900-1901 against Rs. 5,97,501 in 1944-45.[81] The tribute which was given to the British Government by the State was fixed at a rate of Rs.. 1039-10-5 in 1803. This fixed amount was given upto the merger of the State and there was no increase to it. So the increase in tax collection was filling the private treasury of the ruler for personal use.

Thus the burden of land tax on the peasantry along with uncertainty of tenural right only deheartened the peasantry from undertaking any development in land. The State was mopping up its surplus leaving little only for its subsistence. Even natural calamities failed to deter the chiefs to raise land tax. While the States tribute to British Indian Government remained static for the entire period till its merger, the dues on the people increased. It left a huge amount in the hands of the chief for enjoyment and to strengthen law and order administration with more men and better equipments to put down the people's discontent. With the prices of agricultural commodities not increasing much, the peasants had to part with a bigger share of their produce to pay the rent, leaving little for their own use. This sub-human condition of life gradually created environment of protest and movement later.

Cesses

People of Talcher were overburdened with rent tax. Whenever the

80. Collected from the Administrative Reports of Talcher during the years 1927-28 to 1940-41.

81. Orissa Records, Sambalpur Papers, Acc. No. 97OS, *op. cit.*

king wanted, he could impose the tax. Besides land rent there were numerous other taxes, fees and cesses such as the forest cess, education cess, health cess, chawkidar tax etc. and various miscellaneous cesses including road cess, sugarcane cess, ceremonies cess, court building repaircess etc. which were collected from the people. More than seven annas[82] were collected for every one rupee of land revenue for these purposes.

Although, many States were not having the customs duties, Talcher went one step ahead in imposing the customs duties on its subjects. Mayurbhanj was not having this type of duties and in a reply to the letter of *Raja* of Talcher the *Raja* of Mayurbhanj wrote :

"... I do not think the Mayurbhanj reply will be of much assistance to you, because, as I have already stated, we have no customs duties properly ..."[83]

The tax was very high at Talchare on sugarcane and tabacco. The following cesses were collected for every one rupee of land revenue:[84]

	per rupee of rent		
	Rs.	An	Pi.
1. Miscellaneous cess			
(a) On carrying load outside State	0	0	6
(b) For supplying fuel to palace	0	0	3
(c) For thatching court Building	0	0	3
(d) For carrying load	0	0	1
(e) For thatching State Houses	0	1	3
(f) For provisions for Ruler in time	0	1	0
(g) Misc. bethi	0	0	2
(h) Ceremonies	0	0	6
(i) Supplying rice to palace	0	0	6
(j) Timber for car festival	0	0	6
Total	0	5	0
2. Forest cess	0	1	0
3. School Cess	0	1	0
4. Chawkidar Tax	0	0	6
Total	0	7	6

82. One rupee is equivalent to sixteen annas.

83. Orissa Records, Talcher Papers, Letter of Raja Mayurbhanj to Raja Talcher, Confidential 3600/Baripada, 28 October, 1938 (SRT).

84. Anant Mishra, *op. cit.*, p. 3.

The State's income from this source was almost one-seventh of the total income. The following Table can give us a picture of the collection of cesses.[85]

Year	Miscellaneous	Fuel Cess	School Cess	Total
1933-34	29134-15-2	6525-9-3	6453-14-2	42104-6-7
1934-35	28148-14-6	6047-0-1	6819-8-2	41015-6-9
1935-36	23,302-11-3	5735-15-5	6361-0-6	35399-11-2

Monopoly

Monopolies in certain vital daily necessities of life had raised prices, reduced their quality and provided a handle to petty officials often with the connivance or direct encouragement of the rulers and his officials themselves, to oppress the people. There were monopolies in daily necessities of life such as salt, kerosene, coconut, *bidi*, tobacco, betel leaf, coir, betel nut etc. For the business of these articles the seller had to obtain one *pattah* from the State for which he had to pay licence fee to the State. The seller collected the above fee from the buyer.[86] There was a difference of rate of these articles between Talcher and Angul which is given below:[87]

Article	Price in Talcher	Price in Angul
Salt	Re. 0-1-9 per *seer*	Re. 0-1-3 per *seer*
Kerosene	Re. 4-8-0 per tin	Re. 3-12-0 per tin
Betel leaf	Re. 0-2-6 per *Kada*	Re. 0-1-6 per *Kada**

It clearly shows how an artificial pricing system was imposed in certain items under monopoly system in the State, not connected to its cost price inclusive of transport and internal tax, with the sole object of making huge profit out of these articles. As the British Indian Government had also monopoly in some commodities, it did not intervene in these matters in spite of popular petitions by the people.

Forest Law

The forest law was very strict in the State. Almost all the jungles were under reserve category. Even, the reserve line was extended upto

85. Collected from the Administrative Report of Talcher, 1933 to 1936.
86. *Talcher Prajamandal Itihas Committee* (*Compl.*) *op. cit.*, pp. 6-8.
87. *Orissa States Enquiry Committee Report*, p. 110.
* One Kada consists of 50 number of leaves.

the residential area of the people. The rights of the people for grazing, collecting fuel wood and the use of forest timber for domestic purposes were progressively and seriously encroached upon.[88] Nobody was able to collect wood from the jungle without permit. High fees were levied for the use of forest articles for daily, domestic or agricultural purposes. The cattles and goats of the people that wandered into the jungle were caught and thrown into the *Kanjihouse*.[89] People had to face a lot of trouble to get back their domesticated animals from the *Kanjihouse*. They were also fined for this.[90] On the other hand, the people were held responsible for the fire that broke out in the forest. The nearby people were to extinguish the fire without getting any benefit from the State.[91] They could not even collect the timber from the river during flood. If so, that was deposited in the premises of *Durbar*.[92]

The wild animals used to destroy the cultivation of the people. But nobody could kill them. Due to some standing rules, their hands were tight. In case of shooting of such wild animals, the State used to levy fees on every animal shot in protection of crops.[93] Later on, this had been altered and it had been provided that animals might be shot while actually doing damage to crops but the skins and horns were to be deposited in the *Durbar* as these were the properties of the State; the flesh could not be sold. Professional hunters were to be engaged but the animals were to be handed over to the State. A required fee was to be paid to the State for the purpose.[94] So all these obstructions and hindrances were there to kill wild animals. The king had got some pet tigers and elephants in his zoo. The games of him were left free even if these animals destroyed the corn-fields or killed the domesticated animals of the people. The people had no right to kill a tiger or an elephant.[95] Such was the jungle law prevalent in Talcher.

---

88. *Talcher Forest Manual*, 1928, p. 8.
89. It was a shed set up by the State Authority where all the cows and goats that were caught while trespassing were being put. Ultimately they were released on payment of a particular amount of fine by the respective owners.
90. *Talcher Forest Manual, op. cit.*
91. *Ibid.*, p. 2.
92. *Ibid.*, p. 9.
93. Ramdhyani Report, Vol. I, p. 285.
94. *Ibid.*
95. *Talcher Prajamandal Itihas Committee* (*Compl.*), p. 8.

Palace Expenditure

Palace expenditure should bear a reasonable proportion to the income of the State. What could be the reasonable proportion remained undetermined, leaving it under the whims and fancies of the King and family members without any limit. The Orissa States Enquiry Committee has recommended that the Privy Purse should be limited so as not to exceed one-tenth of the income where it ranges between ten to fifteen lakhs per year and should include the private expenses of the Rulers palace expenses, cars and stables of the Ruler and guests except those which have reference to the performance of public duty which should be clearly defined. In case of Talcher there was deviation from it. The following figures which has been extracted from the Talcher State Administrative Reports clearly show as such:[96]

Year	Total Income	Domestic Expenditure
1927-28	Rs. 3,16,512-11-7	Rs. 42,075-3-7
1928-29	Rs. 2,61,803-15-9	Rs. 44,587-14-1
1934-35	Rs. 3,05,411-13-8	Rs. 48,328-1-7
1935-36	Rs. 3,25,079-14-0	Rs. 50,707-11-11

Without caring for the real collection of revenue of the State, the domestic expenditure of the rulers went on increasing year after year.

Besides the sums earmarked in the State Budget for domestic department, there were various devices which the ruler and his officials had found out by which a good amount of public money was diverted to the private treasury of the *Raja*. The Rulers spent, directly or indirectly, the major portion of the State revenues on themselves, their families and dependants. Sucharu Mali Devi, the eldest daughter of *Raja* Kishore Chandra Birabar Harichandan was enjoying an annual allowance of Rs. 3, 680 from the year 1929-30 to 1939-40 and Rs. 3,600 from the year 1940-41 to 1945-46 from the State Budget, though she was not in any official position of the State.[97] In another case, one Daudjee Lathiwall, a businessman and match maker was asked by the authority to find out a suitable bridegroom for the *Jema* of the royal family for which he was granted a sum of Rs. 500 towards his journey

96. Collected from the Administrative Reports of Talcher for the Year 1927-28 to 1935-36.

97. Orissa Records, Talcher Papers, Audit and Report File 1947-48. (SRT)

expenses from the State treasury.[98] The unpublished budget of 1920-21 clearly shows expenditure on different heads of the Chief as follows.[99]

Domestic Charges	Annual Expenditure in Rs.
1. *Khana Kharcha* (Fooding)	2,400
2. *Raja's* Clothing	300
3. *Raja's* pleasure trip	5,000
4. *Raja's* pocket money	1,200
5. *Raja's* palace lighting	360
6. One Tutor for *Rajkumar's* Education	1,800
7. Extra Tutor for *Rajkumar's* Education	1,200
8. One Tutor for *Pattayat's* Education	600
9. *Jubraj's* Pocket money	360
10. *Pattayat's* Pocket money	300
11. Clothing for *Kumar*	400
12. Entertainment of Guests	1,000
13. Religion Charges	2,817
14. Feed of Horses	1,623
15. Fooding, Motor Car materials, diet expenses of servants etc.	4,800
16. Compounder, Personal Attendant, Cook, *Gaud*, Barbar, *Malis*, Sweeper, Dog Keeper, Light Supplier etc.	800
17. *Rajbati* Establishments and so on ...	

Municipality

The municipality which was established in the first quarter of the twentieth century in Talcher was not at all an institution of self-Government as more than half of its members including the Chairman were nominated by the Chief. Automatically, the Chief's voice was counted there. People's demand for beneficial work in the locality was

98. Orissa Records, *op. cit.*, A note to the Ruler of Talcher by *Jubraj Saheb*, Talcher, dated the 16th December 1943. (SRT)

99. *Ibid.*, *op. cit.*, Budget of 1920-21, Durbar Talcher State, File No. 1, Department G, Diary No. 32, 26 April 1920. (SRT)

not at all admitted. The work was done which only could suit the *Durbar*. The amount shown in the different budgets against the expenditure of the municipality was not real.[100] In fact the amount shown was not invested for the improvement of the locality and the work was unsatisfactory.[101] It was a municipality to put Talcher as a decorative piece to be shown to the outsiders as State capital without serving any real purpose of local self-Government like development of education, sanitation, health, drainage etc.

Health and Sanitation

Most of the people of Talcher had been leading an unhygienic life both in town and mofussil areas since a long time. Heaps of cow-dung and other filth were often found very close to the residential quarters of people who cared very little for the injurious effects these might bring to their health. Even night soil was found on the sides of main roads running through the town. People used to encourage their children to ease themselves on the side of public road. The Medical Department was unable to propagate the idea of leading a healthy life amongst the people. People were hardly made aware of the basic principles of hygiene. There had been atmospheric pollution due to the existence of several coal mines and industries in Talcher. But no action had yet been taken to this effect.

Like the British Government, the *Durbar* of Talcher thought the expenses on health and sanitation to be useless expenditure. So the budgetary allocation on this head remained meagre and token. People still relied on traditional Indian treatment and medieval belief of worshipping the disease-god. Whatever health-care was available, it was for the people in the royal capital only.

There was only one hospital situated in the headquarters of Talcher State. Later medical aid centres and dispensary at Kaniha were opened. But all these medical institutions were badly equipped and at times patients did not get medicines. The Sub-Divisional Hospital at the *Sadar* lacked sufficient number of medical staff to look after a good number of patients.[102] The usual practice of the Chief Medical Officer

100. Orissa Records, Sambalpur Paper, Acc. No. 967S, Resident for the Eastern States to Secretary of Crown Representative, Camp Darjeeling, No. R. 9-36/45, 23 October 1945. (OSA)

101. *Ibid., op. cit.,* Cal. No. R. 9-36/45J, 4 March 1947.

102. Orissa Records, Talcher Papers, Notes on Five Year Reconstruction Plan, Development Scheme, File 1/DI-5/48. (SRT)

or other doctors who remained in charge of the Hospital was to attend the *Durbar* every day evening, wasting away the time there and spending the whole evening hours to please the authority. There was lack of good hands in the hospital either due to lower pay or loose administration.[103] The single hospital in the town was not enough for a largely populated area like Talcher. The village people were not covered under any health scheme. They still depended upon the local *Vaidya* and *tantrik* rites to cure themselves. No provision was there for an ambulance car in the *Sadar* hospital for removing any serious patient from the interior to the *Sadar* hospital in case of emergency. 2.5 percentage of the total expenditure of the State was spent in the hospital which was very low.[104]

Leprosy had been a constant menace to the health and well-being of the Talcher people. Proper arrangements were not made for the segregation of infected people from the rest of the population to prevent the spread of the diseases. The leper clinics were found to be moribund and the vetenary departments was very poor.[105] There was cases of small pox, cholera, typhoid, malaria, skin diseases etc. prevailing in the State of Talcher. The atmospheric pollution due to the opening of collieries also caused many diseases in this area. People had been suffering a lot due to it. Vaccination was not popular in the State among the people.[106] There was no provision for sanitary measures in the area during epidemics.[107] So the outbreak of any epidemic used to take a heavy toll of human life without any concern by the feudal chiefs.

Education

Talcher was primarily backward due to lack of education and illiteracy. Had the people been properly educated to understand the sweeping changes coming over the country in quick succession, it would have been less difficult to make the people understand the political creeds and economic implication of various trades.

The education system had not improved upto a standard in this feudatory State for quite a long time. Upto the end of nineteenth

103. Orissa Records, Talcharpapers, *op. cit.*

104. Orissa Records, Sambalpur Papers, *op. cit.*, No. 9-36-45, 23 October 1945. (OSA)

105. *Ibid.*

106. L.E.B. Cobden-Ramsay, *op. cit.*, p. 332.

107. *Orissa States Enquiry Committee Report*, p. 110.

century, education was totally neglected but towards the closing years of the century there had been some progress especially in primary education. During the year 1890-91, there was only one vernacular M.E. School, three Upper Primary Schools, thirty-two Lower Primary Schools and one Girls School consisting of a strength of 80,80,491 and 21 of students respectively.[108] The total attendance in all these institutions was 672 out of a population of 52,674.[109] The next year there was an increase of six more L.P. Schools and the strength became 697.[110] The literacy rate was very poor in this State. According to the Census of 1901, out of the total population of 60,432 only 1,275 people were able to read and write and the percentage of literate on the total population was only 2.1.[111] The State received grants from the Government and enjoyed assistance from Government Educational Officers for the improvement of Primary Education.[112] The Guru Training School was entirely maintained and managed by Government Agency.[113] Besides, a good amount of education cess was being collected from the people every year. But educational improvement from the State side was not satisfactory.[114]

Talcher like other feudatory States was steeped in darkness. The State authority had no interest to educate the people for its allround improvement because education would open the door of modernity for these people which would be detrimental to feudal interest. The primary education without any distinction whatsoever might have been made free and compulsory in the State. Most of the people of Talcher were poor. They could not, after completion of education of their children in Upper Primary or Lower Primary Schools, afford to send their children to the High School at the headquarters. The Middle School in the State was converted to a High School in 1913.[115] That was the only High School in the State upto the merger. Later on it was shifted to a long

108. Orissa Records, Talcher Papers, Report on the Progress of Education in Orissa Tributary Mahals for the Year 1891-92, drawn by Joint Inspector of Schools, Orissa Division. (SRT)

109. *Ibid.*

110. *Ibid.*

111. L.E.B. Cobden-Ramsay, *op. cit.*, p. 37.

112. *Ibid.*, p. 334.

113. *Ibid.*, p. 107.

114. Orissa Records, Talcher Papers, Development Scheme, File No. 1-DE 5/48, Five Year Reconstruction Plan, pp. 12-13. (SRT)

115. *Ibid.*

distance from Talcher proper. This actually suited the chief's family and his cousins and the moneyed men who had got privileges to go there. The students in general faced a lot of trouble during hot, summer, winter and in rainy season who went there on foot. Students from distant villages could not join the school. Though there was hostel accommodation, it was available to those who could afford to stay. There was general complaint of the difficulties of getting good drinking water and fetching daily requirements by the boarders living close to the School. In addition to these, there was no play ground for the students which was highly resented by them. It was suggested to shift the High School to a place just on the out-skirt of the town where the students might find their necessities within easy reach.[116]

Being the President of the Governing Body of this School, the Chief was always interfering in its internal affairs. Before the establishment of this School, people either from royal blood or some moneyed people could go for higher study. *Raja* Kishore Chandra took his High School education at Ravenshaw Collegiate School, Cuttack.[117] The entire money for the *Raj Kumar's* education was spent either from the State finance or debited to General Administration or civil list. Between 1942 and 1948 the amount for this purpose was more than Rs. 30,000.[118]

During time of Kishore Chandra an outward improvement was shown in education which was a public show only. Financial assistance was given to educational institutions from the State treasury outside the State in the British territory or outside Orissa. It is reported that on one occasion he sent Rs. 266 to the Principal, Rajkumar College, Raipur towards this State share for the cost of entertaining the Viceroy in his College.[119] On the other hand, there was lack of proper attention towards education inside the State. The money which should have invested in education was not spent.[120] The income derived from the School cess was more than the expenditure incurred on these schools. The school houses were repaired by the forced labour of the people.[121]

116. Orissa Records, *op. cit.*

117. G.S. Mishra, *op. cit.*, p. 155.

118. Orissa Records, Talcher Papers, Administrator, Talcher to the Special Officer, Orissa State, Cuttack Letter No. A-1-4/48-5178, Talcher 26 November 1948. (SRT)

119. *Ibid.*, Confidential Letter of Raja Talcher to T.L.H. Smith Pearce, Principal, Rajkumar College, Raipur, D.O. No. 13/Con., 1 February 1935. (SRT).

120. Orissa Records, Sambalpur Papers, Acc. No. 967S, *op. cit.*, Cal. No. R-9-36/45J, 4 March 1947.

121. *Orissa States Enquiry Committee Report*, p. 110.

The intention of the kings not to expand modern education was obvious as they did not want the students to get modern knowledge and become forerunners of the national consciousness and anti-feudal democratic movement in the State. But to insulate the people from contemporary currents by chocking the educational facilities in the State was a dream that shattered in the post-World War I years. The attendance of girl students was not at all satisfactory.[122] A statistical figure given in the Appendix will give a clear cut picture of education in the State.[123]

In 1934-35 one upper primary school was established for the *harijans*. Only *harijan* students could read there. This was established as there was differences among various castes in the State and *harijan* students were debarred from attending other general schools.

For the spread of Sanskrit education in the State, the *Durbar* actually did a little for it. The State showed that two Sanskrit *Tols* were in existence in the State. But the *Karmakand Vidyalaya* only started after 1939-40. It was alleged that for some years after 1930 the Sanskrit *Tols* were abolished. The *Durbar* was collecting cess from the *Brahmottar Lakhraj Holders* for the spread of Sanskrit education. Though there was provision for giving stipend and scholarship to the students for Sanskrit education, nothing was given to them. Although the *Lakhraj Holders* used to pay their cess, no student got stipend for Sanskrit Study.[124] The ruler pocketed the money thus collected for educational purposes.

Transport and Communication

In the feudatory State of Talcher, the river Brahmani and the State roads formed the means of transportation and communication. There was a little number of *pucca* roads which only helped the royal family for the smooth running of their vehicles. Most of the roads which went to the moffusil areas were muddy and dirty. The bullock carts were to run in these roads, if necessary when they touched the *pucca* roads the poor farmers had to pay road tax or penalty.[125] Besides, the river Brahmani was used for farming and the people had to pay the charges

122. Orissa States Enquiry Committe Report, *op. cit.*

123. See Appendix J.

124. Orissa Records, Talcher Papers, D.P. Tripathy, Administrator, Talcher to the District Magistrate, Dhenkanal, Letter No. 5393 Talcher, 8 December 1948. (SRT)

125. Orissa Records, Talcher Papers, Report on the Five Year Reconstruction Plan, *op. cit.*, (SRT)

for it. No vehicles from the side of the State was utilised for the common mass for transportation. The only train which used to run from Talcher to Puri could not be utilised by many common people as the station stood far away from the town. Though a train line passes through the town area, the State authority did not take any interest to construct a station or a passenger halt in the nearby of the Talcher locality.[126]

Personal Life of the Chiefs

The personal life of the Chiefs of Talcher was quite different from that of the life of the commoners. They maintained a life style much higher than that of subjects which created a great wall between the ruler and the ruled. Besides their private expenditure which has been discussed earlier in this chapter the Chiefs always tried to live a luxurious life beyond compare. They could marry as many times as they wanted and could keep concubines (*Dasi*) as many as they liked which was not found in the society. If any girl caught their fancy, she was brought to the palace as *dasi*. While *Raja* Krishna Chandra (1752-1765) had two wives,[127] Bhagirathi Harichandan (1778-1846) had three wives and many *Dasis*.[128] Bhagirathi had got special consideration for the children of the *Dasis* whom he granted landed property, financial benefits and other accommodation from the State.[129] Dayanidhi Harichandan (1846-1873) had three wives and two of his brothers had five wives.[130] Besides, the *Raja* had two *Dasis* whom he had given two villages.[131] Almost all the *Rajas* had a good number of *Dasis* in the royal palace. It is observed that some *Rajas* married again and again just to become father of a son which they desired most. During the royal marriage, a lot of money was being spent which was a day dream for the commoners. The birth ceremony, thread ceremony, marriage ceremony of the children, and other expenditure for them whose number was always very high due to many wives and *Dasis* of the Chiefs was going on lavishly and the amount was being spent from the State treasury. During the time of Kishore Chandra, a good number of ceremonies were held in the royal palace. For the comforts of the guests vast arrangements were made including construction of

126. Orissa Records, Talcher papers, *op. cit.*

127. G.S. Mishra, *op. cit.*, p. 74.

128. *Ibid.*, pp. 95-96.

129. *Ibid.*

130. *Ibid.*, pp. 119-120.

131. *Ibid.*

permanent conference hall, *mandap*, guest houses in the State and many bungalows inside the Ranipark.[132] All these were done from the public exchequer at the cost of developmental activities for the common men.

There was a big palace meant for the *Raj* family in Talcher which had got several rooms, conference hall, guest rooms and so on. Every year there was extension of the building expenditure on repairing and maintenance works. Besides that, another palace was constructed for the second son of Kishore Chandra at a place called Scotlandpur of Talcher. Kishore Chandra had got a building at Puri near Narendra Pokhari. He had got another house at Tulsipur of Cuttack known as Talcher *Kothi*. Prior to the purchase of this small palace at Cuttack, Kishore Chandra tried to seek permission from the Political Agent, Sambalpur but the latter denied it and did not give permission.[133] But the *Raja* could manage to purchase it later on. Besides he had got many buildings outside Talcher and Orissa where he used to stay during his tour period.

All these palaces had their own staff of various types and needed huge amount towards their salary, maintenance of the buildings and expenses for the inmates. All these came from State treasury.

The Chiefs were very pleasure loving and for this purpose a good amount was spent. Kishore Chandra from 1891 to 1945 spent a lot that way. A natural zoo called 'Ranipark', an important pleasure garden covering an area of 64 square kilometres was constructed just behind the royal palace to preserve wild animals of different varieties. About 2.5 lakhs of rupees was spent then and more was spent later.[134] The administrative reports for the year 1934-35 and 1935-36 of the State recorded that there was purchase of wild animals from different parts of India and outside India like Assam, Africa, German etc. The animals included Tiger Cubs, Leopards and Leopard Cubs, Bears, Hyena, Bisons, Camels, Antilop, Kudu, Sable, Bush back, White-deer, follow deer, Hog deers, Ring-tailed monkey etc. A group of people were engaged for the maintenance of it. The amount of fooding of the animals was huge. The king, members of the royal family or the royal visitors and State guests only enjoyed the park. During the visit of the foreign

132. G.S. Mishra, *op. cit.*, p. 172.

133. Orissa Records, Talcher Papers, Cobden-Ramsay, Political Agent, Sambalpur to Feudatory Chief of Talcher, Letter No. 7 G/153, 7 February 1915. (SRT)

134. S.B. Roy, *op. cit.*, p. 53.

dignitaries, there was facility to observe the wild life from close quarters. They could easily be hunted by these Britishers who used to pay visit to the State. In return, the throne of the Raja became more secured.[135] The entire huge expenditure was not meant for the benefit of the people rather it was for the self-amusement of the Chief.

On another side of the palace, there was a bird sanctuary covering an area of 90,000 square feets. Besides the birds of Indian origin, Kishore Chandra had purchased many more from China, Japan, Java and Malaya like Cocktail, Arquspheasan Reeve Pheasant, Chue Pheasant, Swinhol Pheasant, Monal Pheasant, Peacock Pheasant, Gold Pheasant, Diamond Dove, White Crasted Kalij Pheasant etc.[136] For this, also, the money was spent from the treasury. This not the tale of a nature-lover but madness of a royal chief to show off before outsiders and provide the British Officers enjoyment for his own purpose at State expenses.

A group of people was always there to whom the *Raja* used to listen. They praised high of the king before him and had rewards for it.[137] His own cousins also got this privilege from the *Raja* Kishore Chandra, had accommodated all of them in good posts though they did not deserve it. Even he had constructed a colony known as 'Samant Quarters' spending sixty thousand of rupees at that time from the State treasury for the residential purposes of his royal blood and fellowmen.[138] But the poor peasantry and the common people did not get a thatched shed to live at the State expense even at the time when they became homeless due to fire or turnado.

The Pattayat, the second son of Raja Kishore Chandra whom he liked more than the eldest one, went to the apex of administration during his father's reign.[139] He had accumulated wealth by setting up of a match factory, opening of a business shop on his name as 'Pramod Store', and many other businesses.[140] One can well imagine how this man could have devoted time for the welfare of the administration who was indulged in this private business. Even advance was being taken from the Talcher State Treasury to invest in the State Departments

135. S.B. Roy, *op. cit.*, p. 63.

136. *Ibid.*, pp. 98-99.

137. *Deshakatha,* 3 February 1931.

138. S.B. Roy, *op. cit.*, p. 113.

139. Orissa Records, Sambalpur Papers, Acc. No. 967S, No. R 9-36/45, *op. cit.*

140. Orissa Records, Talcher Paper, Administrator Talcher to Government of Orissa, Home Department in its Ref. Letter No. 19124/ST/25 November, 1948 on Private Properties of Ruler. (SRT)

consisted of brick moulding, workshop (furniture making), printing press and cloth shop. But the entire benefit was going to the ruler's pocket. Thousands of rupees on coal royalties was also swallowed by the ruler of Talcher every year, but, on the other hand, the peripheral development of Talcher remained a distant dream. The East India Syndicate, a coal company gave only an amount of Rs. 76,671-5-3 as mining royalty to the State in the year 1945-46.[141]

Jubilee Festival

Jubilee festivals were being celebrated with pomp and ceremony in the *Durbar* of Talcher. There were three such occasions which were held in 1911, 1921 and 1931 during time of Kishore Chandra.[142] In every ten years of the reign of the ruler this festival was being arranged by the followers of the *Raja* and his *Durbar* only to show the efficiency of the *Raja*, and eulogise his proper and good administration to the public, which was a mere farce. *Rasad*, *Bheti* and many gifts were being presented to the *Raja*. A great amount of money was being spent. The very first occasion was organised when the State was under pressing economic difficulties.[143] The subjects used to present the *Raja* a letter of congratulation for his administration which was actually made by the followers. But in return the people got nothing.[144] Satirically, people gave their opinion to observe the Jubilee celebration of the Raja every year.[145]

A good amount of money was given to the relatives of the rulers as allowances. The dynastic rule of Talcher shows that most of the people, either the relatives of the ruler or the people having royal blood, were enjoying administrative powers as well as financial help throughout the administration till its merger. Even some of them had been sanctioned grants throughout their life time. The sanctioned budget estimated for the years 1942-43 to 1947-48 showed that the allowances payable to *Raj Kumars* was debitable to the civil list as follows:[146]

141. Orissa Records, *op. cit.*, Political Agent to Ruler of Talcher, Mining Royalty, File No. 2/Admn. Report of Talcher 1945-46, Talcher, 31 July 1946. (SRT)

142. *Deshakatha*, 9 June 1931and G.S. Mishra, *op. cit.*, p. 176.

143. *Deshakatha*, *op. cit*.

144. *Ibid*.

145. *Ibid*., 1 June 1931.

146. Orissa Records, Talcher Papers, No. A-I-4 D.P. Tripathi, Administrator, Talcher, to the Special Officer, Orissa States, Cuttack, Allowances to relatives of the Ruler, Letter No. A-4/48-5178 Talcher, 26 November, 1948. (SRT)

Year	Sanctioned civil list provisions	Sanctioned allowances to Raj Kumars out of the civil list
1942-43	Rs. 69,661-5-6	Rs. 9,900/-
1943-44	Rs. 70,917-5-6	Rs. 16,200/-
1944-45	Rs. 94,917-13-3	Rs. 11,100/-
1945-46	Rs. 74,996-0-0	Rs. 22,800/-
1946-47	Rs. 89,158-8-0	Rs. 21,600/-
1947-48	Rs. 1,02,577-8-0	Rs. 27,600/-

Though the royal family members were in possessions of a good amount of landed properties, residential buildings, pleasure gardens, valuable ornaments, gold, money etc , the feudatory Chief of Talcher had favoured them more in granting money from the State treasury. The exact date of commencement in most of the cases is not available. After the merger of the State a list was sent to the Comptroller, Orissa State for his reference.[147] It stated :

	Name	Relation to the present Ruler	Amount paid per annum	Period
1.	Rajmata Kishori Manjari Devi	Mother (Granted since 1912)	Rs. 10,200/-	Till her Life time
2.	P.C. Dev, Pattayat of Talcher	Brother	Rs. 6,000/-	In perpetuity.
3.	Samant Keshab Chandra Mandhata	Near relative	Rs. 860/-	In perpetuity.
4.	Hadibandhu Singh	Near relative	Rs. 388-4-0	In perpetuity.
5.	Mahesh Chandra Samant	Near relative	Rs. 741-15-6	In perpetuity.
6.	Kailash Chandra Samant	Near relative	Rs. 180/-	In perpetuity.
7.	Umesh Chandra Samant	Near relative	Rs. 356/-	In perpetuity.
8.	Suresh Chandra Samant	Near relative	Rs. 356/-	In perpetuity.
9.	Sucharumali Devi	Sister	Rs. 300/-	Till her Life time

147. Orissa Records, *op. cit.*, Administrator, Talcher to the Comptroller, Orissa States, Mayurbhanj House, Puri Letter No. A. 1-4/48-5014 Talcher, 24 November 1948. (SRT)

10.	Paramananda Samant.	Illegitimate son of late Raja Rama-chandra Dev.	Rs. 590/-	Granted Since 1907
11.	Khitish Chandra Singh	Relation	Rs. 53/-	In perpetuity.
12.	Gour Chandra Das and so on.	Relation	Rs. 36/-	In perpetuity.

Some amount was given from the State Treasury to the people who went on praising the king and his administration through their articles, poems, periodicals published in different times. An amount of Rs. 50 was given annually to Sashibusan Rai for his contribution towards his writing on Talcher King's administration.[148]

The administration of the rulers of Talcher was far from being satisfactory. The people were exploited in the name of justice. They had no liberty in any of the fields. The officials were tyrants to their fingertips with the burden of inequitable taxation. People were deprived and exploited economically, and socially humiliated. The peasants were compelled to do forced labour for the State officials for more than one hundred days in an year. Then, even he was called up at any time for any work of the *Durbar*. At times, he was beaten, fined or even imprisoned. The British Government was a passive onlooker. People demanded justice from the ruler. In course of time, there was indignation among the people which ultimately resulted in the formation of people's movement which aimed at the release of the people from the political anomalies that prevailed in Talcher State. There was seething discontentment amongst them which burst out in the form of risings from time to time.

◆

148. Orissa Records, *op. cit.*, Audit Report 1947-48. Order and Report File, Audit Department Talcher. (SRT)

IV

People's Revolt in Talcher : Early Phase

The history of the heroic resistance movement of the people of Talcher took the same course as was taken by its counterparts in other areas of modern Orissa. The anti-feudal risings in Talcher State dated back from 1898. There were many sporadic uprisings between 1898 and 1932 which raised the banner of revolt against unreasonable enhancement of rent and assessment of new *abwabs* so common in the feudatory States at that time. Though these movements failed after sometime, yet its contribution to the growth of popular consciousness against unjust feudal exploitation and for a wider and stronger organisation of the people for the purpose could not be belittled. No movement can be a failure. It only becomes a stepping stone for the future wider movement.

People's Revolt : Early Phase

The first discontentment was rooted among the people in the year 1898.[1] As *Raja* Kishore Chandra was a minor the State was under Court of Wards. Damodar Patnaik was acting as the manager of the State.[2] Arrangements were made for the marriage of Kishore Chandra next year with pomp and ceremony. For this purpose the manager collected *Rasad* from the people. With this a cess of five annas per rupee land revenue was collected from the people as *magan*.[3] There was an agitation against this cess headed by leaders like Govind Sahu of Deulbera, Govind Sahoo of Talcher Town, Daitari Samantaray of Ghantapara and Mohan Dullavram.[4] People came forward to support the cause. But the agitation was suppressed by the Deputy Commissioner of the British territory of Angul.[5]

---

1. Anant Mishra, *op. cit.*, pp. 1-2.
2. G.S. Mishra, *op. cit.*, pp. 157-58.
3. *Orissa Review*, January 1989, p. 19.
4. Anant Mishra, *op. cit.*
5. *Ibid.*

In 1908 there was a second rising against the excess rent and the Chief was forced to give some concessions.[6] Subsequently, in the next year in 1909 there was another rising. The *Durbar* decided to impose a cess of five annas per one rupee land revenue instead of *beggar* and *Rasad*.[7] This was vehemently opposed by all. Leader like Purandar Pani of Bijigol came forward with the slogan against *bethi* and imposition of new cess. Meetings were organised in various parts of the State. Banamali Param Guru of Jagannathpur and Sudarshan Dhar of the same village became the President and Secretary respectively of the organisation. Purandar Pani became the Vice-President.[8] Secret meetings were held against the maladministration of the State. There was mass awakening. On the other hand, repressive measures were taken by the Chief.[9] The above leaders were arrested. The movement failed to achieve its objective and collapsed. Here we find the prototype of a *Prajamandal* that came up later. It is not known whether the uprising of 1909 was in any way influenced by the so-called Morley-Minto reforms granted to the people of the British Indian territories and denied to the people of princely States.

Another rising was seen in the State when the miscellaneous cess was levied in 1911.[10] The State imposed about seven *annas* per one rupee land revenue as miscellaneous cess which included forest cess, school cess, religious cess, *ratha* cess, personal cess etc. Besides, *magan* and *rasad* were also collected for the occasion of the jubilee celebration of the *Raja* in that year.[11] People under the leadership of Purandar Pani, Banamali Param Guru and Sudarshan Dhar protested against it.[12]

This agitation was more widespread and stronger than the previous ones. But the followers of the chief and the *Sarbarakars* and *Behera Pradhan* who were enjoying rent free land from the *Durbar* betrayed the people. Actions were taken against the people who participated in the movement. The leaders were fined heavily. The lands which were given to them as *Sarbarkari* and *Bhogara* were confiscated. The failure of 1911 uprising emboldened the king to collect miscellaneous cess

6. Anant Mishra, *op. cit.*, pp. 2-3.
7. *Ibid.*
8. *Ibid.*
9. *Ibid.*
10. *Deshakatha*, 27 April 1931, and *Orissa States Enquiry Committee Report*, p. 7.
11. *Deshakatha, op. cit.*
12. Anant Mishra, *op. cit.*, p. 4.

from the people to celebrate in Talcher the occasion of the grand *Durbar* of Emperor George V held at Delhi in 1912.[13] Dissatisfaction grew among the people. They made representation to the authorities for redressal of their grievances. The *Raja* did not listen to it. The representation of grievances was considered seditious. The people refused to pay extra and illegal tax. Purandar Pani, Banamali Param Guru and some others were tried in 1912 under Section 124 A.I.P. for petitioning the political agent against the ruler and against the taxation policy of the State.[14] The Political Agent invariably sent back the representation to the ruler without any consideration. The result on each occasion had been the severe punishment of those who had dared to make the representation.[15] Sadananda Pradhan and others had to furnish security for good conduct for their offences to protest against *bethi* and taxation.[16] The cases of the people in some instances were referred to *Dharmaadalut*. The intention was only to create confusion among the people, among the castes and among the leaders. This agitation was cruelly suppressed by force.[17]

The war years saw comparative lull in people's activities. In 1922 a similar rising occurred in the State.[18] The thread ceremony of *Pattayat* Pramod Chandra Dev, the youngest son of the *Raja* was being celebrated in that year. People were forced to do *bethi* and supply *Rasad* to the *Durbar* for the said purpose. *Magana* was collected in huge quantity from the people. But the villagers of Nalam and several others with the leadership of Natabar Sunder Ray, Bankanidhi Bhakta Ballav and Raghunath Pradhan opposed this type of imposition and protested against it.[19] Many villagers from village Nalam were arrested by the *Raja* and kept in the prison where they were beaten mercilessly. Leaders were humiliated in such a manner that they had to remain silent. However this was curbed down ruthlessly.[20] But the general effect of all these ruthless suppression of popular discontentment was an impending crisis. With the gradual development of greater and greater self-confidence amongst the tenants and the gradual impact of the

13. *Deshakatha*, 9 June 1931.
14. *Orissa States Enquiry Committee Report*, p. 103.
15. *Ibid.*, p. 111.
16. *Ibid.*, p. 103.
17. *Orissa Review*, January 1989, p. 19.
18. R.N. Rath, *op. cit.*, p. 16.
19. P.M. Pradhan, *op. cit.* p. 43 and p. 51.
20. H.K. Mahtab, *History of Freedom Movement in Orissa,* Vol. III, p. 95.

growth of national movement under Gandhian leadership all over the country could not isolate Talcher from the rest of the country.

Thus, the next rising of 1932 was comparatively more fruitful and effective in creating positive impact on the State Authorities of Talcher.[21] People of village Jhula Khuntia and nine others decided not to pay extra taxes, cess or do any more *bethi* in the State. They also put forth their grievances before the political agent. Dhobei Chual Singh and Brindaban Pradhan took the lead in this agitation.[22] The people of these villages denied to join the *Hathi Kheda Bethi* at Gengutia. For this reason, Chual Singh was imprisoned for one year.[23]

These risings though suppressed, failed to wipe out popular discontentment. Suppression of every movement only created the condition for a vigorous determined next movement. With the continuance of tyranny and maladministration of the *Durbar*, the fire of resistance and revolt only spread wide among the populace. The twenties and thirties of twentieth century were different from pre-world war days. With the Gandhian leadership, the national movement had entered an agitational path and in the thirties there was the Congress programme of civil disobedience. Such a turn of national movement whose spark had already reached Talcher, must have emboldened the people of Talcher State.

In 1936 some of the people including school and college students opposed the set up of *Dharma Adalat* which aimed at bringing differences and fractions among the people by casteism.[24] In 1938 the High School students went on a strike. The *Durbar* gave notification that all the school students must wear *Khaki* half pants and shirts. These were only available in Pramod Store, a shop of the *Pattayat*. Naturally there was a sudden, artificially created huge demand of the dress with an aim to profit the member of the royal family. The entire business was managed by the *Pattayat* privately. The students vehemently protested against such an order of the ruler.[25] The ruler was forced to withdraw the order. This retreat was a moral booster for the people.

---

21. H.K. Mahtab, *Odisa Itihas*, p. 517 and *Orissa States Enquiry Committee Report*, p. 7.
22. P.M. Pradhan, *op. cit.*
23. Anant Mishra, *op. cit.*, p. 9.
24. *Ibid.*, pp. 10-14.
25. *The Samaj*, 29 June 1938.

During this period, the 'New Orissa Theatre', of Banchhanidhi Mohanty and Gourang Das staged patriotic plays at Talcher. The songs were also full of patriotism. These plays added fuel to the fire of the agitation and mass awakening gradually grew among the people. A good number of students, farmers, labourers, middle class people and service holders gradually began to understand the realities of time.[26] Talcher, henceforth, would never remain the same again.

Labour Union

In 1937, the labourers of the Coal Mines of Talcher started secret movements to form a labour union.[27] The aim of forming this union was to fight against the tyranny of the King. Communist leaders like Bhagabati Panigrahi, Sarat Patnaik and Laxmidhar Sahoo were leading the movement. Afterwards Pabitra Mohan Pradhan and Maguni Chandra Pradhan of the *Prajamandal* helped them. On 6 January 1940 a Board consisting of seven members was formed in the collieries.[28] In this Board Harmohan Patnaik became the President and Laxman Mohapatra was the Secretary. This Board helped in collecting the labourers at a place at any time for the movement against the maladministration of the ruler. The trade union was not only confined to its own demands but made common cause with the *Prajamandal* against the feudal autocracy. This unity helped a lot to the *Prajamandal* movement later on and the workers had their share of anti-feudal uprising of the forties.

The agitations inside the State of Talcher which were started in different periods since 1898 to 1932 could not achieve their goal due to the suppressive measures taken by the ruler of Talcher. The British Government remained only a passive onlooker. Besides, there was lack of proper organisation and absence of co-operation among the leaders of the State. There was no outside help to fight for the cause of the subjects.

The '*Garajat Praja Sammilani*' which was formed in 1931 was responsible for bringing a sense of unity among the people of the *Garajat* States of Orissa. People were encouraged to fight for the cause of the commoners.[29] Some educated persons of Talcher came forward

26. Anant Mishra, *op cit.*
27. *Ibid.*, pp. 15-16.
28. *Ibid.*
29. L.N. Sahu, *Orissa Garjat*, Cuttack, 1931, p. 18.

to take the leadership of the people bravely. Prominent among them was Pabitra Mohan Pradhan of village Poipal. Though he was a high school teacher under the State *Durbar* he had decided to dedicate himself to the cause of the people since his childhood. He was assisted by Dasarathi Pani, Gouri Shankar Pradhan, Madan Mohan Pradhan, Kritibas Rath and Maguni Chandra Pradhan.[30] The leaders were determined to fight for the benefit of the people of Talcher against the monarchical government of the State. They expected moral help from the National Congress and its leaders in the nearby British Indian territories.

Secret Organisation and Movement

From 1935 to 1937, Pabitra Mohan Pradhan with the help of his friends and other leaders started organising the people secretly. He was working as a teacher in the High School by that time. Every Saturday evening, he used to go to various villages to contact the village heads regarding the future programme. While going round the villages he was telling the villagers about the activities of the Congress and their future role to get freedom from the tyranny of the *Raja* of Talcher. On Saturdays and Sundays, the villagers used to assemble together in different centres like Nadikul, Bajrakot, Derang and Poipal.[31] Newspapers were circulated in these centres. Leaders of different *Parganas* came to the centres on every Sunday and came to know about the activities of the Congress on Indian Independence from the newspapers. Even some people from Pallahara and Bamra took part in this secret discussion and organisation. Bankanidhi Bhakta Ballav* was organising all these secret meetings.[32] Towards 1937 this organisation expanded its base with participation of more villagers. Its centres were opened at Biru, Siipur, Suleipal, Jhula Khuntia, Rengali, Kansamunda, Jarada, Kumunda, Bijigol, Danara, Handidhua, Kankili and Gurujang. The organisation of the colliery areas and Khemei region rested in the hands of Maguni Chandra Pradhan and Madan Mohan Pradhan respectively.[33]

After the creation of the secret organisation inside Talcher State, Pabitra Mohan Pradhan kept in touch with the Congress workers of

30. *Talcher Prajamandal Itihas Committee* (*Compl*), *op. cit.*, pp. 13-14.
31. *Ibid.*
* See Appendix B
32. *Talcher Prajamandal Itihas Committee* (*Compl.*), *op. cit.*
33. *Ibid.*

the nearby British administered areas where the Congress movement was going on. He also had correspondence with the *Garjat Praja Sammilani*, which by this time was formed but remained almost defunct until Sarngdhar Das became its Secretary early in 1937.[34] In an appeal on 20 March 1937, Sarangdhar wanted to convince the people of the Orissa States to be united to fight against the tyranny of the feudal chiefs for the attainment of representative government in the States.[35] He made a second appeal on 27 April 1937 while convening the second session of the *Garjat Praja Sammilani* on 19 and 20 June 1937 and requested the people of the States to attend the same without fail. Of course the date was postponed to 23 to 24 June 1937.[36] Accordingly its second session was held at Cuttack on 23 and 24 June 1937 where an enquiry committee was formed with H.K. Mahtab as its president.[37] The aim of the Committee was to collect detailed information about the circumstances prevailing in Orissa States and the condition of the people of different States under the rule of their chiefs. The Committee conducted their enquiry from 20 June to 30 August 1938 and examined about 2,300 witnesses in several sittings.[38] H.K. Mahtab toured different States where he had the first hand opportunity to study the condition of the States' people. He had approached the rulers to send copies of the Annual Administrative reports about the affairs of the States. But there was no response from the rulers.[39]

The Enquiry Committee recorded fresh, voluminous and authentic evidences at Banarpal, 12 Kilometres distance from Talcher on 26 June 1938.[40] The workers of the secret organisations of Talcher gave witness before the Committee with full particulars. Pabitra Mohan Pradhan and his friends helped this Committee in producing papers before them about the maladministration of the State without the knowledge of the *Raja* of Talcher. The corruption, tyranny, repression and exploitation of the Chief were made public by these witnesses.

---

34. Orissa Records, Talcher Papers, Leaflet, *Odisa Gadajat Praja Sammilani Nibedan*, Oriya, Cuttack, 20 March, 1937. (SRT). See Appendix K.

35. *Ibid.*

36. *Ibid.*, *op. cit.*, Cuttack, 27 April 1937.
See Appendix L.

37. *Orissa States Enquiry Committee Report*, pp. 1-3.

38. *Ibid.*

39. *Ibid.*

40. *The Samaj*, 28 June 1938.

About a hundred people from Talcher gave their opinion before the Committee.[41]

Reaction of Talcher Durbar

The secret organisations and movements of the workers could not be kept secret in Talcher any more. The witness before the enquiry committee and the correspondence with the Congress workers of Cuttack and Angul came to light in course of time. But the name of the workers could not be known. People gradually supported the workers. The *Raja* kept a vigilant eye on their movements. But there was no proof to it as the underground activities had got full approval of the State subjects.

The activities of Pabitra Mohan Pradhan was doubted as he was residing in the school hostel during his service career. He was cautioned not to do any thing against the prestige of the *Durbar*. He was threatened to be killed if he would not avoid the secret organisation. Many people on suspicion were also cautioned, false cases were filed against them and they were brutally tortured.[42] But nothing could prevent them from organising the meetings and the movements inside the State. The open movement at Nilgiri by the people against the tyrannical rule of their chief in June 1938 echoed among the people of Talcher State. They decided to come out their secret cell and organise their movements openly. The State *Durbar* took repressive measures. Attempts were made to arrest Gour Chandra Pradhan, Maguni Pradhan and Dasarathi Pani. Pabitra Mohan Pradhan was put under home arrest.[43] Rest of the leaders were threatened to be beaten. So the prominent leaders decided to go out of the State to nearby provincial areas from where they would be in a position to work freely without any opposition from the ruler of Talcher. Angul, the nearby British territory was naturally selected as the most suitable place to be the makeshift centre of the movement for the time being.

Organising Camps at Angul

Camps were opened at places like Paniola, Natada, Kosala, Santarbandh, Kamsala etc.[44] The leaders like Maguni Chandra Pradhan, Gouri Shankar Pradhan, Kritibas Rath, Adhara Chandra Pradhan,

41. *The Samaj*, 28 June 1938.
42. *Talcher Prajamandal Itihas Committee* (*Compl.*), p. 14.
43. *Ibid.*
44. H.K. Mahtab, *op. cit.*, p. 17, and *Deshakatha*, 19 July 1939.

Kunjabehari Pradhan and many others escaped to Angul before their arrest at Talcher during July 1938.[45] In a night of that month Pabitra Mohan Pradhan also escaped from Talcher to Angul.[46] Subsequently, he resigned from the State service. The leaders decided to carry on the agitation by residing in the above camps at Angul which were lying near the border of Talcher State. Now the movement was carried on openly.

The escape of the organisers to Angul created a flutter in the minds of the people in general. They became very much happy to know the successful escape of their leaders from the clutches of the Raja. They thought of a new world. The long suppressed feeling of the people suddenly found an outlet as they thought of an open movement to achieve their goal. Fear from the *Raja* and his administration gradually disappeared from their minds. They were anxious to be free from the hundred years of ruthless administration of the chief. People from different corners of Talcher started pouring into the camps at Angul. Donations in shape of money and food were sent to these camps from Talcher, Volunteers, thousand in numbers rushed to these camps from Talcher. Men, women, children and old encouraged the organisers to carry on their movement.[47]

Formation of Talcher Prajamandal

On 6 September 1938 an open meeting was held in the village Kosala of Angul organised by the people of Talcher. About six thousand of volunteers joined in it. The meeting was presided over by Pabitra Mohan Pradhan and a Prajamandal was constituted.[48] The following members were elected as the office bearers.

Pabitra Mohan Pradhan	-	President
Balaram Mohapatra*	-	Vice-President
Dasarathi Pani	-	Joint Secretary
Maguni Chandra Pradhan	-	Joint Secretary
Gouri Shankar Pradhan	-	Treasurer
Kritibas Rath	-	Office Secretary
Chandra Shekhar Das	-	Assistant Treasurer[49]

45. *Talcher Prajamandal Itihas Committee* (*Compl.*), pp. 15-16.

46. P.M. Pradhan, *op. cit.*, p. 56.

47. *Ibid.*

48. *Anand Bazar Patrika*, 10 September 1938 (SUA)

* See Appendix B

49. P.M. Pradhan, *op. cit.*, pp. 61-62.

The aims and objectives along with a demand sheet were formulated in this meeting. The copies of the proceedings of the above meeting were circulated in all the villages of Talcher.

Another meeting was held at Kosala of Angul on 16 September 1938. About forty thousand people from Talcher assembled at the meeting. Almost all the *Sarbarakars*, *Mukaddams* and *Garnaiks* had attended it.[50] The proceedings of the former meeting (6 September) were approved unanimously in this meeting. It resolved to carry on the movement till the fulfilment of their demands. With loud cheers the people returned to Talcher and decided to carry on a ceaseless fight for the fulfilment of their popular demands under the guidance of the *Prajamandal*.

The Charter of Demands of Prajamandal

The Talcher *Prajamandal* carried on the agitation with unabated vigour and drew up a list of demands. The charter of demands contained about sixteen items as follows.[51]

(1) the right to form associations, hold meetings and make procession, granting of civil liberties and full responsible government, freedom of press;

(2) abolition of *rasad*, *magan*, *bethi* during ceremonies at *Durbar*;

(3) the enactment and modification of the Tenancy laws; better condition in the collection;

(4) rationalisation of the rent system and the amendment of forest laws, concession in collecting forest products for the poor;

(5) total abolition of forced labour or *bethi* without payment, abolition of miscellaneous cess of five annas;

(6) abolition of monopoly system on Salt, Kerosene, *bidi*, tabacco, betelnut, betel leaf, *tamakhu* etc., free trade on import and export of forest articles;

(7) abolition of fees for social functions like marriages', re-marriage, widow remarriage, atonement for the death of a cow etc., abolition of *Dharma Adalut* or ecclesiastical court;

(8) payment of more salary to the paiks who worked in the police department and abolition of forced labour on them;

---

50. Orissa Records, W.W.C.C., Acc. No. 38, pp. 29-30.

51. *Ibid*.

(9) reservation of 85 percentage of post for the people of Talcher in the coalmines, permission of trade union activities there, rationalisation of pay and introduction of Mining Act by the Government of India. in the Coalmines areas;

(10) introduction of higher education for the lower castes, scholarship privileges and job opportunity on the basis of merit for them should be made;

(11) abolition of professional taxes on blacksmith, goldsmith, oil-men, washerman, confectioner, *hadi* etc;

(12) disallow to the royal blood to do any business inside the State;

(13) payment of proper cost to the land holders of Kankili village whose lands were taken away by the State for construction of an aerodrome fields;

(14) investment of 50 per cent of the total collection of the State for the improvement of education, health, irrigation, roads, bridges etc., to hand over the school cess on the committee of the people;

(15) protection of *Lakhraj* lands and improvement of Sanskrit education for Brahmin students;

(16) to have responsible government through elected people's representatives *i.e.* an adult franchise in the State and this type of government would only be beneficial to both the *Raja* and his people.[52]

A leaflet* in Oriya containing the above demands was circulated by the Talcher *Prajamandal* from its Angul Camp.

An analysis of the charter of demands speaks of the nature and character of the *Prajamandal* in Talcher. There was common demand of all classes and castes about the basic human rights, abolition of obnoxious taxes, cesses and demands, abolition of State monopoly of certain items, rights of local people on their forest and forest products, spending of half of State income in the State in welfare sphere. At the same time, the leaders of *Prajamandal* put up certain class and caste demands to unite all groups in it. The demand of the colliery workers

52. H.K. Mahtab, *History of Freedom Movement in Orissa*, Vol. IV, Cuttack, 1937, p. 17.

* See Appendix M.

were included to bring them to the United front. The demand of the enhancement of the salary of the *Paiks* was put cleverly to make a breach between the lower level of administration, who from class analysis was on the side of the people from the upper one, dominated by people of royal blood, landed elites and their cronies. Even their effort was not to brand it a movement dominated by peasant caste, as certain demands of the Brahmins like protection of *Lakhaj* lands and improvement of Sanskrit education for Brahmin student were included. The question of pros and cons of adding these sectarian demands in the charter of *Prajamandal* should not be discussed as, at that time, the priority was to bring all on a common platform of struggle with a charter of demand in which all castes and classes should have some special interest over and above the common general demand. This was a tactical line of mass mobilisation in the underdeveloped feudal condition of Talcher.

The demand sheet was handed over to the *Raja* on 11 September 1938 which made him quite upset. He wanted to take revenge. On 13 September 1938 Madan Mohan Pradhan a school teacher and an active member of the Talcher *Prajamandal* and Bhagirathi Pradhan, the *Qanoongo* of the State were arrested as they were indulged in Talcher movement. They were threatened to be dismissed if they would go against the State administration.[53] The *Raja* formed another organisation called *Praja Parishad* inside the State with help of some of his followers only to counter the *Prajamandal* headed by Pabitra Mohan Pradhan.[54] He wanted to bring most of the people to his side and called a meeting of the *Praja Parishad* to this effect. But it was observed that majority number of people were in support of the *Prajamandal*, The *Raja* was disappointed. By this time Madan Mohan Pradhan, the active leader of Talcher *Prajamandal*, resigned from his service. Balaram Mohapatra, the Vice-President of *Prajamandal* was dismissed from his job at the State *Durbar*. The leaders from now onwards carried on the movement in the State bravely and quite openly. The mass, enthusiastically, supported the movement and almost all the people joined the *Prajamandal* as active workers. Mass meetings were held in different parts of the State, processions were organised in protest against the despotic administration of the chief and non-cooperation with the administration was successfully organised. This resulted in a mass awakening.[55]

53. *Krushak*, 24 September 1938.

54. *Talcher Prajamandal Itihas Committee* (*Compl.*), *op. cit.*, p. 22.

55. N.K. Sahu and S.C. De, *op. cit.*, p. vi.

By that time the Congress had formed the ministry in Orissa which boosted their morale and enthused them to go for bigger and bigger struggle in future days. The Congress involvement in States' Peoples' Movement in Orissa despite the clear direction from AICC further linked the movement in the State to the wider national movement outside and brought them to realise the various dimensions of their struggle.

Measures Taken by Raja

The *Raja* of Talcher resorted to all sorts of repressive measures for suppressing the movement. He started a reign of terror. The *Durbar* issued notices banning *Khadar* and Gandhi caps. People wearing Gandhi cap and wearing *Khadar* dress were arrested and punished under law.[56] By another notification the Talcher *Prajamandal* and its branches had been declared unlawful under Criminal Law Amendment Act No. XIV of 1908 and the members of those associations had been asked to withdraw their membership within 18 September 1938.[57] These notifications had created stir among the people.

The State authority of Talcher arrested many agitators and even expelled large number of people from the State. People suspected to be actively associated with *Prajamandal* were interrogated and their houses were searched. Innocent persons were fined and subjected to physical torture. The assembly of more than five persons was declared illegal. False cases were instituted against the suspected participants of the movement. The labourers who eked out a miserable living were compelled to execute bonds for the discharge of forced labour. The properties of the agitators were unlawfully forfeited by the State. The people who defied the law were flogged, fined heavily and sent to the prison in large scale. Even some leaders of the *Prajamandal* were caught behind by some hired miscreants from the camps of Angul, brought to Talcher and thrown behind the prison where they were brutally tortured.[58]

The repressive measures could not check the people's upsurge in the State and more numbers of people jumped to the fire of the movement. Future plan and programmes were always sorted out in the camps of Angul through meetings. Accordingly, meetings and

56. *Anand Bazar Patrika*, 18 September 1938 (SUA)

57. *Ibid.*, and *Krushak*, 24 September 1938.

58. *Talcher Prajamandal Itihas Committee* (*Compl.*), p. 23.

processions were organised inside the State territory defying the prohibitory order of the *Durbar*. Parallel 'Panchayat' administrations were carried on in the villages.[59] Most of the cases were settled amicably in presence of both the parties and leaders of the *Prajamandal*.[60] The people refused to pay any illegal tax or render any forced labour. At last, the chief took the help of the armed police. Finding the armed force inadequate, he requisitioned the British forces. On 20 September 1938, in the dead of the night, these armed forces rushed into some villages namely Bantol, Kakudula, Baghoabole, Ghantapara, Kankili, Deulbera and Handidhua. The villagers were molested in different ways. It was alleged that a vehicle carrying the police force was stranded in the sand. The villagers were forced by the police to do *bethi* on pushing back the vehicle to move. But they refused to do so and consequently it took the form of civil disobedience.[61] The angry police forces molested and assaulted men, women and children and looted their houses.[62] On 21 September the police opened fire on the agitating people of village Chandrabil causing the death of Bika Nayak and serious injury to five others.[63] These injured persons included Rathi Behera, Bali Sahu, Jogi Behera, Baishnab Behera, and Magta Moharana.[64] All of them were admitted to Angul hospital. The police also raided other villages like Seepur, Gurujang, Poipal and Kankili.

The chief appealed to the people of Talcher in a proclamation on 22 September 1938 to withdraw themselves from the movement. In the appeal he said :

> "My dear innocent subjects, you have created anarchy and terror in the State at the persuasion of some selfish revolutionists. Many of you are ignorant of the reason or purpose for which you are doing so. It is known to me. From the very beginning of the agitation, I am having frequent opportunities of discussing with a great majority of you regarding the movement. I am fully convinced of the correctness of this decision of mine. Now in the present circumstances, before requesting His Majesty's force

59. *Talcher Prajamandal Itihas Committee* (*Compl.*), p. 23.
60. *Krushak*, 24 September 1938.
61. Orissa Records, Talcher Papers, Enquiry Report of the Senior State Officer, Talcher to the Administrator, Talcher, 26 February 1948.
62. *Ibid.*, W.W.C.C., Acc. No. 38, p. 33. and Krushak, 24 September 1938.
63. N.K. Sahu and S.C. De, *op. cit.*, p. vi, and Muktipatha, 5th Issue, 30 September 1938 (SRT) See Appendix N.
64. *Krushak*, 24 September 1938.

through the Honourable Political Agent for helping me in the situation, I again appeal to you through this proclamation to give up the spirit of violence you have so far inculcated and to leave the self-seekers whose evil pursuasions have turned you astray. I am also asking you that you cannot accuse my *Durbar* of any harm or loss which you may sustain in future if you neglect to comply the declaration of my *Durbar*.

Now I ask you to come away immediately from the evil guidance of the persons who have engaged you and have instigated you to the ruinous path against the *Raja*, his administration and the paramountcy and *Ranee Seheba*. We are even ready to forgive you, it is sufficiently known to you that my palace gates and my *Durbar* are always wide open for such forgiveness.

22nd September, 1938 Raja Kishore Chandra Birabar Harichandan, *Durbar*, Talcher".[65]

The appeal failed to cool down the mass temper. Many of them, mostly the villagers were afraid of the torture of the police and they ran into the forest to hide themselves. Some of them went to Angul, Pallahara and Bamra to take refuge. Due to absence of the workers, the work at coalmines hampered.[66] On the other hand the ruler brought help from the neighbouring States to stop the activities of the *Prajamandal* workers in Talcher. Freedom of press was curtailed in the State. Apprehending encouragement of lawlessness and disaffection among the people against the ruler through the press, the entry of the *Samaj*, the daily newspaper and '*Krushak*', the weekly newspaper of the Congress Socialist Party, were banned in Talcher.[67]

But the growing public spirit of the workers, the awakening political consciousness of the masses and the spirit of the time combined with the undoubted grievances of the people and their natural aspiration for self-expression and self-determination generated spirit of defiance and resistance. For the smooth conduct of the movement in Talcher, people were provided with pamphlets, circulars and leaflects by the Talcher *Prajamandal* which contained guidelines to the people, encouraging them for further movement. A vernacular pamphlet named *Muktipath** was published by Talcher *Prajamandal* from its Angul camp at different

65. Talcher State Gazette, 22 September 1938. (SUA)
66. Anant Mishra, *op. cit.*, pp. 17-19.
67. Home Political (Internal) File No. 32/7/38 (NAI)

times and circulated among the people of Talcher advising them about their future course of action. It served as the organ of the *Prajamandal* in Talcher. The indiscriminate firing on peaceful crowd gave a new turn to the people's movement which adopted the means of non-cooperation. *Satyagraha* was launched in Talcher on 5 October 1938.[68] As the first step, about twenty number of *Satyagrahis* came forward and marched through the villages like Jagannathpur, Bantol, Kukudula, Baghoabol and Talcher *garh* with the slogans of 'Mahatma Gandhi Ki Jai' and 'Talcher *Prajamandal* Jindabad'. While continuing their peaceful march, they were arrested, beaten in the custody and sent to jail.[69] This was being followed by another group consisting of the same number of *Satyagrahis*. The *Prajamandal* instructed the people to get themselves ready, in a group of at least twenty from each village to join the *Satyagraha* movement in Talcher, so that there would be continuity in the movement without any break.[70] The *Satyagraha* volunteers were trained in Angul camps. About fourteen hundred *Satyagrahis* started agitation on batches in Talcher through non-violent means for about two months. The slogans which they uttered were mainly connected with non-payment of heavy, excessive, uneconomic and illegal medieval feudal dues, responsible Government and abolition of forced labour. But the *Raj Durbar* interpreted these slogans to be revolutionary.[71]

The *Satyagrahis* opposed the activities of police force inside the State. They carried on meetings after meetings and took out procession in defiance of the State's prohibitory order. Many volunteers were arrested and sent to jail.[72] Mobilization among the people went on for non-payment of land revenue as a result of which most of the lands were confiscated.[73] The *Satyagrahis* wherever found were dragged to the police station and were brutally tortured. The Talcher jail was overcrowded with these *Satyagrahis* and there they were meted out with inhuman punishments. More than a thousand *Satyagrahis* became

---

* Given in Appendices Oi and Oii.

68. *Anand Bazar Patrika*, 16 October 1938. (SUA)
69. *Muktipath*, 7th Issue, 6 October 1938. (SRT)
    See Appendix P.
70. *Ibid.*
71. *Anand Bazar Patrika*, 16 October 1938. (SUA)
72. *Ibid.*, 7 October 1938. (SUA)
73. Orissa Records, Talcher Papers, Court of the State Magistrate, Case No. 40 of 1938-39. (SRT)

prisoners in Talcher jail which had the capacity to keep very few persons. Their food and shelter was quite insufficient in the jail. Each of them was beaten mercilessly. They were forced to sign in blank papers.[74] Some were tattooed with the letters like 'Ni and 'Ha' singifying the word *Nimak Haram*' on their arms with the help of hot irons.[75] Some also had been branded on their buttocks. Number of ways were devised to harass and inflict punishment on those subjects who dared to defy the authority of the State and participated in the agitation against the misrule of the chief. Outside the jail, the volunteers were also tortured. The houses of the organisers were broken with the help of elephants or were burnt.[76]

Bethi was now being realised with the help of armed police, to construct and repair roads in spite of the special cess collected earlier for that purpose at the rate of five annas per rupee of rent.[77] The *Durbar* again had imposed three fresh taxes on people which involved of one for meeting the agitations, another for meeting the cost of military force brought to quell the agitation and the third one for repairing roads. One, who would not pay would be disallowed to reap the harvest from the field.[78] Simultaneously, rampant loot and arson also went on unabeted. All these repressions were made by the State authority to break the backbone of the people's movement. Leaders were also arrested from outside Talcher. Dasarathi Pani, Secretary of Talcher *Prajamandal*, Kritibas Rath and Gouri Sankar Pradhan were arrested at Angul under extradition warrant under Sections 431 and 109 of the Indian Penal Code.[79] Inspite of arrests, firing, torture, loot and arson the people did not give up their fight. By this time Srimati Sauridevi, wife of Bankanidhi Bhakta Ballav of Talcher *Prajamandal* who was in jail, had been elected the new dictator, to lead the people's movement in Talcher in absence of the organisers.[80] The matter took a serious turn and all eyes, including Mahatma Gandhiji's were then focused on Talcher. Gandhiji was always in touch with the affairs of

74. *Krushak*, 15 October 1938.
75. *Harijan*, 20 May 1939. (OSA)
    Nimak Haram is an Oriya word meaning ungrateful.
76. P.M. Pradhan, *op. cit.*, pp. 66-67.
77. *Anand Bazar Patrika*, 2 November 1938. (SUA)
78. *Ibid.*
79. *Ibid.*
80. *Ibid.*, 17 December 1938. (SUA)

Talcher through various channels. In accordance with Gandhiji's advice the representatives of Talcher *Prajamandal* met Hare Krishan Mahtab, the eminent Congress leader of Orissa at Cuttack to represent their case before him.[81] Mahtab was also advised to proceed to Angul and Talcher the next day to study the situation and submit his report to Gandhiji.[82]

Hare Krishna Mahtab and Girija Bhusan Dutta, a Congress M.L.A. were always taking interest in the people's movement of Talcher and they were giving their valuable advice to the organisers of *Prajamandal*. In the presence of both the leaders, the organisers of Talcher people's movement and more than five hundred important workers sat together at Angul to discuss the inhuman torture of the Talcher Chief. As the people of Talcher were unable to tolerate the repressive measures of the ruler, an alternative novel course of action was badly necessary. In the meeting Hare Krishna Mahtab was entrusted to meet Gandhiji and seek his advice on the issue.[83] Accordingly Mahtab went to Gandhiji to narrate the oppressive rule of the Talcher Chief. Gandhiji advised him that the people of Talcher should leave for any British territory like Angul which would attract the attention of the British Government and it might pressurise the Talcher *Durbar* to redress the grievances of the people of Talcher.[84] Gandhiji also reported to have written a letter in this connection to Girija Bhusan Dutta.[85]

Mass Exodus from Talcher

The people of Talcher finding the repression of the ruler too severe resorted to mass exodus (hizrat) from Talcher under the leadership of Pabitra Mohan Pradhan and other leaders of *Prajamandal* and on the advice of Mahatma Gandhi.[86] This exodus commenced from 8 November 1938 and on this very day villagers from twenty-five villages had almost evacuated from Talcher State,[87] By the end of December 1938, it was estimated that about thirty thousand* of people out of the total population of seventy thousand had evacuated from

81. *Anand Bazar Patrika*, 7 October 1938 (SUA)
82. *Ibid.*
83. N.K. Sahu and S.C. De, *op. cit.*, p. VI.
84. *Ibid.*
85. *Talcher Prajamandal Itihas Committee* (*Compl.*), *op. cit.*, p. 25.
86. N.K. Sahu and S.C. De, *op. cit.*,
87. P.M. Pradhan, *op. cit.*, p. 69.

* The number was 26,000 published in *Harijan* of Mahatma Gandhi.

about fifty number of villages.[88] They took refuge in several camps at the British territory of Angul which included Kosala, Kamasala, Natada, Changudia, Santarbandh, Bhalugadia and Paniola.[89] There refugee took shelter for about eight months. They had left their ripe paddy fields and *rabi* crops which were attached by the *Raja*. Their properties were confiscated.

There was acute problem of food and water in these refugee camps.[90] But the people could sustain it. On the other hand the number of refugees increased day by day.[91] The Congress Government of Orissa took steps for their shelter, health, hygiene, drinking water etc. The increase of their number became a problem for the Government of Orissa to give them proper shelter.[92] They were living in huts of leaves in open space defying the ravages of the winning hill. About 4,000 huts had been erected to house the refugees.[93] The refugees had to loose the crops for two years. They had exposed themselves to the bitter winter and then to the scorching sun of summer under the chequered leaf-shades hurriedly built by themselves.

The way of life in these camps was quite ideal. People from different castes were living together as co-fighters for a common cause. They had forgotten casteism and thought of a model society. Gandhiji had advised to start *Satyagraha* in British Orissa only. It was followed in these refugee camps which were supervised by Girija Bhusan Dutta, representatives of Angul, Laxmidhar Roy Choudhury and Saibani Dei.[94] Flag hoisting, meetings, newspaper reading, political teaching to the refugees and the methods of successfully organising the agitation were the daily discussions of the camp routine. There was *Panchayat* administration in the camps. Branches were opened for education, health, food, trade, relief work etc. There was a camp-chief and a dectator who took the entire responsibility of the camp life.[95]

---

88. *The Statesman,* 12 January 1939. (SUA)
89. *Anand Bazar Patrika,* 4 December 1938. (SUA)
90. *The Statesman, op. cit.*
91. *Orissa Legislative Assembly Proceedings,* Vol. IV, 18 March 1939, pp. 167-70. (OSA)
92. *Anand Bazar Patrika,* 4 December 1938. (SUA)
93. *Ibid.*
94. Orissa Records, W.W.C.C., Acc. No. 38, pp. 31-32.
95. *Talcher Prajamandal Itihas Committee* (*Compl.*), *op. cit.*, pp. 23-25.

Official and Non-official Help to the Camps

The refugees, who stayed outside Talcher in the camps of Angul, underwent great hardship and forgot their cultivation, properties and life at Talcher. Forty-six per cent of the total population of Talcher, men, women and children left their hearth and homes had decided that they would rather die than return to the State where life, honour and property were all unsafe. They came among with tears in their eyes and babies in their arms knowing not what would happen to them, as they were desperate and determined.[96] This was an unprecedented event in the annals of the States' Peoples' Movement in India and consequently, attracted attention of the leading politicians of India and some in England. The Congress and Socialist leaders of the province fully supported the agitation and denounced the oppression of the ruler of Talcher.

Hare Krishna Mehtab, the eminent leader had expressed his great concern and criticised the callousness of the *Raja* of Talcher regarding the exodus of people from his State. He was surprised to see how the exodus of a large number of people from a small State like Talcher was treated so lightly by the Talcher *Durbar*.[97] A photograph of the refugees of Talcher was published in the press and many of them were said to have on the verge of starvation.[98] But the chief of Talcher denied even the truth of the photograph in the press for which he had received a well-deserved snub from the Editor of the *Stateman*.[99] Gandhiji had stated that this denial was a shameful perversion of truth.[100]

The people of Orissa in general expressed their warm sympathy for the cause of the people's movement in Talcher. At a large public meeting held at Town Hall, Cuttack on 18 December 1938 with Naba Krishna Choudhury, M.L.A., Orissa in the Chair, it was decided to boycott the matches manufactured at the factory of Talcher and also to organise help for the large number of refugees who had come out of Talcher due to confiscation of ripe crops by the State and also various other grievances.[101] News reached Sambalpur that the subjects of Talcher

---

96. M.N. Das, *op. cit.*, p. 289.
97. *Anand Bazar Patrika*, 12 December 1938. (SUA)
98. *The Statesman*, 12 January 1939. (SUA)
99. *Harijan*, 18 February 1939. (OSA)
100. *Ibid.*
101. *Anand Bazar Patrika*, 19 December 1938. (SUA)

State had left the State and taken shelter in Angul refugee camps. The people of Sambalpur decided to render necessary help to them and a sub-committee was formed in a meeting on 18 December 1938 for raising funds to provide relief to the refugees.[102] Many national and provincial leaders from Congress, Communist and Socialist creed actively associated themselves with the movement in the State and advised them from time to time. Prof. N.G. Ranga, M.L.A. of Madras and a renowned Congress peasant leader of national repute came to Cuttack on 8 January 1939 to discuss with the leaders of Orissa about the State's problem.[103] He visited the refugee camps at Angul and appealed the Congress leaders for help in providing the refugees with immediate necessities by starting 'State Refugees Relief Fund'.[104] He held the opinion that the return of the refugees to the States could not be effected without the desirable gesture from the Raja by way of ending the repression and satisfying the minimum demands of the people. Mahatmaji brought these facts to the notice of the outside world through his paper *Harijan*.[105]

> He wrote, "The movement for liberty within the States is entering a new state. History is going to repeat itself. Talcher and Dhenkanal have led the way in repression. It is no small matter that 26,000 out of 75,000 all told have migrated from Talcher to British Orissa. Prof. Ranga has published horrowing details of the suffering of these refugees. This narrative is supported by Thakkar Bapa, the great social reformer and philanthropist, who responds to the call of distress no matter from what quarter it comes. They have been in exile for two months. I had hoped that they would have returned to their homes. But there seems to be no peace for these people as yet.
>
> It is not possible for Orissa alone to tackle the relief work. The Government of Orissa has not much money to spare. I hope that the Marwari Relief Society will take up the relief work bearing in mind that labour should be found for the refugees."[106]

Thus Miss Agatha Harrison, Secretary of the Indian Conciliation Group in London and member of the British Parliament came down to

---

102. Orissa Records, W.W.C.C., Acc. No. 13, p. 75.
103. *Ibid.*, *op. cit.*, Acc. No. 38, p. 40.
104. *Harijan*, 23 January 1939. (OSA)
105. S.N. Patnaik, *op. cit.*, p. 144.
106. *Harijan*, 28 January 1939. (OSA)

Angul and spent about four months in the refugee camps. With the help of Hare Krishna Mahtab, she tried to bring about a conciliation in matters of Orissa States through the intervention of the Political Department of the Government of India. She assured the refugees of Talcher of proper redress regarding their grievances.[107] After her departure she spoke in the British Parliament about the Talcher problem.[108] C.F. Andrews, a noted philanthropist, who visited Orissa and had seen the miserable conditions of the people in camps during that period, discussed the State's problem with the local political leaders. He had also narrated the problem of the refugee of Talcher before the British authority at New Delhi and gave publicity in London and America.[109] Captain Woods of the Salvation Army interviewed the *Raja* of Talcher, the leaders of the camps and other important persons in an attempt to effect a compromise in the refugee situation. His attempts, however, proved abortive as the *Raja* refused to agree to the cancellation of extradition warrants or to allow the tenants to participate in the State's administration.[110]

Mahatma Gandhi advised the Orissa ministry and the leaders of Congress Party in Orissa to visit the refugee camps regularly and find out a solution of their problem. Regarding this in *Harijan* dated the 4th February, 1939 he stated :

"Thus the ministers in Orissa may not sit comfortably in their chairs, if they do not succeed in sending 26,000 refugees of Talcher to their homes with an absolute assurance of safety and freedom of speech and social and political intercourse. It is insufferable that the Congress, which is today in alliance with the British Government, should be treated as an enemy and an outsider in the States which are vassals of the British".[111]

Almost all the Congress leaders including Biswanath Das, the Prime Minister of Orissa had been to the camps to come across their problems. The Congress ministry had given financial help to these camps for construction of thatched sheds. Provision of drinking water, public health and sanitary measures were taken up by the Government of Orissa. It also provided to set up nine police stations, appointed

107. Orissa Records, W.W.C.C., Acc. No. 38, p. 42.

108. *Talcher Prajamandal Itihas Committee* (*Compl.*), *op. cit.*, p. 28.

109. *Ibid.*

110. Orissa Records, W.W.C.C., Acc. No. 38, p. 47.

111. *Orissa Review,* January 1991, p. 4.

additional district magistrate and many doctors in the camps.[112] Gandhiji had sent the eminent social worker and philanthropist A.V. Thakkar as his representative, who stayed with the refugees in the camps of Angul for a few months.[113] On his appeal, the Marwari Relief Society was providing monetary help and rice to the refugees in the camps. He had also made an appeal to different societies through press for the help to these camps.[114] Aid was provided to these camps through private and charitable organisations. Jugal Kishore Birla and *Gandhi Seva Sangha* started relief work.[115] The volunteers of *Gandhi Seva Sangha* taught the refugees in these camps few self-employment skills like hand-spinning, weaving, preparing leaf-plates etc. which not only reasserted the self-confidence of those people to survive but also brought a sense of unity of the living in feudatory States people, with the anti-British Congress activities in the national scene.

Gopabandhu Choudhury and Rama Devi of All India *Charakha Sangha* with their volunteers worked out a good number of relief work in the refugee camps. Besides the All India *Harijan Sevak Sangha,* All India *Krushak Sangh*, Christian missionaries etc. did a lot of work in the camps.[116]

Journalists and press reporters of different dailies and periodicals came to these camps to have a glimpse of the movement. They congratulated the refugees for their unity against a tyrant. Even the representatives of the Anglo-Indian daily, *The Statesman,* praised the refugees for their brave work and they condemned the *Raja* of Talcher for his misdeeds. The king's maladministration was published in various newspapers.

When the mass exodus began the ruler of Talcher took an attempt to make a confusion among the refugees. Hooligans were hired and sent to the camps of Angul to create disturbances. Some sheds of the refugees were set on fire. About five hundred huts were burnt to ashes.[117] Extradition warrants were issued against the leaders who had left Talcher. Almost all the leaders of the People's Movement of Talcher were kept inside Cuttack jail. Dasarathi Pani, Kritibas Rath and Gouri Shankar Pradhan were arrested in the first week of November 1938 at

112. *Orissa Legislative Assembly Proceedings, op. cit.*
113. *Ibid.*
114. *Anand Bazar Patrika,* 25 March 1939. (SUA)
115. *Orissa States Enquiry Committee Report,* p. 111.
116. *Talcher Prajamandal Itihas Committee* (*Compl*) *op. cit.*, p. 27.
117. *Anand Bazar Patrika,* 13 March 1939. (SUA)

Angul under extradition warrant, but the provincial government refused to hand them over to State authorities. Pabitra Mohan Pradhan and Maguni Chandra Pradhan absconded and went underground.[118] Oppressive measurers were resorted to inside Talcher. Their crops were taken away by authority for non-payment of rent.

On the other hand, the Ruler was giving an impression to the world outside that there was no trouble in his State and that no tenant of his State had actually left Talcher.[119] He had circulated a bulletin in this regard. Gandhiji commented, "I have a Talcher Bulletin sent to me by Thakkar Bapa for me to laugh or weep over".[120] However the *Durbar* made it clear that it would not yield. The political department stood firm that it would not advise the Talcher *Durbar* to come down in the matter. The refugees also stood firm not to return to Talcher unless their demands were fulfilled. The number of refugees from Talcher State assumed such proportion that new camps were opened in Dhenkanal to provide shelter to the displaced agitators.[121] Due to the constant flow of the refugees to the camps their number was always varying,[122] but it was too big a number to manifest the seriousness of the whole issue.

Hannessey-Mahtab Pact

The refugee problem of Talcher drew the attention of political leaders and the British Government. To bring a solution, a meeting was arranged at Angul on 21 March 1939. Mr. Ansorge, Revenue Commissioner of Orissa; Major Hannessey, the Assistant Political Agent of Orissa States; Captain Woods of the Salvation Army, H.K. Mahtab, Major Greogory of the Military Intelligence Department and two members from each of the refugee camps participated in that conference.[123] They discussed about an agreement on the terms of a compromise to be effected between the ruler of Talcher and the subjects of the State. H.K. Mahtab narrated the demands and problems of the refugees of Talcher and their conditions to return to the State. Major Hannessey gave his comments on it. A Pact consisting of nine points

118. *Anand Bazar Patrika,* 2 November 1938.

119. *Orissa Legislative Assembly Proceedings, op. cit.*

120. *Harijan,* 18 February 1939. (OSA)

121. Orissa Records, W.W.C.C., Acc. No. 38, p. 47.

122. *Orissa Legislative Assembly Proceedings, op. cit.*

123. Home Political, File No. 18/4/39 Confidential D.O. No. 1163-C, 3 April 1939 (NAI) and Orissa Records, W.W.C.C., Acc. No. 38, p. 47.

was signed among them which is commonly known as Hannessey-Mahtab Pact.[124] The terms of the Pact were :

"1. Reduction of miscellaneous cess from five annas to three annas per rupee of rent, and an undertaking that after the settlement to be started about next November, the combined rent and cesses will not be higher than the Angul rent and cesses with the same classes of land.

2. The abolition of monpolies on the necessaries of life except hides, skins, horns, *ganja*, opium, *bhang* and liquors.

3. State administrative machinery should not be used for enforing fines, etc. levied by ecclesiastical courts and *Panchayats*.

4. Compulsory labour (*bethi*) should be abolished except when necessary for public purposes and then on payment of wages at ordinary rates.

5. Abolition of special tax (poll tax) on industrial castes.

6. There should be no victimization of refugees on their return to the State.

7. Constitutional reforms enabling the people to participate in the administration through their representative will be introduced as soon as the schemes are approved by the political department.

8. There shall be no interference with freedom of speech and meetings provided that there is nothing subversive or disloyal to the Ruler on his administration in those speeches or meetings.

9. People should be allowed to kill wild animals in the State on their own property without penalties or fees".[125]

But the Raja of Talcher refused to honour the above Pact. The conference ended in a failure as the *Raja* was disinclined to accept the proposal of the terms.[126]

The Rulers of other States of Orissa played a vital role in the case of this Pact. They persuaded the *Raja* of Talcher not to accept it as this would hamper his prestige as well as of them.[127] It would be the

124. *Anand Bazar Patrika*, 22 April 1939. (SUA)

125. *Harijan*, 22 April 1939 (OSA)

126. Orissa Records, *op. cit.*, and *Anand Bazar Patrika*, 29 May 1939. (SUA)

127. *Talcher Prajamandal Itihas Committee* (*Compl.*), *op. cit.*, pp. 35-37.

beginning of limiting feudal authority in Orissan States. The *Raja* on the other hand thought that his denial of the Pact would bring down the refugees morally. They would be forced to return to their homes. He also, expected that the people in thousands would return as the cutlivation season was ahead and moreover, they would have been demoralised under pressing financial condition. But that was a day dream of the chief at Talcher. The refugees were determined not to return to Talcher rather they would prefer to die in the affair of Talcher Administration to bring an amicable settlement between the Ruler and his subjects. It is really surprising to note that the chief could dare to refuse the Pact even when responsible British Officers were the signatories to it.[128] This exposed the British concern for peace and normalcy to be a hoax and they were still siding with the rulers against the subjects. Just a warning by the British Government would have made the *Raja* to accept the Pact, but the former remained silent diplomatically.

Nothing definite could be achieved in that conference. The Ruler played a mischief and did not make an open declaration to this effect. Gandhiji thought that Major Hannessey had the authority of the *Raja* of Talcher to sign the Pact. But it was strange enough that the *Raja* refused to do so.[129] The *Raja* also did not follow the terms of the Sanad given to him by the Viceroy of India on 26 February 1937. Clause 6 of the said *Sanad* provided that the *Raja* was bound to act in accordance with such advice as might be given to him by the Agent to the Governor-General, Eastern States, or such other political officer as might be vested with authority in that behalf by H.E. Viceroy. But the *Raja* of Talcher did not follow it in case of the Pact given to him by Major Hannessey, the Assistant Political Agent of Orissa. Gandhiji was deeply concerned with the delay in carrying out the Pact regarding Talcher. "Delay is not only dangerous", he observed, "it is criminal".[130]

The People's Movement of Talcher acquired a new position towards the end of April 1939. The refugees at Angul camp pressurised the Political Agent, Orissa States to consider their grievances and bring a solution to it. Pressure from all sides heaped on the Political Department. Gandhiji severely criticised them, for their indifference to

---

128. C.U. Aitchison, *op.cit.*, Vol. II, p. 328.

129. *Harijan, op. cit.*

130. *Ibid.*

the sufferings of the people of Talcher. He took up the issue with Lord Linlithgow, the Viceroy of India.[131] The Political Department advised the Ruler of Talcher to adopt conciliatory attitude and the *Raja* agreed to it. Gandhiji advised the agitators to withdraw *Satyagraha* and to start constitutional agitation for the redressal of their grievances. H.K. Mahtab, who acted as the political representative of Gandhiji, communicated this message to the refugees. Before the declaration of the Ruler on some grievances, a negotiation committee was formed.[132] H.K. Mahtab, representatives of the refugee camps, the Resident of Eastern States, the Political Agent and some British Officers who attended this conference discussed to find a solution to Talcher problem. Accordingly, after more than a month, it was announced by the Resident that the Ruler of Talcher was ready to accept all the points of Hannessey-Mahtab Pact except the reduction of cess which would be left for the Resident's decision.[133]

The *Durbar* issued its declaration on 1 May 1939.[134] But neither it fulfilled the terms of the Hannesey-Mahtab Pact nor it accepted the views of the solution committee. To the surprise of all, it did not contain the concessions promised as a result of which the attempt at a conciliation failed. It was observed that the Raja as well as the political department were not sincere to implement the Pact. The announcements included :

"1. *Miscellaneous Cess* : The State is ready to give to its people redress on any just and reasonable grievances...

2. *Monopolies* : Monopolies over betel, tabacco, leaves, salt, kerosene, *bidi*, soda, soap have been abolished, Monopolies over Opium, *Ganja, Bhang,* Hides, Horns, Liquors have been retained...

3. *Religious Fees* : Old religious fees have been abolished. It is optional for people to either approach the ecclesiastical court or *Panchayats* or civil court in social and religious disputes. The Panchayat's decision will be confirmed by the Ecclesiastical court. Appeals against the decision of the Ecclesiastical court will be referred to ruler. The people who are not interested to appeal before the *Dharma Adalut* can go to the *Dewani Adalut*.

---

131. H.K. Mahtab, *Sadhanar Pathe*, pp. 193-94.

132. *Talcher Prajamandal Itihas Committee* (*Compl*), *op. cit.*

133. *Orissa Review*, August 1989, p. 129.

134. Orissa Records, Talcher Papers, Talcher State Gazette, Extraordinary, State Durbar, Talcher, 1 May 1939 (TPRR) See Appendix Q, the Oriya Version of the Gazette.

4. *Liberation of Bethi* : *Bethi* or unpaid labour has been abolished. Payments for *Bethi* when called for in the interest of *Raja, Raj* family and public purpose are made at ordinary rate. People prefer to take remission of animals killed. That was treated as a payment in kind.
5. *Poll tax* : There is no special tax (poll tax) on industrial castes existing in the States....
6. *No Victimisation on Return* : No reprisal or victimisation on refugees on return to the State will be allowed. Amnesty orders have been already issued asking people to refrain from frequenting the camps and to settle peacefully and unconditionally in the State.

   Persons against whom extradition warrants are outstanding will be released and pardoned and warrants will be cancelled and no reprisals will be taken against them provided that they are willing to furnish the security for good behaviour in the State courts for a limited period. Such securities will not be unduly large and should not be fortified without good reasons.
7. *Constitutional Reforms* : Constitutional reforms have been granted by setting up *Byabastha Parishad* (Order, 1939) enabling people to participate in the administration through their representatives.
8. *Freedom of Speech* : There is no-restriction over freedom of speech or meetings when they are within the law and when there is nothing subversive or disloyal to the Ruler, his family and his administration in those speeches and meetings.
9. *Protection of Crops* : People have the right to kill the wild animals from their stalling crop. This privilege cannot be extended to cases where professionals are engaged for killing wild animals. In that case provision has been made for payment of fees or sale proceeds of remissions as may be convenient to the people".[135]

The above terms in the declaration made by the *Raja* could not satisfy the people nor the advisors outside the State. The Talcher *Prajamandal* rejected the *Raja's* proposal as there was no clear picture on *Bethi* and *Byabastha Parishad.*[136] C.F. Andrews asserted that he

135. Orissa Records, Talcher Papers, Talcher State Gazette, *op. cit.*

136. *The Statesman*, 9 May 1939. (SUA)

could see nothing in the long statement made by the ruler of Talcher except a black refusal to meet the situation. "The terms that the Ruler of Talcher now put forward", said Mr. Andrews, "were quite different. This extraordinary proposition was actually put forward by the *Raja* ten years after India's own signature to the convention abolishing forced labour".[137] There was disagreement by the refugees relating to *bethi*. The question of road repair or, in lieu thereof, the levy of road cess as was the case in British India was under consideration. The forced labour was to continue in the interest of the *Raja* and his family relatives. The refugees contained that this declaration definitely retained *bethi* in spite of the repeated declaration by the British Government that it would not be in force in India.[138]

Regarding the setting up of *Byabastha Sabha* as a measure of constitutional reform the refugees objected to the proposal of the election of representatives by caste representation. They wanted a scheme approved by the Political Department and the people's representatives and that the principle of popular control on the administration of the State should be incorporated in the reform. C.F. Andrews proposed that under the establishment of ecclesiastical courts the Ruler of Talcher might imprison or confiscate the property, or fine heavily any one who wished to be free from intolerable caste restrictions.[139]

The Ruler, on the other hand, gave some relaxation regarding the formation of the *Byabastha Parishad*. In an order known as '*Byabastha Parishad* Order, 1939' the king made some remission according to which the *Parishad* would consist of one President and twenty members of different communities roughly according to the population basis not depriving any community or group of communication from representation.[140]

The people and the refugees of Talcher were not at all satisfied. They appealed to the Government of Orissa to make further representation to the India Government on the subject.[141] As the concessions did not satisfy the refugees, they continued to stay in the camp at Angul. Yet, it is a milestone in the path of development of the

137. *The Statesman, op. cit.*

138. *Ibid.*

139. *Ibid.*

140. Orissa Records, Talcher Papers, Talcher State Gazette, State Durbar, Talcher 7 May 1939. (TPRR)

141. *The Statesman, op. cit.*

State people's movement in Talcher. The ruler, who for such a long period was callous to the people's demand, had to come down to accept a few demands though not all. The British game of supporting the king internally and openly paying lip service to the sufferings of the people was then exposed and under popular pressure it had to ask the ruler to accept some provisions of the understanding. At the same time, it hightened the mass spirit and they were so enthused that they declined to accept the truncated declaration of the king reaffirming their decision to continue the struggle further till they achieved the total package of the Pact. It speaks of the confidence and determination of these people.

The rejection of the announcement put the *Raja* of Talcher into a great trouble. His cleverness did not work out. He was afraid of the people. He begged help and support from the Political Department. The Government of Orissa was not satisfied with him as he had spoiled the chances of a satisfactory settlement. Thinking the cases against the leaders of Talcher to be false, the Orissa Government agreed to free the political prisoners. On 12 May 1939 extradition warrants were withdrawn from forty-three *Prajamandal* leaders including Dasarathi Pani.[142] In Talcher and other *Garjat* States the warrant still prevailed so. The leaders decided to organise the movement from British administered areas like Angul. Pabitra Mohan Pradhan, Maguni Chandra Pradhan and some others, who earlier went underground, helped the organisers at Angul camps in disguise.

Efforts from all corners continued to solve the problem of the Talcher refugees. The Congress Government of Orissa and the Congress leaders also took initiatives to solve the problem. Gandhiji vehemently criticised the policies of the Ruler of Talcher. He also held the paramount power responsible for Talcher problem.[143] In his '*Harijan*' of 20 May 1939, Gandiji under the title "Talcher Again" had stated :

"Talcher promises to be much worse than Rajkot. In Rajkot it was the Ruler's word that was broken. In Talcher it is the Paramount Power's. In Rajkot the State atrocities were not the subject of scrutiny. In Talcher the sorry condition of the numerous refugees is almost everything. Hence delay is criminal and may mean loss of one year's crop to several thousand cultivators. The other relief promised by the political agent, Major Hannessey, relates to paltry things so far as the

142. *The Statesman*, 13 May 1939 (SUA)

143. *Anand Bazar Patrika*, 20 May 1939 (SUA)

Ruler of Talcher is concerned; but they are serious enough for the people.

It has been whispered to me that I have been guilty of injustice to Major Hannessey and hence to the paramount power by attributing to them breach of promise; for it is said, Major Hannessey promised nothing, he merely undertook to convey to the Ruler the wishes of the people concerned. It is further said that even if it is proved that he made any such promise he did so without authority.

I cannot admit either of the pleas. Major Hannessey signed the document without any reservations. Sri H.K. Mahtab describes the tragedy with a wealth of detail which compels conviction. He has been an eye-witness of the events narrated by him. So far as I am aware Major Hannessey himself has never denied or has not been given an opportunity of denying the allegations made about him.

There seems to be no doubt that the Ruler of Talcher is in no mood to do justice to his people unless he is made to according to the *Sanad* I have already reproduced in these columns. The representative of the Paramount Power can even require the smaller States of Orissa to perform acts in the interest of their people. Can there be any doubt as to the necessity of redressing every one of the injustice mentioned in the memorandum signed by Major Hannessey?

Indeed redress has been long over due. Why is the ruler being humoured by the Political Department in his wholly indefensible attitude? Why is the welfare of several thousand refugees being lightly regarded? Is not the prestige of the Paramount Power being used to sustain the admitted evils? Surely there is some things radically wrong somewhere in all this".[144]

In the same issue, Gandhiji, also, narrated the entire repressive majors taken by the *Raja* of Talcher on the people who were on agitation, on the title, "Confusion worse confounded".[145] The history of the People's Movement and the mass exodus was also described in it. Pandit Jawaharlal Nehru in a statement said : "Among all the States in India, the Orissa States stand out today in their agony at Talcher of broken promises and wandering starving refugees.[146]

144. Harijan, 20 May 1939. (OSA)

145. *Ibid.* See Appendix R.

146. *Anand Bazar Patrika*, 30 May 1939. (SUA)

All the efforts of Gandhiji and other Congress leaders of the State as well as outside urged upon the Viceroy of India to interfere in the affairs of Talcher. The Viceroy decided to come down to Orissa to know at the spot of the problems of the refugees. He was convinced that the Ruler of Talcher had mishandled the matter.[147] The *Raja* became apprehensive that the State would be confiscated in case he did not settle the problem of the refugees before the tour of the Viceroy to Orissa. With that in mind, the *Raja* issued another proclamation on 23 June 1939 with regard to the constitutional reforms in the presence of the Political Agent at Angul.[148] According to the proclamation, the State machinery would not be used either for collection of fines imposed by the ecclesiastic courts and *Panchayats* or for implementing the decision of such courts in the State. *Bethi* was abolished and would be confined to the requirement of the ruler. Killing of wild animals who destroyed crops was permitted.[149] Most of the demands were fulfilled by this declaration. As many of the important grievances remined unredressed, the workers were dissatisfied. Assurance was given that the rest would be fulfilled soon and the ministry of Orissa was a witness to it. Most of the Congress leaders including Gandhiji were not satisfied over the declaration. Gandhiji had sent a message regarding his dissatisfaction to the Viceroy.[150]

Gandhiji was always in touch with the affairs of Talcher which was going on by that time. Advising the leaders of Talcher movement Gandhiji said :

> "I am advising Travancore, Rajkot and to a certain extent Talcher, as I have been constantly guiding them. But even with regard to them I have been tendering my advice which is for them to accept or reject".[151]

The proclamation reached the refugees camp on 25 June 1939. The organisers of Talcher *Prajamandal* with Pabitra Mohan Pradhan in the chair made detail discussion on this issue. With the advice of Gandhiji and with full assurance of the Congress leaders and the ministry of Orissa about the fulfilment of other demands very soon, the organisers decided to ask the migrants to return to their respective

147. P.M. Pradhan, *op. cit.*, pp. 83-84.

148. *Ibid.*

149. *Talcher Prajamandal Itihas Committee* (*Compl*), *op. cit.*, pp. 38-40.

150. *Ibid.*

151. *Harijan*, 24 June 1939. (OSA)

villages. Accordingly, the refugees started going back to their homes on 26 June 1939 with their hearts filled with joy.[152] The refugee problem had temporarily become less acute not because of the ruler's concession, rather due to the approach of the paddy season.

The policy of appeasement of the chief of Talcher could not, however, satisfy the people as their primary demand for grant of civil liberty and representative system of administration had not yet been granted to them by the *Durbar*. The warrants and cases pending against the leaders were not withdrawn by the State. So these leaders could not return to Talcher and had to chalk out their future programmes by remaining at Angul camps as before.[153] *Prajamandal* committees were established in each village of Talcher and constructive activities were carried on in the field of education, health, irrigation, *Harijan* welfare, settlement of disputes through *Panchayats* etc. *Rajdurbar* and the royal courts were defied. The villagers were advised to boycott the foreign goods and rely on self-employment.[154] It seemed as if the *Prajamandal* had stolen the Congress programme and implementing it with a different name. The head office of *Prajamandal* continued at Angul. Pabitra Mohan Pradhan prepared constitutional reform scheme and sent copies of it to the President of Eastern States Agency, the Political Agent of Orissa States and the *Yubaraj* of Talcher for consideration.[155] Finally in August 1939 all the warrants were unconditionally withdrawn by the *Durbar* and the leaders could enter Talcher.[156]

Now onwards, the People's Movement in Talcher took a different course though there was a temporary peace in the State. Before any final step could be taken by the authorities to solve the problem on a permanent basis, the Second World War broke out and the Congress ministry in Orissa was out of office. The second half of 1939 saw an unusual calmness in the State. The people's agitation had lost much of its force and ferocity. The end of the first phase of the movement, 1930-39, marked a change in the outlook of the people in the State of Talcher as well as other States including British India. People achieved some economic concessions. The revolt shook off the fear of the ruler and his arbitrary rule from the minds of the people in the State. People

152. *Talcher Prajamandal Itihas Committee* (*Compl*), *op. cit.*

153. *Ibid.*

154. *Ibid.*

155. H.K. Mahtab, *History of Freedom Movement in Orissa,* Vol. IV, *op.cit.*, p. 28.

156. P.M. Pradhan, *op. cit.*, pp. 85-86.

of the State became conscious politically and they were united to fight against injustice prevailing in the society. All of their demands were not fulfilled and the British Government was condemned and held responsible for it. Taking the opportunity of the beginning of the war, the British Indian Government's involvement in it, and the Congress ministry's resignation, the ruler again came forward to forget his past commitments and thought it a golden chance to reassert his authority which he agreed to surrender partly to the people. He was more than eager to face any challenge to the established privileges he used to enjoy unhampered earlier. Thus, whatever was gained by the people's struggle was now on the verge of total washout. The administration was not streamlined and the old grievances of the people still remained very much in the agenda of the forties.

◆

V

The World War II and the People's Movement

The outbreak of the World War II on September 1, 1939 was a turning point in the Indian national movement in general and State People's Movement in particular. The constitutional progress made under Indian Council Act of 1935 was given a death blow with the beginning of the World War. The Indian National Congress which accepted offices in various provinces under the provision of the Act lost no time in denouncing the British Indian Government's decision to commit India on the side of the allied powers without consulting the Indian public opinion. The Congress ministries in various provinces tendered their resignations.

The complicated political situation in the country provided a golden opportunity to the native Indian rulers to strengthen their oppressive hands in their territories. The declaration of war created an abnormal situation in the country and even the nationalist-leaders took sometime in deciding their future course of action under the changed situation. The Government of India introduced emergency measures curtailing the civil liberties of the individuals in its territories. Taking clue from it, the native rulers lost no time in banning all the political organisations including the *Prajamandals* in their States. Instructions were issued to the rulers of the States to quell any type of disturbances. The organising leaders were thrown into prison and their properties were forfeited. But the repressive measures failed to dampen the fighting spirit of the people. Even during the war years, the people had upheld the banner of agitation which became vigorous, during the 'Quit India Movement'.

The people of Talcher, who migrated to nearby provincial territories had undergone untold miseries and sufferings besides the economic loss. The refugees started to return back to Talcher from 26 June 1939.[1] After the lifting of the extradition warrants from them in August

1. *Talcher Prajamandal Itihas Committee* (*Compl.*), *op. cit.*, p. 40.

1939, the leaders returned back to the State. But the office of the *Prajamandal* was still functioning at Angul. On their return they found a revengeful attitude of the State administration in Talcher. In their absence and because of joining the *Prajamandal* against the existing Government the lands and *Sarbarakaries* of some members were taken out. Some were heavily penalised by way of imprisonment, forfeiture of property and payment of fines. The land products were looted by some hooligans with the instigation of the State authority. The Talcher *Durbar* made a general declaration for the refugees and agitators who were still outside the State to come back to their respective villages and not to continue the agitation in the State.[2] Those who did not respond to it lost their *Sarbarakaries*. Though the *Prajamandal* claimed that more than hundred *Sarbarkars* suffered, the *Durbar's* office found that as many as 45 *Sarbarakars* had been evicted from their respective *Sarbarakaries* for their joining political agitation and absconding from their respective villages and showing disloyalty to the *Durbar*[3] The State *Durbar* was of the opinion that as the *Sarbarakar* was a servant and representative of State in the village and he enjoyed the '*Malikana*' charge for collection of revenue, he must not show disloyalty or revolt against the *Raja*; should not fail to pay the total revenue of the village and should stay in the village permanently by building a dwelling house etc.[4] Besides, *Sarbarakar* enjoyed the State *Jagir* land called *Bhogra** on payment of rent thereon for the duties imposed on him for being the *Sarbarakar*. Some had actually joined the people's movement in the State and went to Angul to protest against the repressive measures taken against them by the State administration. They were evicted simply for joining the political agitation in the State.

With the declaration of World War II the hands of the feudal chiefs were further strengthened. The chief of Talcher took the advantage of it. Repressive measures again was taken by the *Durbar*

2. Orissa Records, Talcher Paper, Talcher State Gazette Notification, 18 September 1939. (TPRR)
3. Orissa Record, Talcher Paper, Report of the Senior States Officer on the Petition filed by President, Talcher Prajamandal, Talcher 15 January 1948. (SRT)
4. *Ibid.*

* *Bhogra* lands were service tenures and the *Sarbarakar* held it on his being appointed as *Sarbarakar*, a State servant. He got five per cent of the collection made and also held some rent paying lands which passed into the possession of each new *Sarbarakar* on his succession or appointment to the post. The *Sarbarakar* held the '*Bhogra*' for the time being who paid rent for it.

against the people who involved themselves in the people's agitation either in the past or at that time. During the exodus from Talcher to Angul camps some *Dhobis*, Barbers, *Dakuas*, *Panias*, *Paikas* and *Chaukidars* were alleged to have helped the agitators in their camps and left the State for the exodus camps.[5] Such social servants who had full sympathy with the agitators and joined them and caused inconvenience to the people in rendering social services were considered by the State authority to be notorious in abetting the agitators and were dismissed from their respective *Jagir lands*, which they had been enjoying from the time of their fore-fathers and new persons were appointed in their places.[6]

The lands of the people were attached and sold in public auction for absconding from the State and avoiding warrants of arrest for cases started against them under the sections of Indian Penal Code and Defence of India Rules. Even poor tenants on whom the *Durbar* had kept an eye were evicted from their holdings due to arrears of rents.[7]

There were many cases which were filed before the *Durbar* during the year 1939-40. Chandra Sekhar Rajballab, Ramchandra Sahoo and some twenty-eight other tenants of Biru made petitions before the *Durbar* alleging looting of their properties and selling their movable properties at the lowest price. Sambhu Biswal and Baidhar Sahoo of Danara also lodged complaints for the same reason. Kashinath Santra of Baghuabol brought an allegation that his properties were looted, his home was demolished and he was made a street beggar as all his movables were taken away by the *Durbar* as he joined the *Prajamandal*. Bhagirathi Pradhan of Rangabeda alleged that during the agitation of 1938-39 some people snatched away a gold chain weighing 6 *tolas* from his daughter-in-law's neck. He reported this matter before the police which took no action.[8] In all these above cases it was found that no action had been taken for the safety of the people and the decision of the cases went against the petitioners.

In the beginning of 1940 repressive measures of the State *Durbar* became severe in its attempt to quell agitation. These measures included:

5. Orissa Records, Talcher Papers, Report of the Senior State Office, *op. cit.*
6. Ibid. op.cit. Memorandum filed by President, Talcher Prajamandal before the Chief Administrator, Talcher, and Special Commissioner, Orissa State, 9 January 1948, pp. 25-27. (TPRR)
7. *Ibid.*
8. *Ibid.*

"1. Personal and house searches of those suspected to be furthering *Prajamandal* activities.

2. Prohibiting the assembly of more than five persons.

3. Stopping of the enrolment of *Prajamandal* members."[9]

The adoption of such measures on the part of the State *Durbar* made the subjects all the more determined to rally under the '*Prajamandal*' and to carry on their struggle with an untiring spirit. The leaders of the *Prajamandal* fought with the earnest endeavour to strengthen their organisation in order to carry on a relentless struggle against the tyrannical lords of the States.

The workers of the *Prajamandal* were always harassed in the State. Number of false cases were instituted against the people who were suspected by the authority to be the leading participants in the agitation. The village servants who eked out a miserable living by the sweat of their brows were compelled to execute bonds for the discharge of forced labour. Labourers in coal mines were forced to sign bonds of loyalty.[10] The Talcher *Prajamandal* had vehemently opposed this provision as the village servants went to serve the villagers themselves.

The Defence of India Rules had strengthened the power of the *Raja* of Talcher. Number of ways were devised to harass and inflict punishment on the subjects who dared to defy the authority of the State and participated in the agitation against the misrule of the chief. Certificate cases were instituted for realisation of arrear of land rents from the defaulters immediately. Talcher people resolved to continue their agitation and their *Prajamandal* continued to function from its office at Angul. In January 1940, Pabitra Mohan Pradhan, President of Talcher *Prajamandal* submitted a representation to the Political Agent, Orissa States, narrating the oppression of the State officials on the *Prajamandal* members.[11] Subsequently in February 1940 the Talcher *Prajamandal* sent a memorial to the President, Eastern States Agency and the Viceroy of India, containing the following demands :

"1. Reformation of *Praja Parishad* or the People's Assembly.

2. Complete abolition of miscellaneous cess.

3. Right to kill wild animals who destroyed crops etc..."[12]

9. Orissa Records, W.W.C.C., Acc. No. 32, pp. 2-3.

10. P.K. Jena, *op. cit.*, p. 227.

11. Orissa Records, W.W.C.C., *op. cit.*

12. *Ibid.*

But as the *Raja* was very loyal to the British regime, the Government did not take any action against him. The promises made by the ruler in his declaration was not translated into action. As such, the feeling of the people grew bitter against the intention of the chief as they interpreted the declaration to be a measure adopted by the *Raja* to hoodwink and misguide the people. Pabitra Mohan Pradhan vehemently criticised the *Raja* and condemned the British Government as it stood only a passive onlooker. The 'Martyr's Day' was observed at Kosala Camp of Angul on 1 March 1940 and a meeting was held on the same day where some important resolutions were passed.[13] These included fight for the return of *Sarbarakaries, Bhogra* and tenure lands; restoration of properties confiscated during the last agitation; abolition of miscellaneous cess etc.[14]

During the middle of 1940 enrolment of *Satyagrahis* and workers began in the State on the face of opposition from the *Durbar*. More and more people joined in the peoples' movement of Talcher. Meetings were held in different places to strengthen and expedite the struggle. The leaders accused the *Durbar* of broken promise and bad faith and the British Government of inaction and passive support to the King in this act. The authority of the State was in search of ways to put the organisers into trouble and arrest them. In that year, heavy showers in the early part and drought in the later period caused the destruction of paddy and other crops in the State. There was least arrangement of water supply for irrigation purpose. The aweful sight of the damaged standing crops added to the misery and starvation of the people more and more. There was no remission of land revenue for these affected people. Proper attention was not given for their improvement.[15] People suffered much due to the natural calamity and apathy of the State administration. On 20 August 1940 the Talcher *Prajamandal* organised a public meeting at Kosala Camp of Angul.[16] The inactivity of the State authority of Talcher was condemned in this meeting. It was also unanimously demanded to bring independence of judiciary and executive in the State, introduction of relief measures in drought affected areas and remission of land rents. The people requested and urged the State *Durbar* and the Political Department to set up an impartial enquiry

13. Orissa Records, *op. cit.*, Acc. No. 30, pp. 6-8.
14. *Ibid.*, Acc. No. 32, p. 3.
15. *Talcher Prajamandal Itihas Committee* (*Compl.*), *op. cit.*, p. 41.
16. Orissa Review, August 1989, p. 135.

committee to see the quantity of crops destroyed and to remit the land revenue accordingly. To solve the problem of hunger, the State *Durbar* was requested to introduce constructive work, in which the people could earn their bread.[17]

The mass exodus of the Talcher subjects in the mid-thirties still made the British Government apprehensive of its recurrence. The Political Agent preferred handling the situation through his Assistant Political Agent. The issue of the crop failure was becoming a weapon of mass mobilisation by the *Prajamandal* and the people's discontent and consequent anger alarmed the British Government. It used the State machinery to propagate that the issue of crop failure as raised by *Prajamandal* was false, non-issue and exaggerated. The *Prajamandal* activities connected with organising the people on the issue were arrested, tried in the court of law and were convicted.[18]

The Talcher *Prajamandal* completed its second year anniversary on 6 September 1940. In that function a resolution was adopted demanding relief measures to be adopted in the State. Neither the Political Department nor the State *Durbar* gave any concession to the people and all the proposals of Talcher people were rejected outrightly. At last people elected a non-official enquiry committee to measure the extent of crops destroyed and senta report to the political department for necessary consideration and action. Madan Mohan Pradhan was elected as the Chairman of the committee and Dasrathi Pani, Maguni Chandra Pradhan and Gouri Sankar Pradhan as members.[19] All these persons were the members of the executive committee of Talcher *Prajamandal*. The committee began its work in November 1940, verifying the damaged crops from village to village.[20]

Being informed of the activity of the committee, the Assistant Political Agent, North Orissa States paid a visit to Talcher on 12 November 1940 to see the loss of crops in the drought affected areas.[21] Being escorted by the State Magistrate and some other officials he visited some villages in which destruction were meagre. Hearing the inspection and arrival of the Assistant Political Agent, Pabitra Mohan

17. Annual Report of Talcher *Prajamandal*, 6 September 1940 to 6 September 1941 by K.B. Rath, General Secretary, Talcher 23 September 1941, pp. 2-4. (NMML)
18. Orissa Records, Talcher Papers, Enquiry Report of the Senior State Officer, Talcher to Administrator of Talcher, 26 February 1948. (SRT)
19. *Ibid*.
20. *Ibid*.
21. Anant Mishra, *op. cit.*, p. 40.

Pradhan, the President of Talcher *Prajamandal* wrote to him for an interview and the request was granted. The interview took place in the open square of a damaged crop field. The opinions regarding the destruction and amount of crops of a certain plot of land varied between the people, Political Agent and the President, and a hot discussion went on. The Assistant Political Agent did not agree to accompany the President in his tour.[22] Then the committee asked for an interview with the Assistant Political Agent but was flatly refused and a 'correspondence war' started between them. However, the committee went on with the work, but to its utter surprise, the Assistant Political Agent instructed the *Durbar* to arrest the leaders. In order to put a dead lock to their activities and to that of the *Prajamandal*, the State Police arrested all the members of the committee on 27 November 1940 and put them under custody.[23] Pabitra Mohan Pradhan, who was in the British territory of Angul was arrested there by a requisition warrant (E.D. Rollact of 34 and 35) and sent to Talcher jail.[24]

A false charge under Defence of India Rules was framed against them. As the President and the office bearers of the *Prajamandal* were arrested, new election for President and other office bearers took place. This new elected body made its first attempt to defend the persons whose cases were tried in the court of *Sadar* Sub-divisional Magistrate.[25]

Formation of New (Temporary) Prajamandal

The formation of the new and temporary *Prajamandal* took place in January 1941 comprising mostly of youths and energetic people from the State. The followings were elected as the office bearers of the new *Prajamandal*.

1. Sri Kalandi Charan Pradhan - President
2. Kritibas Rath - Joint Secretary
3. Bichhand Pradhan - Joint Secretary
4. Kashinath Samantray - Treasurer
5. Sudhkar Rath - Advisor
6. Gouri Shankar Pradhan - Advisor

22. Annual Report of Talcher Prajamandal, *op. cit.*
23. *Ibid.*
24. Orissa Records, Talcher Papers, Register of Undertrial Prisioners in Talcher Jail of 1940s, Warrant No. 56. (TJRR)
25. Annual Report of Talcher Prajamandal, *op. cit.*

Besides the office bearers, leaders like Bankanidhi Bhakta Ballav and Chandra Sekhar Das who were still absconding also helped the *Prajamandal* in disguise.[26] This second line of leadership was helped by other stalwarts like Anand Chandra Pradhan, Pabitra Behera, Sudarsan Pradhan, Maheswar Pradhan, Dukhabandhu Sahu, Phiringi Pradhan, Kalia Das, Madan Sundar Pradhan, Parsuram Pradhan, Baikuntha Sahoo and many others.[27] This *Prajamandal* with the help of the youths arranged a good number of meetings inside the State and at Angul. After its formation, the *Prajamandal* first convened a mass meeting in January 1941 and there, it explained and appealed the people to engage themselves in constructive efforts, such as, excavation of ponds, water reservation for irrigation purpose, spinning cotton, plantation, education, rural upliftment etc. Enthusiastically people from all quarters of the State responded to this appeal. The work was a great success.[28] Small pox, Cholera and diseases among the cattle were rampant and took a heavy toll of lives but no medical aid from the side of the State was available. Leaflets containing the autocracy of the chief of Talcher, his oppression and collection of high rents from the people forcefully were distributed by them at Angul on 7 January 1941. A memorandum to this effect was given to the Political Agent by the *Prajamandal*.[29] The people demanded before the *Durbar* for the adoption of relief work in the village. On the other hand, the State authority took revengeful measures. False cases were instituted against the workers of the people's movement. Most of them, who came to the Talcher Court regarding their cases were taken away by the agents of the *Raja* and kept in the prison. Later on false cases were filed against them. These prisoners had to suffer in the prison. They were humiliated, tortured brutally and punished heavily. The supporters of the *Prajamandal* also could not escape from it.

This was strongly objected by the *Prajamandal*. In May, it criticised the Talcher *Durbar* not to keep its promises made by the *Raja* previously regarding the constitution of '*Byabasta Parishad*'.[30] In this institution, there was no democratic election rather nomination from among the supporters of the ruler. The *Prajamandal* also opposed the tyrannical

26. *Gadajat*, Special Issue, 1989, pp. 12-14.
27. *Ibid.*
28. Annual Report of Talcher Prajamandal, *op. cit.*, pp. 7-8.
29. Orissa Records, W.W.C.C., Acc. No. 30, p. 35.
30. Administrative Report of Talcher State, 1940-41, p. 2.

rule of the *Raja* and his method of arresting the people to stop the people's movement in the State was vehemently condemned. The ruler thought that the workers and their families would be harassed and would be compelled, under circumstances to give up the attitude of joining the movement.[31]

The Talcher *Durbar* chalked out its plan to bring to an end the people's movement. False cases were instituted against the leaders and workers of the *Prajamandal*. Warrants were issued to arrest the *Prajamandal* workers, those who absconded their properties were attached to the State or sold to the third parties. On 3 February 1941 the Sub-Divisional Magistrate of *Sadar* ordered for issue of warrants of arrest against Sudhakar Rath bailable for Rs. 500 for his production before 26 February 1941. On refusal, the court ordered on 11 October 1941 to attach the movable and landed properties of Sudhakar Rath.[32] His landed properties situated at Bontol, Nuagan, Khulua, Lingarakata and Jagannathpur covering about twenty acres were confiscated by the State.[33] Likewise the people associated with the movement like Kritibas Rath, Kashinath Santra, Upendra Pradhan, Dukhabandhu Sahoo, Mukunda Sahoo, Bichhanda Pradhan, Surdarsan Pradhan, Magta Pradhan, Pabitra Pradhan, Bankanidhi Bhakta Ballabv and Bandhu Sahoo also lost their lands which were attached to the State.[34]

In its meeting of the 26 May 1941, the *Prajamandal* passed a resolution for the redressal of the real and genuine grievances of the people on or before the ruler's Golden Jubilee which was to be celebrated on 9 June 1941 and in which people might take part if their demands were fulfilled. In that meeting the leaders vehemently opposed the establishment of *Bybastha Parishad* by the ruler which was not at all a democratic organisation as the *Durbar* disallowed majority people's representation to participate in it. The meeting also denounced the establishment of two such types of institutions, one each at Talcher and another at Kaniha where most of the members were nominated by the *Durbar*.[35] But the *Durbar* did not pay any heed to this resolution of the *Prajamandal*, as a result of which people did not co-operate with

31. Annual Report of Talcher Prajamandal, *op. cit.*, p. 6.
32. Orissa Records, Talcher Papers, Criminal Case No. 1/193 of 1940-41, Talcher *vs.* Sudhakar Rath and others, Case u/s., 124 A.I.P.C. (SRT)
33. *Ibid.*
34. *Ibid.*, *op. cit.*, S.N. Sharma, Senior State Officer, to the Magistrate Class I Sadar/ Kaniha, Letter No. 164-169, Talcher 27 October 1948. (SRT)
35. *Ibid.*

the Jubilee celebration.[36] Thus the King lost a golden opportunity of soliciting the popular support on the basis of solving few demands of the people and it was more opportune as the Congress had not yet given the call for any great struggle, as the one that came in August 1942.

Any man who worked in the name of *Prajamandal* was threatened. Leaders like Dasarathi Pani was arrested on 17 January 1942 and Madan Mohan Pradhan and Maguni Chandra Pradhan were arrested on 19 January 1942.[37] False charges were issued against them. But nothing could prevent them from raising their voice against the tyranny. The political prisoners opposed every work of the *Durbar*. Though the chief kept a good number of people in the prison, his plan of suppressing the voice of the people could not be successful. More and more young men and energetic leaders came forward to carry on the people's movement in the State. At last, the *Raja* and his youngest son, the *Pattayat* were forced to meet the leaders inside the Talcher Jail with a package of new deal.[38] The *Raja* met the prisoners and gave them a proposal that he would first set free Pabitra Mohan Pradhan who would bring a peaceful atmosphere in the State. After that the rest will be freed from the jail. As the second step, he also suggested that the State administration would run according to the advice of the *Prajamandal*. Accordingly two small committees would be formed. Pabitra Mohan Pradhan would lead the committee from the side of *Prajamandal* whereas the Pattayat would represent the State in it. These committees would finalise the problems of the State administration and steps to be taken to solve it. In case of differences, the Political Department of the Government or the Resident would give the final decision.[39]

The proposal given by the *Raja* and his son was not bad but there was doubt about their integrity to implement it honestly. Though the *Prajamandal* leaders had no faith on any assurance given by the ruler due to their past experience, they still decided to give the *Durbar* a chance for reconciliation. The political leaders in the jail agreed to

---

36. Orissa Records, *op. cit.*, S.N. Sharma, Senior State Officer, to the Magistrate Class I Sadar/Kaniha, Letter No. 164-169, Talcher 27 October, 1948. (SRT)
37. *Ibid.*, op. cit., Register of Undertrial Prisoners in Talcher Jail, Serial No. 59, 60 and 61 respectively. (TJRR)
38. *Talcher Prajamandal Itihas Committee* (*Compl.*), *op. cit.*, pp. 44-46.
39. *Ibid.*

accept the proposal. Accordingly, Pabitra Mohan Pradhan was set free on 29 January 1942.[40]

Pabitra Mohan Pradhan was ordered to stay inside the municipal area of Talcher and disallowed to go outside. With the help of other leaders, he made one parallel Government in the State. His residence was converted into an office of the people. Any difficulties found among the people was referred to this office. The cases of conflict were solved without any delay. People did not like to attend the royal court. The decision of this office was gladly accepted by both the parties.[41] This was not tolerated by the chief as it directly challenged the authority of the *Durbar* and hampered its economic interest. The Political Department of the British Government also opposed it. Again, Pabitra Mohan Pradhan was arrested on 26 March 1942 and put in the Talcher Jail.[42] Fabricated and false cases were filed against him which was supported by the Resident of Orissa. The process of bringing peace and tranquility to the State in a phased manner was frustrated and the people now came to see it for themselves and blamed the *Durbar* for breaching the truce understanding.

The valiant spirit of the agitators, however, could not be curbed by the repressive measures meted out to them by the chief and his agents. The participants faced the torture inflicted on them with courage and forbearance and carried on the revolt in the State with undoubted vigour. They condemned the brutal policy of the chief in unequivocal terms and deplored the royal effort to counter the *Prajamandal* by the puppet institutions in the form of '*Praja Parishad*' and '*Byabastha Parishad*' that acted as handy tools for the advancement of the sinister designs and selfish interest of the *Raja*. The arrest of the popular leaders greatly agitated the people inside the State and the institution of false cases against them evoked strong resentment among all the sections of people of Talcher. Spontaneous protest movements accompanied by sporadic violent incidents occurred when the Quit India Resolution was passed by the AICC.

Quit India Movement and its Reflection in the States' Peoples' Movement

After the failure of the Cripps' Mission, the Congress thought to

40. *Talcher Prajamandal Itihas Committee (Compl.), op. cit.*
41. *Ibid.*
42. Orissa Records, Talcher Papers, Register of Undertrial Prisoners in Talcher Jail, Serial No. 76. (TJRR)

launch a new mass movement in India to ventilate the grievances of the people against the British Raj. Gandhiji made it clear that like other movements, this would also be on the basis of non-violence. On 14 July 1942, the working committee in their meeting at Wardha passed a long resolution known as "Quit India Resolution" which stated :

> "Events happening from day to day and the experience that the people of India are passing through, confirm the opinion of Congressmen that British rule in India must end immediately, not merely because foreign domination, even as its best, is an evil in itself and a continuing injury to the subject people, but because India in bondage can play no effective part in defending herself and in affecting the fortunes of the war that is desolating humanity. The freedom of India is thus necessary not only in the interest of India but also for the safety of the world and for the ending of Nazism, Fascism, militarism and other forms of imperialism and the aggression of one nation over another..."[43]

The Working Committee referred the matter to the All India Congress Committee scheduled to be held on 7 August 1942.[44]

In their concluding speeches Maulana Abul Kalam Azad, the Congress President and Gandhiji made it clear that their next steps would be to approach the Viceroy as representing the British Government and to appeal to the heads of the principal united nations for an honourable settlement which, while recognising the freedom of India, would also advance the cause of the United Nations in the struggle against the aggressor Axis powers.[45] When the resolution of the Working Committee was published it created an electric atmosphere in the country. People did not pause to consider what were the implications but felt that the time had reached to launch a mass movement to make the British Quit India. The historic 'Quit India' Resolution was passed on the evening of 8 August 1942 by the All India Congress Committee which caused an unprecedented upsurge in the whole country.[46] Early in the morning of 9 August 1942, all important Congress leaders of the country including Orissa were rounded

---

43. M.A.K. Azad, *India Wins Freedom*, New York, 1960, p. 91.
44. P. Sitaramayya, *History of the Indian National Congress,* Vol. II, Bombay, 1946, p. 341.
45. Jawaharlal Nehru, *The Discovery of India*, Delhi, 1989, p. 478.
46. M.A.K. Azad, *op. cit.*, p. 97.

up by the police. The Orissa Government banned AICC and the allied organisations in the province.[47]

Immediately after the people took to 'Direct Action' at various parts of British India. The people in the feudatory States were similarly affected by the August movement.

The message of August revolution did reach them through various channels. The Congress had got a fair number of member and sympathisers in feudatory States apart from Congress-socialists. There in the Quit India Movement the State people saw a golden opportunity to sack off the autocratic feudal rule along with the end of their protector's empire. They thought that the pre-occupation of British Indian forces to deal with the violence in their areas would leave the State Police alone to meet the exigencies inside the States. Thus, by sheer number and organisation, they could outmatch the State force and would be successful in their struggle of liberation. The king would be, rather, compelled to enter into an understanding with the *Prajamandal* to secure his position. The people rose in rebellion against the State authorities. As the people of India were determined to achieve their independence at any cost, the people in the States also became more violent to bring the administration to their side from the chiefs. The most spectacular movement took place in Talcher which was more widespread and deep-rooted. The workers of Talcher *Prajamandal* who devoted most of their time in silent constructive work during the World War II now jumped *en mass* to the flow of the movement.[48]

The primary cause of the entire people's movement was against the maladministration of the *Raja* of Talcher. During Second World war he got a bright chance of suppressing the people by brute force. The chief had his own calculation. He cleverly calculated the British interest in suppressing any voice of dissent, whatever might be the justification, during the war years. So the British Government would not allow the *Prajamandal* to continue any type of agitation against the feudal autocracy even if the *Raja* of Talcher would dishonour the understanding an year earlier. The British would not displease their loyal royal friend, who lost no time in sending assistance to the war efforts of the British Indian Government. So, again the situation was coming back to the earlier time of royal oppression and arbitrary rule and the war only gave him a chance to take back what little medieval

47. *Amrit Bazar Patrika*, 10 August 1942.

48. S. Mishra, *Swadhinatara Jayajatra*, Oriya, Cuttack, 1984, p. 108.

autocratic prerogative he reluctantly surrendered earlier. But the spirit of Quit India had gone deep into the veins of the dumb millions, who confronted the *Durbar* with heroic spirit as their counterparts against the British in provincial territories. Almost all the leaders were inside the jail where they were brutally tortured. Despite heavy precautionary measures, Pabitra Mohan Pradhan, the leader of Talcher *Prajamandal* escaped from Talcher Jail on 31 August 1942.[49] He went underground and a reward of ten thousand rupees was declared for his arrest.[50] Later on he had joined the movement led by Baishnab Charan Patnaik at Dhenkanal and skilfully organised the people's movement in Talcher.

The escape of Pabitra Mohan Pradhan from the jail made the people's movement violent and sporadic. Rumour spread throughout the State that the authority had killed him inside the jail. There was apprehension that the other leaders might be killed in the prison. So the people in thousands went to Talcher *Garh* to break the walls of Talcher jail to free all the prisoners. But the workers of *Prajamandal* stood on the way and prevented the people from doing such thing.[51]

No information was available of the whereabouts of Pabitra Mohan Pradhan. An emergency meeting was held by the *Prajamandal* at Paniola Camp of Angul on 2 September 1942.[52] It was unanimously decided to fight openly against the tyrannical rule of the *Raja* of Talcher and liberate Talcher from his clutches. It also adopted resolution to fight against the British imperialism. Now there was open affirmation of *Prajamandal* to the fight against British imperialism along with feudalism. This qualitative leap was possible due to the organisational activities of Congress, Congress-socialists and Communists to link the national struggle going all over India to the regional struggle of the State people against the *Raja*. The *Prajamandal* declared an open fight against the Talcher *Durbar*. Bichhanda Pradhan was elected the dictator of this programme. Pabitra Mohan Pradhan who earlier went underground was giving advice to *Prajamandal* from his place of hiding supposed to be on the bank of Brahmani.[53] It was decided that the people *en mass* would attack the *Durbar* on 6 September 1942 and would establish a peoples' Government.

49. P.M. Pradhan, *op. cit.*, p. 88.
50. N.K. Sahu and S.C. De, *op. cit.*, p. x.
51. B. Mohanty, *Swadhinata Sangram O Odisa*, Oriya, Cuttack, 1973, pp. 116-117.
52. *Talcher Prajamandal Itihas Committee* (*Compl.*), *op. cit.*, pp. 49-50.
53. *Ibid.*

This time the people's movement became violent one. The workers got the permission to attack the palace and the royal court of Talcher. Immediately, they went to their villages to prepare themselves for the fight.

They had endured all sorts of torture of the State authorities and then the time had come to retaliate the State violence with whatever weapon they had got. 'Do or Die' was their slogan. Practically the entire administration of Talcher had collapsed from the day the people had attacked to break the walls of Talcher jail on the issue of missing of Pabitra Mohan Pradhan on 31 August 1942.[54] This was just a reflection of the national movement in a national setting. The declared Congress policy under Gandhian guidance of non-violence was quitely replaced by a violent course of struggle during the August Revolution. The same was the case in Talcher. The people no longer were prepared to accept the royal oppression just lying low. Now violence of the State would be combated with popular violence.

The Talcher *Prajamandal* defied the *Durbar* Government and organised a parallel independent Government. In true sense, the entire State excepting its headquarter town came under the control of the *Prajamandal* Government. The Ruler had little administrative control in the State. *Prajamandal* committees were formed at the village, block, *pargana* and sub-divisional levels. A central committee was formed to look after these committees.[55] All the State administrative organisations and sub-organisations were disallowed to function in the State. The Government agencies and their representatives were not allowed to enter the village. Their offices and official records were destroyed. The *Sarbarakars, Choukidars*, block officers and circle officers surrendered their dresses, badges and all the official records before the State Government and burnt them with their own hands. This was being followed by the officers of police, revenue, excise and forest department.[56] They left their jobs and joined the people's movement. The *Sarbarakar* of village Seepur was murdered by the people as he denied to obey the new system of people's Government.[57] The *Prajamandal* militia collected all the arms, ammunitions, rifles etc.

54. *Talcher Prajamandal Itihas Committee* (*Compl.*), *op. cit.*, pp. 52-53.

55. *Ibid.*

56. *Ibid.*, p. 54.

57. Orissa Records, Sambalpur Papers, Acc. No. 1026S, Letter from A.N. Mithchell, Political Agent, Orissa State to Raja of Dhenkanal, D.O. No. 515/I, 8 September 1942. (OSA)

which were there in the Government as well as private offices in the State. All the Government houses, bungalows, police stations, forest offices, quarters etc. were burnt in different places in Talcher. The communication system was totally disrupted. People destroyed roads and bridges, removed railway lines, cut off telegraph lines and looted post offices.[58] The *Prajamandal* workers pursuaded the railway and coal-mine workers to join them in order to paralyse the mines and industries in the State.[59] It would curtail the profits of the *Raja* from mineral activities inside the State.

After formation of Panchayat Administration in every village with the help of volunteers of the people's movement a peasant militia called *Krisak-sena* was formed. It decided to force the *Raja* to hand over the administration into the hands of the people and a popular Government would be established in the State democratically. All the family members of the peasants in every village voluntarily involved themselves in this militia. Every member of this group had to keep food for himself at least for three days. They were armed with crude weapons. A Red Cross Society was with them for the treatment of any casualty. The organised bands of peasant militia marched from almost each village of the State towards Talcher on 6 September 1942.[60] But heavy showers of rain obstructed their way. The same day they derailed 42 train engine and removed 20 yards of rail track.[61] On the next day, 7 September 1942, about eight thousand agitators of Talcher armed with guns, spears, axes and bows planned to attack the palace of the *Raja*, break-open the jail and assembled at Hatatota under the manogroves near Talcher *Garh* and surrounded the palace in a semi-circular way.[62] The royal force would have been easily outnumbered but they were reinforced by British Army. Twelve rounds were fired resulting in one death and two wounded and arrest of 243 people's volunteers.[63] The people were determined not to withdraw before occupying the palace. But the Talcher *Durbar* stood firm against the

---

58. Orissa Records, Sambalpur Papers, *op. cit.*

59. *Ibid., op. cit.*, Situation Report No. 452-P/42, 8 September 1942.

60. Orissa Records, Talcher Papers, Enquiry Report of Senior State Officer, Talcher to the Administrator, Talcher, 26 February 1948. (SRT)

61. *Ibid*, Sambalpur Papers, Acc. No. 1026/131, C.P. Hancock, Resident to Political Agent, Sambalpur, No. C-2(10)-C/42, Express Letter 11 September 1942. (OSA)

62. *Ibid.*

63. *Ibid.*

mob.[64] Leaflets from aeroplane were distributed dissuading the people and for creating a fear-psychosis among the people.[65] As it created no effect among the violent agitators, they used smoke screen and teargas shells. It was quite impossible for the authority to fight with them on ground due to the comparative large number of agitators. Finally, the authority took to machine gunning from air to disperse the mob.[66] Fifty rounds of ammunition in all were used in three times till complete dispersal of the crowed.[67] This caused the death of four persons, hundred were wounded and more than three hundred were arrested.[68] The peasant militia who were practically armless in comparison with the Government force had then to give way after strubborn opposition and they fled away in a stampede as a result of the orderly and planned attack of the superior official force. The angry people destroyed police outposts and looted the post office at Seepur, twenty miles north of Talcher on 8 September 1942. They destroyed the Nandira bridge and some culverts on the way. This mob also looted the Government postal money kept in Seepur Police Station. They burnt the primary school of Bijgol and injured the father of the *Sarbarkar* of Seepur who protested their move.[69] Even the village servants '*Paiks*' of the same village Seepur joined the agitation of the people of Seepur, Seeling, Karnapal, Biru, Parabil and Gaham on 8 September 1942. They actively involved themselves with the angry people who burnt the police records of Seepur *Thana*, police and choukidar dress, broke up the police station, looted money from the post office iron-chest and cut out telephone lines. For these reasons *Paiks* like Kusa Samal, Natha Swain and Bhadra Mohant etc. of Seepur had been dismissed from their posts and consequently the *jagir* lands had been taken away from them and given to others who were newly appointed in their places.[70] On 9 September 1942 many bridges, culverts and about nine telegraph lines

64. Orissa Records, Sambalpur Papers Acc. No. 1026/111, Letter from *Raja* of Talcher to Raja of Dhenkanal, No. 466 p/42, 10 September 1942. (OSA)
65. *Ibid.*, Talcher Papers, Enquiry Report of the Senior State Officer, *op. cit.*
66. Orissa Records, Sambalpur Papers, Acc. No. 1026S, Raja of Dhenkanal to Resident of Eastern States of Orissa, No. 452-P/42, 8 September 1942. (OSA)
67. *Ibid.*, Telephone Message from Royal Air Force, Cuttack to the Resident Eastern State Agency, Calcutta, No. C-2(9)-C42-1909, 9 September 1942. (OSA)
68. *Talcher Prajamandal Itihas Committee* (*Compl.*), *op. cit.*, pp. 64-65, the persons who were shot dead from the air were Basudev Sahoo of Danara, Krutarth Pradhan of Danara, Matia Shool of Handidhua and Bhajana Nayak of Brahman Bahal.
69. Orissa Records, Sambalpur Papers, Acc. No. 1026/131, *op. cit.*
70. Orissa Records, Talcher Papers, Enquiry Report of Senior State Officer, *op. cit.*.

were damaged and pulled down fifteen miles north of Talcher Town.[71] It seemed that Talcher had taken a page from the history of ongoing 'Quit India' agitation that was going on all over the country.

On the other hand, the authority took revengeful attitude towards the people. The *Durbar* was able to suppress the stubborn rising of the people with the help of the British forces and recovered the administrative control of the State. Some leaders were imprisoned and some remained underground. They continued to organise the people against the State and British Government. But the Viceroy of the State forces led to ruthless suppression and a reign of terror was let loose on the people. Looting and arson of the villages were systematically conducted when troops marched through the villages to demoralise the people. Mass fines were imposed and realised by force from the villagers causing untold suffering and loss for the people.[72] Large number of *Prajamandal* workers and freedom fighters were confined to prisons where they were inhumanly tortured which caused the death of Rabichandra Pradhan of Langijoda and Baji Sethi of Seepur in the jail.[73]

When the political movement was going on during 1942 and the States peace and order was at stake, the Talcher *Durbar* for the maintenance of law and order passed an Ordinance in an extraordinary issue of the State Gazette on 8 September 1942.[74] This order empowered the *Durbar* to impose collective fines on the villages which were party to the creation of disorders and lawlessness. By the strength of this Ordinance the *Durbar* imposed collective fines on 35 villages of the State, as the inhabitants of the villages according to the opinion of the *Durbar*, were concerned in commission of offences prejudicially affecting the smooth running of the State administration and also reported to have taken important part in destruction of Railway lines, Telephone lines, Telegram lines, bridges, culverts etc. An amount of Rs. 25,500 of fine was imposed on the following villages:[75] Gaham, Parabil, Biru, Seeling, Nalam, Titirima, Puipal, Karnapal, Seepur, Rengali, Rangabeda, Jaroda, Sanatribid, Bolangi, Ghontinali, Kakudia, Changudia, Kansamunda, Boinda, Santrabandha, Kumunda, Suluda,

71. Orissa Records, Sambalpur Papers, *op. cit.*

72. *Ibid.*

73. *Ibid.*, Talcher Papers, Enquiry Report of Senior State Officer, *op. cit.*

74. *Ibid.*, Talcher Durbar Extraordinary Gazette Notification, Talcher 8 September 1938. (TPRR)

75. *Ibid.*, Enquiry Report of the Senior State Officer, *op. cit.*

Danara, Kalamchhuni, Ghantapara, Handidhuna, Deulbera, Bantol, Jagannathpur, Kukudula, Baghoabol, Kankil, Hensmul, Karnapur and Gurujang. These villages had to bear the revenge of the ruler by paying a collective fine of Rs. 25,500. Besides Rs. 5,325 and Rs. 1,275 were collected as individual and departmental fines from many persons.[76] The amount was forcefully collected and deposited in the State treasury. The *Prajamandal* of Talcher later on contradicted the official report and alleged that beside these 35 villages, collective fines had further been realised from other 81 villages. The report on the collection of fine was also much less than the actual collection which was about Rs. 79038-5-2.[77]

Many false cases were instituted against the people who participated the 1942 movement in the State. In the case of *Nizigarh* town some people were fined heavily on political grounds. Among them, Gourang Das, Kalandi Kaviraj and fifteen others were convicted for attempting to break open the jail and the *Raja's* palace.[78] The *Prajamandal* lodged a complaint to conduct an open enquiry by the State into the looting, extortion, demolitions and misappropriation so that the affected subjects might be restored the value of their looted and destroyed properties and the convicted person must be penalised.[79] The so called officers with the help of the State Police Force and with the instigation of the *Durbar* used to go to different villages and looted individual houses. They demanded exorbitant fines and when the people could not pay it they attached their houses and took away the movables, livestock and valuables. The dwelling houses of some of the workers who participated the movement were demolished and raised to the ground. During 1942 agitation the properties worth of Rs. 700 of Bhagirath Pradhan of Rangabeda was stolen and this was reported in the Kaniha Police Station, but no action was taken.[80] This clearly showed that the agents of the *Durbar* often played a vital role in creating anti-social work to curb down the agitation. The State administration was an active abetter and supporter to the incidents. The Talcher *Prajamandal* had

76. Orissa Records, Sambalpur Papers, Acc. No. 1026/220, Raja of Talcher to Political Agent, Sambalpur D.O. No. 445, 15 October 1942. (OSA)

77. *Ibid.*, Talcher Papers, Memorandum filed by President, Talcher Prajamandal, *op. cit.*, pp. 21-22.

78. *Ibid.*, *op. cit.*, Criminal Case No. 51/6 of 1942-43, Talcher Durbar 14 October 1942. (SRT)

79. *Ibid.*, Memorandum filed by President, Talcher Prajamandal, *op. cit.*, pp. 28-29.

80. *Ibid.*

represented to have an open enquiry to these looting, demolition and stealing of valuable wealth of the people which was not accepted by the State authorities.[81]

Repressive measures continued in vigour by the Talcher State *Durbar*. The British Air Force and the Army were with the ruler who was creating havoc in the minds of the people. British Army was involved in looting, molesting the innocent and collecting fines forcibly from the people. A reward of ten thousand rupees was announced to arrest Pabitra Mohan Pradhan.[82]

Besides the ordinary *raiyats*, some States semi-officials like *Sarbarakars, Jagirdars, Lakhrajdars* were also found taking part in the agitation. Some of them were dismissed from the services, some were fined and some were compelled to sign bonds. A good number of people were arrested. Depressed classes like *Pan, Dom, Hadi, Kandara, Sawars* had been exempted from paying fines and were rewarded as they had not taken part in the people's movement of Talcher.[83] The clever *Durbar* was able to divide the common people, separating the depressed classes from the upper classes and utilising the former against others, utilising the age old Indian caste division in the society. Due to ignorance and social oppression, these unfortunate lower castes sided with the ruler, who in their traditional estimation was a part of divinity and would do good to them. It is only a game of 'Divide and Rule, which Britishers were applying all over India in various forms. Naturally, the danger of August Revolution engulfing the entire British Indian Government led it to move immediately to the assistance of the *Raja* of Talcher and in the process the title of *Raja Bahadur* was conferred on the ruler of Talcher in 1942 as a personal distinction in recognition of his work in August disturbance of 1942.[84]

It was the people of the State of Talcher with the help of Dhenkanal people led all other States of Orissa in their agitation against the State authorities in 1942. It was one of the five places of India, according to Sir Alan Hartley on the question of Pandit H.N. Kunzru in the debate in the central council on the States on 25 September 1942 where

81. Orissa Records Talcher Papers, Maguni Chandra Pradhan, Secretary, Talcher Prajamandal to the Prime Minister of Orissa, in his letter on 24 January 1948. (SRT)

82. *Utkal Prasanga*, August 1972, p. 56.

83. P.M. Pradhan, *op. cit.*, pp. 88-90.

84. Orissa Records, Sambalpur Papers, Acc. No. 970, Political Agent, Orissa State Agency to Secretary to Resident, Eastern State Agency, Sambalpur, D.O. No. pp. 1-5, 14 February 1946. (OSA)

machine gunning of masses from the air had to be resorted to for quelling the 1942 agitation.[85] The State officials of Talcher *Durbar* thought that with the mass arrest of the *Prajamandal* workers the storm had subsided. But it was not so. Even the fire resorted to by military police could not check the intuition of the people to become free from the feudal order. It was only a lull before the storm which broke out in the State with all its fury later.

On the face of the ruthless military force, the people's movement could not proceed any longer and *Prajamandal* decided to postpone direct confrontation. It was just a replica of what happened to the great August Revolt within a year. Of course, underground activities still continued unabated. Some prominent leaders still absconded. A secret armed squad was organised. The volunteers of the squad had equipped themselves with guns and other weapons to face the British forces employed by the State in the villages. They had to stay inside the forest and took recourse to guerilla warfare.[86] They kept themselves aloof which was unknown to the State *Durbar*. During night they used to go to the villages to encourage the people to have patience, courage and zeal against the chief and the British. They punished the government officials, agents and followers of the *Raja* both physically and financially. Partly due to such tactics, the oppression made by the officials of the *Durbar* was reduced to some extent.[87] The role of the Armed Squad was made known to the chief of Talcher some time later. Towards the end of May 1943, while the tired volunteers of the secret Armed Squad were asleep in the night, they were *gheraod* by the military police and reserve army. There was exchange of continuous firing among the two forces causing the death of leaders like Maheswar Pradhan and Padia Behera of Talcher *Prajamandal*.[88] Some other militants including Phiringi Pradhan, Mukunda Sahoo, Kalia Das and Jadunath Pradhan were severely injured.[89] The squad was dissolved later on. Of course this secret squad helped the Talcher *Prajamandal*

---

85. File No. 3/18/45, Home Political (Deposit) (NAI) The other places where machine guns from air resorted to were Cirick in Patna district about 12 miles of Bihar Sharif; Bhagalpur, near Ranghat of Nadia District and in between Pasraha and Mahesh railway halt in Monghyr District.
86. P.M. Pradhan, *op. cit.*, pp. 43-44.
87. *Talcher Prajamandal Itihas Committee* (*Compl.*), *op. cit.*, p. 59.
88. *Ibid.*, p. 65.
89. *Ibid.*

to gather its strength in future. It stood on the way of tyranny and maladministration of the chief for about eight months.

In the history of the revolutionary movement in India we find the role of a group of armed nationalists who were called by the Government as terrorists written in golden letters. When the unarmed people were suppressed, the people had no physical strength to combat the armed brutes, at that time these groups played a pivotal role in keeping alive the line of hope of liberation of the masses, inflict psychological fear in the minds of the British Officers and agents and by their self-sacrificing deed rouse the people again from slumber to action. The armed actions of Bhagat Singh and his group in HSRA in late twenties, Surya Sen and his associates in Chittagong in early thirties and many more martyrs amply portrays the truth. The armed volunteer squad of Talcher did the same in its sphere and though was active only for eight months, it wrote a page of its own in the history of the States' peoples' movement in Orissa.

By June of 1943 almost all the agitations all over Orissa were suppressed. In Talcher the State *Durbar* with the help of the British Officials started ruthless oppression. Most of the leaders went underground. The leaders and organisers of the people's movement who absconded were the main targets of the State authorities. Subsequently they were arrested and put in the prison. Even the life of Pabitra Mohan Pradhan was in grave danger. He was absconding at that time. Under such circumstances he had to leave Orissa and joined the Indian National Army of Netaji Subash Chandra Bose as member of the suicidal squad.[90] Of course, Sri Pradhan's joining INA was not corroborated by any other documentary evidence. The other leaders were put behind the bar.

Thus, by the end of June 1943 the people's movement in Talcher lost its vigour. The 1942 movement in the State which was quite violent showed the *Durbar* and the British Government its popular strength and support for the establishment of a democratic people's representatives Government inside the State in particular and in the country in general. Due to the superior military force of the authorities, because of the participation of the British Indian Force and the violent method adopted by the *Prajamandal* which perhaps did not touch all the people in the same way resulted in the collapse of the movement of that time. The demands of the people were not accepted by the State

90. S.N. Patnaik, *op. cit.*, p. 178.

Durbar and it remained adamant due to the British support during the war years. The British Government was very kind enough to award the chief, Kishore Chandra with the title of '*Raja Bahadur*' for his ability of suppressing the people's agitation in the State and for controlling the difficult situation. In a grand Durbar in 1942 held for presenting the chief the *Sanad* of '*Raja Bahadur*' Col. Hancock, the resident for the Eastern States in his speech stated :

> "The present Ruler, whom I am delighted to looking so hale and strong today succeeded to the *Gadi* while a minor in 1891. He was installed in 1901 and has, therefore, ruled for 41 years. And it was an age when many another man would have been unequal to the test that a few week ago he was confronted by violent crowds misled by agitators who certainly had not the true interest of India at least. The *Raja Saheb* trusting in affection and good sense of his people went alone and unarmed amongst them; he made his dispositions with energy, skill and courage and it is for that reason that today and at this moment I present him the *Sanad* of the title of "*Raja Bahadur*" conferred upon as a personal distinction by "His Excellency the Crown Representative".[91]

Though there was no development in the relation between the *Raja* and the subjects, the rising proved that the people once backward and underdeveloped had become conscious of their rights and were not prepared to accept the autocratic rule as done in the past. If necessary, they could be equally violent to assert their rights.

The August rising could not be called a fiasco as it paved the way for the future events to mature leading to the total collapse of the British rule along with its dependants in the feudatory States. The great Gandhian struggles of 1920-22 and 1930-34 had not immediately achieved what it aimed at that particular time. Gandhi's call to give 'Swaraj within one year' in 1930 did not materialise. Even the earlier one's Swadeshi movement of 1905-08, failed to annul the partition of Bengal. Yet these are not failures, but steps towards a grand success. The Talcher struggle of 1942 had brought the people to a place where their enemy was not the King alone but its backers, the British Imperialism. They saw the clear signs and realised due to grounds prepared by the *Prajamandal* that the democratic institutions in the State could not be inaugurated in isolation to the absence of the same

91. Orissa Records, Talcher Papers, Polonissa, Sambalpur to Raja Sahib, Talcher State, 10 November 1945, File No. 18/45-46. (SRT)

in national level. The Congress Government that came to power in various provinces failed to function properly and had to resign after the outbreak of the war, gave its own lesson to these people.[92] The Congress Ministry in Orissa tendered their resignation on 4 November 1939 and great enthusiasm prevailed among the people at this dramatic action of the ministry. It received the sympathetic support from all the corners of the State.[93] Of course, the programme during 1942 in Talcher had its source of inspiration from the August Resolution of AICC and many Congress leaders were active in the struggle, especially the Congress-socialists and Communists. The Congress and Socialist leaders of British Orissa were involved in the movement of Talcher during 1942. Nabakrishna Choudhury, Nityananda Kanungo, Rajkrishna Bose etc. were the leaders who actively supported the cause of the people's revolt in Talcher. It now linked more with national developments outside the State than before. Due to the total suppression of the movements, arrest of almost all leaders and few remaining underground the movement could not continue further. In the national level also the Quit India Movement lost its edge after one year of its inauguration. It also influenced the local scene. There was a perceptible lull in the political activities in the State till the end of Second World War. The workers of *Prajamandal* devoted themselves to constitutional work in their villages till the end of war. This lull was only providing a respite from the exhaustion of a violent struggle and preparing for a final one to make a frontal assault on feudalism for their rights and dues lock, stock and barrel.

◆

92. Orissa Records, W.W.C.C., Acc. No. 32, p. 8.

93. *Ibid.*

VI
Towards Victory, 1946-48

The collapse of Quit India Movement and the end of World War II in May 1945 witnessed a perceptible lull in the political activities in the Orissan States. The State subjects shared the same depression with their provincial counterparts and waited for a new era of resurgence in future time. On one hand, the defeat of Axis powers kindled a new ray of hope for humanity but, on the other, Indian people were still enslaved by the British and were apprehensive of more and more repression from the jubilant, victorious British power. So the people of the feudatory States as well as others were getting ready for a final round of struggle with the British. At that time the feudatory States of Orissa were celebrating the Victory of British power over Japanese militarism, German Nazism and Italian Fascism with great pomp and ceremony. They thus tried to impress upon their subjects the futility of any struggle against the feudal lords who had got the friendship and support of the victorious British Indian Government. The victory celebration in the feudatory States was just a veiled threat and warning to the *Prajamandals* and a way of intimating the British master of their loyalty to them.

The Durbar of Talcher, where the Quit India Movement was most severe and violent amongst all other Orissan States lost no time in issuing a notification to observe 'Thanks Day' and Public Holiday on 19 and 20 August 1945 respectively in the State. To commemorate the occasion festive arrangements were made for dance, music, merry making and distribution of sweets in the State.[1] Letters were issued by the *Durbar* to all the Heads of the Departments to decorate all official buildings with flags and illumination.[2] In this occasion funds were raised by the *Durbar* from different institutions like the Collieries to

1. Orissa Records, Talcher Papers, Talcher State Gazette, Extraordinary by P.C. Dev, Dewan, Talcher, 18 August 1945 (SRT)
2. *Ibid.*, *op. cit.*, Dewan to All Heads of Departments, Letter No. G/127/ Talcher 18 August 1945. (SRT)

celebrate the victory of the Allied powers in the State in a big manner. The managers of the M & S.M. Ray Colliery, B.N.R. Colliery and Villiers Colliery were supposed to give each an amount of Rs. 260, Rs. 167-8-0, and Rs. 197-8-0 respectively to the *Durbar* in this connection.[3] Besides, others also gave in kind to the State for it.

The feudatory chiefs, who were the stooges at the hands of the British, could not know that the death bell had already knocked at the door. The fall of Nazism and Fascism made the imperialism to count its last days. The victory of the allied powers also symbolised the victory of democratic aspirations over autocracy. The western powers fought the war with a slogan to safeguard democracy for the world. Naturally, with the end of World War II, again the demand for democratic institutions raised its head determinedly and the imperial west had no answer to the popular demand but to concede independence to the colonial people within a short time. They took various steps to hand over power to the Indian people.

The arrival of the Cabinet Mission in 1946 and the following political developments in the country as a whole had considerable repercussion in the affairs of the Orissan States. The discussions about impending Indian independence made the people of Orissan States more apprehensive of their own future after the British withdrawal and induced them to go for the struggle with renewed vigour and spirit. The State people revived agitation demanding popular government in the States. It was supported by the *Garajat Chatra Sammilani*, the Orissa and Chhatisgarh council, the press and different political parties. By that time; the Congress Ministry headed by H.K. Mahtab had already been formed in the province in April 1946 and it extended its hands for the cause of the people's movement in the States.[4] The Government of India also advised the rulers of Indian States including the Orissan States to look to the welfare of the State and its people. In a letter to the *Raja* of Talcher the President of Eastern Agency, Calcutta wrote :

> "I recommend to you to try and make the task a happy partnership between the Ruler and Ruled. Consult the best interests of your people and seek to command their loyal collaboration and good will. They are your own people, your own partners and make

3. Orissa Records, Talcher Papers, Raja to Manager of 3 collieries, Letter No. G/124-26 Talcher 18 August 1945. (SRT)
4. Orissa Records, W.W.C.C., Acc. No. 35, p. 54.

their best interests. Your first and foremost concern when I am sure they will respond in full measures for they too have their citizen duties and responsibilities to the partnership"[5]

After the end of the World War there was, still, maladministration in the States. In 1945 the *Raja* of Talcher, Sri K.C. Dev died and the old system of *bethi*, *begar* and *magan* was still continuing in the State. The *Pattayat*, Sri P.C. Deb, was of the opinion to raise a public subscription to make the funeral ceremony of his late father. He had suggested the *Juvaraj Sahib*, the present *Raja*, that he should take up the work in his own hand and do everything.[6] This proved the intention of the royal family of Talcher on the collection of *Magan* during any ceremony. *Bethi* was also prevailing in other State like Narsingpur. On the recommendation of R.K. Ramdhyani, His Excellency the crown representative, who was appointed as special officer to enquire land development system in Eastern State Agency, decided in 1944 that *bethi* or forced labour should be abolished from the States. The Narsingpur *Durbar* initiated that they had abolished this system from their State; but it now appeared that 'forced labour' in disguise of 'voluntary service' was still in existence.[7] Though there was restriction on *bethi*, *magan* etc. by the Central Government, yet it was still in force in the States of Orissa even after the Second World War. The social condition of the subjects actually did not improve.

The Central Government, after the World War had reached the conclusion that the ban on the All India Congress Committee and any existing bans on Provincial, District or lower Congress Committee or on the All India Spinners' Associations etc. be removed. They had accordingly requested the Provincial Governments to take necessary action to this end.[8] But this order was not implemented in most of the States of Orissa. Maguni Chandra Pradhan, a prominent *Prajamandal* worker of Talcher had made a petition to the Political Agent, Eastern

5. Orissa Records, Sambalpur Papers, Acc. No. 1164S, Eastern State Agency, Calcutta to Political Agent, Orissa, An advance copy of Speech of the Hon'ble President for *Raja*, Talcher, D.O. No. R. 13-10/45 P. dated 13th March 1946. (O.S.A.)
6. *Ibid.*, *op. cit.*, Dewan Bahadur P.C. Dev Talcher to Secretary Eastern States Agency, Sambalpur, No. P1-60/45, dated 9th November 1945. (O.S.A.)
7. *Ibid.*, *op. cit.*, Acc. No. 966S. Secretary, Eastern States Agency to *Durbar* of Narsingpur No. M.1-17/46-1058, dated 10th August 1946. (O.S.A.)
8. Orissa Records, Sundergarh Papers, Acc. No. 27318S, Political Agent, Pol. Orissa, Sambalpur Express Letter to all Durbars No. P.1.53, dated 28th September 1945. (OSA)

State Agency, Sambalpur on 17 March 1947 regarding the illegal arrest and harassment of his seventy year old brother, Upendra Pradhan by the Talcher State police for his association with such a society.[9] The political prisoners who were arrested during 1942 movement and in the Second World War were set free when the Congress formed the Interim Ministry in 1946 at the Centre. But, in the State of Talcher the authority did not release the prisoners. About four hundred workers of the Talcher People's Movement were still inside the prison. The warrants were still in force for those who were absconding. Towards the last part of 1946 prisoners were released and warrants were withdrawn. But warrants against Pabitra Mohan Pradhan was not lifted.[10]

Talcher *Durbar* still behaved as it had done in the past. No concession in civil liberty was granted to the people. Entire power remained in the hands of the royal family. Some of the clauses mentioned in the Talcher State Gazette issued by the *Durbar* during 1945-46 Stated :

"1. . . . .

2. The executive authority of the State shall be exercised by the Executive Council, which shall consist of the Ruler as President, the Diwan as Vice-President and two other members.

3. The council shall exercise such authority as the Ruler may decide to delegate to them under the Rules of Administration.

4. The Diwan and the members of the council shall be appointed by the Ruler on such terms and conditions as may be agreed upon.

5. The members of the council shall individually exercise such authority as the Ruler may decide to delegate to them under the rules of the administration.

6. Diwan would do all except civil list which are reserved for Ruler.

7. All appointments to the State service (except civil list) would be made by Ruler.

8. . . .

---

9. Orissa Records, Sambalpur Papers, Acc. No. 1234S, File No. J-2-9/47, dated 13th June 1979. (OSA)

10. *Talcher Prajamandal Itihas Committee* (*Compl.*), *op. cit.*, pp. 60-64.

9. The Ruler will make rules for the convenient of management of the administration of the State, including the allocation of the Departments to the control of the individual members of the Council".[11]

At the session of the chamber of princes held in February 1946 resolution were moved and accepted that it desired to reiterate that the Indian States fully share the general desire in the country for the immediate attainment by India of her full stature, and would make every possible contribution towards the settlement of the Indian constitutional problem. It further moved a resolution that most States had already adopted statutory provisions guaranteeing the Rule of Law and the Security and protection of person and property within their territories. No person should be deprived of his liberty and should enjoy the right of free expression of opinion, the right of free association and combination, and the right to assemble peacefully without arms. All persons should be equal before law and there should be no *begar*. This session also made resolution on proper justice and impartial administration in the States.[12] But these resolutions made no change in the prevalent situation in the States. This was only accepted in theory but in practice the reverse was done in the States. There was dissatisfaction due to the tyrannical rule in the State.

At the seventh session of the All India States' Peoples' Conference met at Udaipur in December 1945 Pandit Jawaharlal Nehru, the President, declared that its goal was 'attainment by peaceful and legitimate means of full responsible Government by the people of the States as an integral part of a free and federated India.[13] A strong agitation started for the merger of the princely States with Orissa and to that effect a memorandum was submitted to the Cabinet Mission when it came to India in 1946[14]

The goal of achieving independence was the primary aim of the people of India. The State's people also wanted to get rid of the tyranny of the feudatory chiefs. The students on the other hand created

---

11. Orissa Records, Sambalpur Papers, Acc. No. 1164S, Talcher State Gazette of 1945-46 No. 6, Vol. 9 by Talcher *Durbar.* (OSA)
12. Orissa Records, Sambalpur Papers, Acc. No. 1085S, Political Department, New Delhi to H.J. Todd, Resident for the Eastern States, D.O. No. F 23-P(S)/46, dated the 21st February 1946. (OSA)
13. *Orissa District Gazetteers, Dhenkanal,* p. 72 and P.N. Chopra, *op. cit.*, pp. 188-90.
14 *Ibid.*

a panic in the minds of the chiefs through their organisation. At a States' students' conference held at Cuttack on 10 February 1946 speakers criticised the administration of the Orissa States and demanded the release of political prisoners, the restoration of civil liberties and the amalgamation of the smaller States with British India.[15] Later on, a conference of students from the Orissan States had been held at Balasore where the usual complaints were made against various States' administration.[16]

The students of Talcher State also jumped into the fire of the people's movement in the State. With the active co-operation of the *Prajamandal* they established an organisation called the 'Talcher Cultural Club', consisting of members from all corners of Talcher.[17] The King Kishore Chandra was dead by that time but the old way of administration was still going on in the State through his son, *Pattayat* P.C. Dev. The court, which was held in the nights made the people more uncomfortable. This club of the students made extensive propaganda against the maladministration of the *Durbar* through papers, leaflets, drama and national songs.[18] Meetings were organised by the students inside the State. They also circulated copies of the periodical called *Muktiyudha* published by the Communist Party of India, Orissa Branch, in Oriya among the people of Talcher in which the tyranny and oppression of the authority was published.[19] Those who were associated with this cultural club were arrested. Some of them were dismissed from the service by the authority. The cause of the students in particular and the public in general was supported by the people living in the adjoining British territories of Orissa. A public meeting was organised at Sambalpur on 18 February 1946 which was being attended by representatives of many States of Orissa and from different parties like Sarat Patnaik, Dayanidhi Satpathy of Bamanda, Banamali Das of Nilgiri, Brajkishore Patnaik of Athgarh etc. The meeting was presided over by Pandit Laxminarayan Mishra of Sambalpur.[20] Some of these leaders were Communists and some others were Congressites or non-party members. A temporary Committee was formed in the

15. Orissa Records, W.W.C.C., Acc. No. 50, p. 68.
16. *Ibid., op. cit.*, p. 75.
17. Anant Mishtra, *op. cit.*, p. 51.
18. *Ibid.*
19. *Ibid.*, pp. 52-53.
20. Orissa Records, W.W.C.C., Acc. No. 10, pp. 82-83.

meeting consisting of Gour Shankar Raiguru as President, Basudev Mohapatra as Vice-President and Brajkishore Patnaik as the Secretary.[21]

Beside the students and public, the workers wanted to put forth their demands through the people's movement. They also stood against the prevailing administrative system of the feudatory States. A conference of the Orissa States' workers was held at Sambalpur and in that conference resolutions were passed demanding the release of political prisoners, the cancellation of warrants of arrest against political absconders, the establishment of responsible Government in the States based on adult franchise and the abolition of forced labour.[22] Thus, the struggle for the State people's right and development was taking a final vigorous form, keeping pace with the developments outside, in the British Indian territories.

During the lull period that prevailed during the years 1942-46, there had been no leader to organise the people of Talcher for agitation. After June 1946 the *Prajamandal* of Talcher took the labour problem into its hands. In presence of the former Prime Minister of Orissa Sri Biswanath Das a big meeting of the labourers was organised.[23] In that meeting a Trade Union was formed from among the labourers of the three collieries. Binchhanda Pradhan was elected as the President of the Trade Union.[24] Bimbadhar Mohanty and Narayan Chandra Pradhan, two juvenile youth leaders actively assisted in organising the trade union in full spirit. During the war years they had kept contact secretly with the Congress leaders for the purpose of the formation of a trade union which later was successfully formed. This trade union gave its full co-operation to the Talcher People's Movement after the Second World War.

The post-Cabinet Mission period brightened the prospect of independence and made the people of the State's active to secure their future. During 1947 the people's movement in the Orissan States was revived with unabated vigour. That was the period when the independence of the country was on the cards. Still, the problem of the future of the princely States was in the agenda. There was the apprehension of these States remaining independent of the future independent India. Again the activities of the Communists made

21. Orissa Records, W.W.C.C., *op. cit.*

22. *Ibid.*, Acc. No. 50, pp. 70-71.

23. *Talcher Prajamandal Itihas Committee* (*Compl.*), pp. 75-77.

24. *Ibid.*

Congress leaders to think again on reorganising the *Prajamandals* and struggle for their merger with India. In order to regularise and coordinate the people's movement in different States an attempt was made to reorganise the *Prajamandals* by H.K. Mahtab, Radhanath Rath, Sarangdhar Das and Kailash Chandra Mohanty.[25] *Prajamandals* were set up in those States where they were not existing earlier. In the meantime, in order to have a systematic and concerted action with the ultimate aim of achieving their object, the States' people of the eastern regions of Central Province, Orissa, Bengal and Assam constituted jointly an organisation under the name of 'The Orissa and Chattisgarh Regional Council' with Sarangdhar Das as Chairman and Madan Mohan Pradhan as Secretary.[26] In its first session held on 1 March 1947, the Council urged upon the rulers of the States to transfer all powers of administration to the people's representatives in their respective States or group of States or to negotiate and amalgamate in consideration of language, culture, geographical continuity and economic necessity with the neighbouring province.[27] The Rulers of the States apprehended potential resistance from this political organisation of the people and themselves tried to break it up by means of divide and rule policy. The State of Nilgiri led the way in this respect. The rulers set up parallel *Praja Parishad* to counteract the works of the *Prajamandals*, consisting of persons owing allegiance to the rulers. Those were the puppet organisations consisting of 'yes-men' of the *Raja* such as *Sarbarakars*, State employees, dependants of the ruler and anti-*Prajamandal* workers.[28] By this way, they tried to draw away the people from the people's *Prajamandals* but failed. The Rulers' organisation tried to secure its affiliation to the Regional Council but did not succeed.[29]

By this time on 25 April 1947 a meeting of the leaders of *Prajamandals* of all the *Garajat* States of Orissa was held at Choudhury Nivas of Cuttack. About forty-nine members of different State *Prajamandals* of Orissa were present.* Under the Presidentship of Judhistir Mishra resolutions were passed condemning the proposal of

25. N.K. Sahu and S.C. De, *op. cit.*, p. x.
26. *Ibid.*, and H.K. Mahtab, *op. cit.*, p. 131.
27. R.N. Rath, *op. cit.*, p. 15.
28. N.K. Sahu and S.C. De, *op. cit.*, p. xi.
29. *Ibid.*

* See Appendix S for the Signatories of the Meeting.

forming the Eastern States Union, condemning the high handedness of the feudatory chiefs and so on. Wide discussions were conducted on the organisation of *Prajamandals* and its stand in the present politics. While some members were in support of merging the *Prajamandals* with the Congress, majority were of the opinion that this organisation should maintain its independent identity in the State and continue its activities.[30] The rulers of Orissa and Chattisgarh States started thinking in terms of a federal union since the announcement of Cabinet Mission proposal. They held a secret conference at Puri from 9 July to 14 July 1947 and passed several reactionary resolutions some of which were about the formation of a federation of Orissa and Chattisgarh States and administrative coordination with British Indian Province or with a bigger State like Hyderabad.[31] But by July 1947, already the decisions were taken on Indian independence and the impractical propositions cut little ice with the national leaders, who were bent on annexing these territories to the British Indian areas after independence.

The Orissa and Chattisgarh Regional Council of the Tenants met at Cuttack on 10 August 1947 which was attended by about 22 members of the different State *Prajamandals* and demanded merger of the Orissa States with the province of Orissa.[32] Resolutions were passed condemning the Eastern States Union Act of 1947 and urging the inclusion in the province of the States bordering Orissa on a linguistic basis, calling upon the States' people to resist the undemocratic acts of the rulers, giving an ultimatum to the Rulers that unless the people's demands were conceded they would launch a movement and formed a sub-committee of the *Rulers* and requesting the rulers to release all the political prisoners.[33] The stage was set for confrontation. The people were in no mood to relent and the time was in their favour. The rulers were fighting with their back to the walls. The future of the people of the States now depended on the outcome of the impending struggle.

The attainment of independence in August 1947 brought the problem of merger to the forefront. The feudatory States of Orissa after the withdrawal of the paramount power assumed the attitude of independent sovereign States. The rulers did not institute popular governments. They were not willing to negotiate for amalgamation

30. Minutes of the Meeting (Self Custody).
31. H.K. Mahtab, *Beginning of the End*, Cuttack 1972, pp. 119-25.
32. Orissa Records, W.W.C.C., Acc. No. 28, p. 26.
33. *Ibid., op. cit.* Acc. No. 99, p. 28.

with the Orissa province. So the people of the States had again started to carry on the agitation on the advice of the regional council. They strengthened their organisation by enlisting the services of the students and formed councils of action.[34] In some States people resorted to the action, 'do or die', to establish popular governments and as a sign of determinations, gave their thumb impression with their blood on the pledge.[35] Voluntary forces were recruited in different States with the object of wresting power from the hands of the rulers.[36] The enthusiastic masses joined it in large numbers to give a final death blow to the crumbling foundation of feudalism that oppressed them for centuries.

The people of Talcher and Dhenkanal took a lead in this matter.[37] The warrant against Pabitra Mohan Pradhan was lifted on 29 August 1947[38] after immense pressure from all parts of the country on the ruler of Talcher and he returned to Talcher on 6 September 1947.[39] He was given a worm and rousing reception by the people. Pabitra Mohan Pradhan had condemned the federation of the C.P. and Orissa States and appealed to the Orissa people to extend a helping hand to the States' people struggle.[40] Under his leadership, thousands of volunteers were enrolled with an aim to make determined bid to wrest power from the chief of Talcher by force. He walked on foot all over the State and collected volunteers who joined hands with him and planned to attack the palace of the Talcher Chief. In many other States, also, agitation continued with a great zeal. In Dhenkanal a volunteer force was organised to force the ruler to grant responsible Government. The State Krushak Sangha of Patna started a no tax campaign. It issued an ultimatum for acceptance of their demands such as abolition of forced labour, grant of full rights over trees to the tenants etc.[41]

In Nilgiri a parallel Government known as the *Azad* Nilgiri Government was formed and started functioning from Balasore with Kailash Chandra Mohanty as President and Sarangdhar Das as advisor.[42] The aborigines of Mayurbhanj gradually deserted the *Prajamandal* and

34. H.K. Mahtab, *History of Freedom Movement in Orissa,* Vol. iv, p. 144.
35. Orissa Records, W.W.C.C., Acc. No. 28, p. 26.
36. N.K. Sahu and S.C. De, *op. cit.*, p. v.
37. *Ibid., op. cit.*, p. xi.
38. P.M. Pradhan, *op. cit.*, p. 248.
39. *Talcher Prajamandal Itihas Committee* (*Compl.*) *op. cit.*, p. 62.
40. Orissa Records, W.W.C.C., Acc. No. 28, pp. 25-28.
41. *Ibid.*
42. *Ibid.*

joined their own organisation entitled '*Adibas Sava*' formed by Sonaram Majhi on the issue of adequate representation in the Constituent Assembly and the Interim Government.[43] There were cases of clashes and police firing in Narshingpur and the ruler attempted to suppress the agitation.[44] The *Prajamandal* workers of Athmallik resolved to form village defence committee and volunteer corps for protection against any attack by the aboriginals.[45] The ruler of Bamra induced the aboriginals not to co-operate with the caste Hindus and instigated them to rise against the people of Orissa who were trying for amalgamation of the State with Orissa. The *Prajamandal* members successfully induced the people of the State to resign from the State sponsored *Prajamandal*.[46] The people's movement in Bamra, Talcher, Khandapara, Dhenkanal, Nayagarh, Sonepur, Narsingpur, Athmallik and Keonjhar demanded immediate transfer of power to the people. The Communist party requested its volunteers to co-operate with the people's movement in Orissa States in their agitation for the establishment of a responsible Government by creating a joint front with the Socialist of the province.[47] Thus a picture of hectic political activity emerged in all the princely States.

The agitation of the States' people and the action of the regional council gave rise to strong reaction from the rulers. Consequent upon such renewed movement, rulers of some feudatory States designed to perpetuate their sovereignty over the people of the States. Almost all the rulers formed parallel *Praja Parishads* as a counter-move against the *Prajamandals*. Several rulers of the Eastern States Agency decided that the Indian States Department should not have the right to intervene in the civil and criminal jurisdiction of the B and C class States numbering 17 as they were already under a common High Court. It was further decided to reinforce the States Joint police force by recruitment of Gurkhas and Pakistanis to round up all popular leaders in the event of an agitation of a violent situation.[48] In addition to the States Police, the Eastern States Joint Police Force were requisitioned which was also found insufficient to meet the demands of the States.

43. Orissa Records, W.W.C.C., Acc. No. 47, p. 107.
44. *Ibid.*, p. 108.
45. *Ibid.*, Acc. No. 28, pp. 25-28.
46. *Ibid.*
47. *Ibid.*
48. *Ibid.*, pp. 98-99.

On the other hand, as an exceptional case, the ruler of Athgarh issued an appeal to all the rulers of the Eastern States union to dissolve the Eastern States Union which proved an administrative failure.[49]

In the annual session of the State *Krushak Sangha* held at Bolangir on 29 and 30 October 1947, the States *Prajamandal* representatives rejected the *Dushera* declaration of the ruler of Patna, condemned Kalahandi State authorities of the federal Eastern States Union and condemned the high handedness of the *Durbar* of Bamra and Sareikala.[50] This made the people apprehensive about the intention of the rulers in handing over power to the people's representatives. The *Prajamandal* workers of the States started a counter move and carried on a no tax campaign throughout the States of Orissa. Rulers were given ultimatums to start popular administration while *Panchayat* rules were actually implemented to a extent in many States.

The people's movement in the States of Orissa got full co-operation and support by all sections. The All India Students' Congress adopted many resolutions in favour of the States movement regarding establishment of responsible governments in the States in its District Conferences of Puri and Cuttack.[51] The Working Committee of All Utkal Students' Federation in a meeting at Berhampur on 12 and 13 October 1947 decided to support the cause of the people's movement in the feudatory States of Orissa.[52] The Working Committee of the Regional Council of Orissa and Chattisgarh States passed resolutions in a meeting held at Balasore on 15 and 16 November 1947 appreciating the actions of the Dominion Government and the Government of Orissa in respect of Nilgiri State, declaring the police firing on the subjects of Baramba and Narsinghpur States as unjustifiable and urging the Government of India Dominion and its State Department to dissolve the Eastern States Union and its joint police force.[53] Due to people's agitation, some of the State rulers declared their intention of transferring the entire administration to the people whereas some other States decided to hand over powers to the people after the formation of an interim Government based on adult franchise.[54] In the State like Khandapara

49. Orissa Records, *op. cit.*, p. 27.
50. *Ibid.*, Acc. No. 47, p. 107.
51. *Ibid.*, Acc. No. 99, p. 2.
52. *Ibid.*, Acc. No. 47, p. 101.
53. *Ibid.*, Acc. No. 28, p. 28.
54. *Ibid.*

parallel Government was started by the people. Its ruler conceded all powers to the interim ministry in the State.[55] The rulers of Bonai, Sonepur, Baramba, Mayurbhanj, Athgarh and Rairakhol handed over all powers unconditionally to the *Prajamandals*. All relations with ruler of Bamra was cut off as he tried to create differences between the people and Adivasis.[56]

The ruler of Athgarh State thus handed over the administration to the popular ministry made from the *Prajamandal* workers consisting of *Biswanath Rath* as Prime Minister and Govind Chandra Mishra and Raghunath Rout as members of the Cabinet.[57] Though the ministry was short lived, it became very popular in solving the people's demands. After handing over the charge the ruler of Athgarh in a letter to the Council of Ministers wrote :

"Honourable Ministers,

It is with great pleasure and pride I welcome you as my ministers today. By making over to you the responsibility of the administration, I feel I have been able to satisfy one of my people's long cherished ambition.

I know you are going over a rosy path to traverse, while internal problems are many, external problem of merger is a critical one before you. While I do advocate the principle of merger with Orissa in its essentials and broad outline, I feel constitutional safeguards are necessary for the people of *Garjat* in such a merger. I hope you shall deal with this problem fairly and squarely to all concerned.

Lastly I hope and I would pray that you shall deal with all the subjects of my State impartially, justly and honourably.

Swami Bidyananda Saraswati
9.12.1947
Ruler of Athgarh State".[58]

Though the ministry of Athgarh State was short lived due to the merger of the States in Orissa Province, it became very popular for a

55. Orissa Records, *op. cit.*
56. *Ibid.*, Acc. No. 35, p. 35.
57. Interview with Sri Biswanath Rath of Athgarh at his Bhubaneswar Residence by the author on 1 November 1992.
58. Original Letter of the Ruler of Athgarh. (Self Custody)
See Appendix T for its Oriya Version.

good number of achievements. The people of Athgarh thus, presented the popular ministry a letter of commendation praising the deeds of their tenure in the office.[59]

The *Prajamandals* of Patna and Dhenkanal declared their intention to take the administration into their own hands if their demands were not fulfilled by December.[60]

Thus a new stage had arrived on the scene of post-independent India. Under the impact of national development and emboldened due to Congress taking over the reign of Central Government and of many provinces, the *Prajamandals* decided to enter into the last struggle for merger of these States into the Indian Union. They rightly thought that the solution did not lay in demanding representative Governments in respective States, which was only a stop-gap arrangement so far as their demands and grievances were concerned. The real answer to all their quarries for all times to come would be their final merger to the Indian Union. Now their target was aimed at that direction .

Talcher

After achievement of independence on 15 August 1947 the feudatory States assumed the attitude of independent sovereign states. The rulers of Talcher and other feudatory States neither granted popular government nor were they willing to merge their States with the province of Orissa. The chief of Talcher was publicly denouncing any agitation at all as he had already established *Praja Parishad* in the State. But he was following the Mayurbhanj model of handing of power to people's representatives in a perverted way whereas the *Maharaja* of Mayurbhanj, an enlightened royal house gave the real power to popular government. The Talcher chief created a hand picked *Praja Parishad* of nominated royalists which failed to draw people's support from the beginning. The people's movement in the State of Talcher like other States of Orissa was carried on with full vigour on the advice of the Orissa and Chattisgarh regional council.[61] The people of Talcher and Dhenkanal took a lead in this matter. Under the leadership of Pabitra Mohan Pradhan, Brajkishore Dhal and Maheswar Sabhahu Singh thousands of volunteers were enrolled with a view to wrest power from the chiefs by force. About twenty thousand volunteers joined hands with Pabitra

59. See Appendix U.

60. Orissa Records, W.W.C.C., Acc. No. 28, p. 28.

61. *Ibid.*, Acc. No. 99, p. 28.

Mohan Pradhan at Talcher.[62] Wearing Gandhi caps each of them had got a stick attached with a rope. They marched on the streets of the State and threatened the *Sarbarakars* and other followers of the king and made several slogans for independence from feudalism. They pledged 'do or die' to establish popular Government in the State. They wanted to mobilise the Eastern States Joint Police Force, the State Police Departments, State Officials and State Workers to join with them against the *Durbar*. Even most of the State officials were not allowed by the *Prajamandal* volunteers to enter into their offices. Many official buildings were occupied by the *Prajamandal* volunteers of Talcher.[63] The impact of the works of these volunteers fell on other States like Pallahara, Athmallik, Hindol, Athgarh, Tigiria, Narsinghpur, Nilgiri, Nayagarh, Khandapara, Ranpur, Sonepur and Boudh. The *Prajamandals* of these States organised volunteer groups like Talcher which went up to more than two lakhs.[64] It was alleged that most of these volunteers created a great upsurge in the States and induced the people to cut off relations with the *Durbar*. They also took an attempt to attack the *Pattayat's* Palace but in vain. There was indiscriminate looting, destruction of properties and breaking dwelling houses by some people who took law into their own hands.[65] This preparation on the part of the people created panic in the mind of the chief of Talcher. Most of the chiefs of Orissa States where these volunteers organised themselves, approached Gandhiji to interfere. Gandhiji referred the matter to Sardar Patel who afterwards advised the leaders of *Prajamandals* to wait till the next decision.[66] Thus, now the cause of State people was heard and taken up by the Central Government.

Merger Movement

After the lapse of Paramountcy, the Indian Government considered the problem of integrating the administration in the States with that of Central Government. There was a wide gap between the *Garjat* States and the British administered *Mughalbandi* territories in Orissa. The feudatory States had never given any importance to administration, economic development and establishment of popular Government. But

62. N.K. Sahu and S.C. De, *op. cit.*, p. xi.
63. V.P. Menon, *op. cit.*, p. 166.
64. P.M. Pradhan, *op. cit.*, Vol. II, p. 9 and P.K. Jena, *op. cit.*, p. 233.
65. Orissa Records, Talcher Papers, Petition filed by Pallimangal Samittee before the Chief Administrator, Talcher, 29 April 1948. (SRT)
66. N.K. Sahu and S.C. De, *op. cit.*

the necessity of a unity of the feudatory States with the British Orissa was felt during last part of nineteenth century when Mr. Cooke, the Commissioner of Orissa pleaded for inclusion of the tributary States under the same law and rules to the other Oriya population.[67]

The Attlee Sub-Committee of the Simon Commission which was set up in 1930 for the purpose of examining the question of a separate province for Orissa, recommended that the Orissa feudatory States should be brought into relationship with any administrative set up for Orissa.[68] The Orissa States Enquiry Committee strongly recommended the amalgamation of the States with the province of Orissa. It also had the opinion for the cancellation of the *Sanads* granted to the rulers and to treat them as landlords of permanently settled states.[69] This had got an impact on the people's movement in the States. The chiefs of the feudatory States took a serious view of the recommendation and played a vital role not to implement the same for a united Oriya province.[70]

In 1940 the Secretary of States for India had himself envisaged that the Orissa States should ultimately have to become an integral part of the province of Orissa.[71] The Political Advisor to the Crown representative in his note on 10 August 1940 expected that "the day may quite clearly come when these small States will disappear altogether and be merged in the neighbouring province.[72]

With the progress of the people's movement in the States, it was felt more and more that merger was the inevitable solution of the problem. The situation had changed with the restoration of popular administration in the provinces in 1946. In Orissa, the second Congress Ministry took office in April 1946 with H.K. Mahtab as its premier who took an attempt for a complete solution of the merger problem.[73] H.K. Mahtab was involved with the State people's problem from the very beginning of their organised movement in the thirties. He was the Chairman of the State Enquiry Committee to look into the grievances of the State subjects and he signed the famous Mahtab-Hannessy Pact after the mass exodus of Talcher subjects to Angul. So his taking the

67. Administrative Report of Orissa Division, 1895. (OSA)
68. V.P. Menon, *op. cit.*, pp. 151-56.
69. *Orissa States Enquiry Committee Report*, p. 59.
70. H.K. Mahtab, *Beginning of the End*, pp. 15-17.
71. V.P. Menon, *op. cit.*
72. Ramdhayni Report, Vol. I, p. 102.
73. H.K. Mahtab, *op. cit.*

Premiership was a great moral booster for the State people in general and for the people and leaders of *Prajamandal* of Talcher in particular. When the Cabinet Mission visited Orissa in 1946, H.K. Mahtab met the Mission on 6 April 1946 and submitted a memorandum published by the Provincial Congress Committee pleading for amalgamation of the feudatory States of Orissa with the province.[74] On 26 April he also wrote to Stafford Cripps in this regard to exercise his influence with the authorities concerned regarding the amalgamation of the Orissan States. But the Cabinet Mission was busy in finalising other important matters and could not look into this specific issue.[75] On 14 May 1946, H.K. Mahtab sent telegrams to Lord Pethick Lawrence, the Secretary of States for India and Lord Wavell, the Viceroy, informing them about the urgent necessity of the merger of the States.[76] He was eager to discuss the matter with the Orissa rulers of the princely States. During May-June 1946 he wrote circular letters to all the feudatory chiefs of the State clarifying his stand on the question of amalgamation and requested them to lend their support but it bore no fruit.[77] The Orissa press and public leaders carried on a vivacious campaign in favour of amalgamation. Many rulers agreed that there should be mutual discussion between the authorities of the States and the province. But they, in general, were hostile to any move for amalgamation of the States with the province of Orissa.[78]

The rulers of the Eastern States like Athmallik, Kalahandi, Nilgiri, Boudh, Sonepur, Dasapalla, Dhenkanal, Nilgiri, Patna, Gangpur, Talcher, Bamra, Ranpur, Khandapara, Kharsawan, Sareikala, Korea, Surguja, Sakti, Kawardha, Khairagarh etc. met in a Conference at Tripura House, Calcutta on 12-17 July 1946 and decided to form a federal union of the Orissa and Chattisgarh States.[79] In his Presidential Address of this meet Raja Narayan Prasad Dev of Boudh stated :

74. H.K. Mahtab, *op. cit.*
75. *Ibid.*, pp. 145-46.
76. *Ibid.*, p. 128.
77. Orissa Records, Sambalpur Papers, Acc. No. 1027S, H.K. Mahtab to Maharaja of Kalahandi, D.O. No. 49(19), HMP 9-10 May, 1946. (OSA)
78. *Ibid.*, *op. cit.*, Maharaja of Kalahandi to H.K. Mahtab, D.O. No. 33, 8 June, 1946.
79. Orissa Records, Talcher Papers, Summary of Proceedings of the Council of Rulers, Eastern States, held at Calcutta on 12 July 1946 and onwards, Confidential, President to Ruler of Talcher State, pp. 2-3. (TPRR)

"There has been a good deal of opposition coming from the Congress Camp in the province of Orissa in respect of our proposed Union. As a matter of fact, it is an open secret that our opposition camp has already started creating some troubles in some of the Orissa States. Although it is a fact that this opposition comes from a few interested persons and has not much popular support behind it, nevertheless, it is for us to consider how best we can achieve our objective and prove to the world that the States do not lag behind the rest of India in bringing about appropriate administrative and constitutional reforms as are called for by the changing times and circumstances . . ."[80]

However, Mahtab continued his efforts for a greater cause. He met some of the rulers of the States at Sambalpur on 16 October 1946 in presence of the political agent and tried to convince them the necessity of their joining with the province of Orissa, but to no effort.[81]

The rulers of the Eastern States again met at the Raj Kumar College at Raipur on 17-23 December, 1946 where the activities of the Congress workers against them regarding the amalgamation of the States in Orissa was discussed.[82] The activities of Sarangdhar Das and other Congress leaders in the States and the spread by them of hatred and disaffection against the rulers were brought to the notice. Many rulers of the States were not in favour of the sway which was going on in the States for the merger into the province of Orissa. They were in search of forming a new type of province which would suit themselves. Of course, they had taken into the account that their stand would not continue. Before the preparation of the rulers' conference at Calcutta in July 1947, the President to the Rulers in the circular wrote :

"I fear this will be the last conference of Rulers at which officers of the Political Department will be present, and as will be realised the last opportunity for them to be of any assistance."[83]

In this circulation, there was proposal for forming the Union of the Eastern States in the ensuing Rulers conference to be held in

80. Orissa Records, Talcher Papers, *op. cit.*

81. H.K. Mahtab, *op. cit.*, pp. 20-23.

82. Orissa Records, Talcher Papers, Summary of the Proceedings of Council of Rulers, Eastern States, held at Raj Kumar College, *op. cit.*, (TPRR)

83. *Ibid.*, *op. cit.*, President Eastern States Agency to Raja H.C. Dev. D.O. No. 1854 Calcutta, 25 June 1947. (TPRR)

Calcutta on 10-12th July 1947.[84] Subsequently the Union was formed and it started functioning from 1 August 1947.[85]

Some rulers also wanted to create confusion to counteract the propaganda for establishing the States as parts of the province of Orissa. The anti-Hirakud Dam Agitation in Sambalpur district was carried at a higher pitch and was helped by the ruler of Patna.[86] He was planning to add Sambalpur and Angul to the Eastern States Union and forming the ancient 'Kosal' territory.[87] This was launched only as a counter blast to the movement of amalgamation. The Government of Orissa charged the ruler of Patna Estate with having inspired the agitation.[88]

Indian Independence and the Merger Activities

After the achievement of independence of India, a separate ministry to deal with Indian States was constituted under Sardar Vallabhai Patel. H.K. Mahtab submitted a memorandum to Sardar Patel which contained various administrative difficulties created by the States territories being interlaced with the province. He suggested to bring communication, education, public health, police, judiciary, excise, forest, agriculture and industry into common administration.[89] But no immediate steps were taken by the States ministry of the Central Government as it was quite busy in solving the problems of Kashmir and Hyderabad regarding integration.

By this time there was a chaotic condition in Orissa. The people's movement was rampant in the States to achieve independence of the States from the hands of the rulers through the *Prajamandals*. Volunteers in thousands had jumped into the fire of struggle as their last attempt of snatching power from the State authorities.

There was lawlessness in the States. The *Prajamandal* of Talcher and other States were agitating to achieve responsible governments in their States even resorting to coersive methods. The rulers were still hopeful of continuing in their seat of power. The Government at the Centre was busy for a quick formation of an integrated India. This was

84. Orisa Records, Talcher Papers, *op. cit.*
85. Orissa Records, Sambalpur Papers, Acc. No. 1189S, Resident, Eastern States Agency to Political Department of Indian Government, Telegram on 8 August 1947. (SRT)
86. H.K. Mahtab, *op. cit.*, pp. 23-25.
87. *Ibid.*
88. V.P. Menon, *op. cit.*, pp. 154-55.
89. H.K. Mahtab, *op. cit.*, p. 218.

the time when nothing was clear in the Orissa politics. There was chaos and confusion in the State.

An unsatisfactory situation was created in the feudatory State of Nilgiri towards the end of October 1947. The chief of the State, it was alleged, formed a party of his own consisting mostly of aboriginals and had recruited some Punjabi and Muslims in his military force. These aboriginals under his instigation to counteract the existing *Prajamandal*, plundered the villages and occupied the cultivated lands. There was complete break down of administration and led to an anarchy in the State.[90] The Government of Orissa reported the situation of Nilgiri to Government of India. The Government of India authorised provincial Government to take over the administration of the State and restore law and order. Accordingly the District Magistrate of Balasore was authorised to take over the administration of Nilgiri. On 14 November 1947 it was accomplished without any trouble.[91]

The Eastern States Union reacted at the incident at the Nilgiri State and stated : "We are afraid we cannot endorse the action of the Government of India, Ministry for States in asking the Orissa Government to take over the administration of the Nilgiri State...". It further said: "We sympathise with the Ruler of Nilgiri in his present difficulties who has obeyed the proclamation of the Central Government, in the spirit of a soldier, "for though the soldier knew, someone had blundered". The contrast between Nilgiri and Kashmir is interesting yet glaring. It is because Nilgiri has no strategic value or campaigns in New Delhi".[92]

Soon after the takeover of the administration of Nilgiri the States ministry convened a meeting on 20 November 1947 to consider the constitutional future of Orissan States. The meeting was attended by the Secretary, the Additional Secretary of the Ministry of States; H.K. Mahtab, the Prime Minister of Orissa and the Regional Commissioner of Sambalpur. Three conclusions were reached. In the first place it resolved that the Eastern States Union should not be recognised by the Government of India, secondly, that B and C Class States should be asked to agree to common administration of certain subjects by the provincial Government and thirdly, that the States Ministry should

90. H.K. Mahtab, *op. cit.*, pp. 27-28.

91. *Ibid.*

92. Orissa Records, Talcher Papers, The Eastern States Gazette, Nagpur, 15 November 1947, File No. 12/47-48. (SRT)

call a meeting of the rulers of 'B' and 'C' Class States at Cuttack sometime in December.[93]

In the meantime, there developed a fraction among the rulers of the Eastern States Union which strengthened the hands of the Political Department. The incident of Nilgiri and the views of the ruler of Athgarh regarding dissolving the Union actually annoyed other rulers.[94] Some rulers met Sardar Patel at Delhi on 1 December 1947 who were told that the Eastern States Union would be dissolved. The 'B' and 'C' class States would be merged in the neighbouring provinces while the 'A' Class States would be grouped with the province for joint administration of certain subjects.[95]

Controversy on Merger Issue

Some confusion and controversy were created on the eve of the merger of the province of Orissa. Obstacles came regarding this issue from the side of some rulers and *Prajamandal* leaders of some States. Different opinions were given by some of the leaders of the movement.[96] Some of the rulers yielded to the people's demand and declared their intention of transferring State administration to the people.

The ruler of Athgarh took initiation in this regard and tried to bring the *Prajamandal* to his side. Some rulers of the States also supported his stand. The rulers of Kalahandi, Bamra, Bonai, Patna and Gangpur were not in favour of merger of their States with the province of Orissa. Out of fear, they had signed the agreement with Sardar Patel but later on after the merger, their intentions were clarified when they instigated their subjects to agitate against the provincial Government against the merger of their States. Anti-merger agitation went on just after amalgamation of Orissan States with the province in the States stated above.[97]

The ruler of Khandapara conceded all powers to the interim ministry

93. V.P. Menon, *op. cit.*, pp. 149-50.
94. Orissa Records, W.W.C.C., Acc. No. 28, pp. 27-29.
95. V.P. Menon, *op. cit.*, pp. 154-55, The States were classified as 'A', 'B' and 'C' on the basis of their revenue. There were 11 'A' Class States such as Mayurbhanj, Patna, Kalahandi, Sonepur, Boudh, Dhenkanal, Gangpur, Nayagarh, Sareikala, Keonjhar and Bamra; 12 'B' Class States such as Athgarh, Athmallik, Khandapara, Narsingpur, Baramba, Bonai, Daspalla, Hindol, Nilgiri, Rairakhol, Talcher and Kharaswan; 3 'C' Class States as Pallahara, Ranpur and Tigiria states in Orissa before its merger.
96. P.M. Pradhan, *op. cit.*, p. 7.
97. *Asha*, 21 January 1948 and *Krushak*, 24 January 1948.

in the State. In Dhenkanal, Talcher, Patna and Nilgiri the *Prajamandal* volunteers demanded full responsible government on the failure of which, they declared their intention to take over the entire administration of the State.[98] This was the time when the ruler of Athgarh, pleaded against the merger of the States with the province who was supported by some rulers. Ruler of Ranpur was in favour of setting up a Union of feudatory States which he suggested during the discussion on merger issue with Sardar Patel. Baramba Ruler was in favour of responsible government in the States whereas the ruler of Kharsawan was wanting to merge with Bihar and not with Orissa.[99] The ruler of Mayurbhanj who was present in the merger meeting on 14th December 1947, kept aloof from the scheme on the ground that he had already granted responsible government.[100] Some leaders of the *Prajamandals* supported this view and were of the opinion of introduction of responsible government in the feudatory States under the existing rulers. These leaders were Radhanath Rath of Athgarh, Pabitra Mohan Pradhan of Talcher, Kapileswar Prasad Nanda of Bolangir, Sidheswar Guru of Raigarh, Bipan Behari Patnaik of Tigiria and Pratap Chandra Patnaik of Baramba States.[101] The Orissa and Chattisgarh States Regional Council was of the opinion of the merger of the States with the province of Orissa and not in favour of responsible government and it sent instruction to the *Prajamandals* to this effect.[102] But Pabitra Mohan Pradhan defied this instruction and asked the *Prajamandal* leaders to meet in a separate conference.[103]

It can be presumed that perhaps Pabitra Mohan Pradhan was not in favour of merger of the feudatory States like Talcher with the coastal areas to make an Orissa province as he apprehended that this feudatory State which was quite rich in minerals and natural resources might be neglected in future. The coastal areas of the province would rise and prosper at the cost of the *Garjat* resources which actually came true after the merger. He might be thinking to make Talcher a prosperous State by keeping the State as a separate province or State

98. H.K. Mahtab, *History of Freedom in Orissa*, Vol. IV, p. 148.

99. Orissa Records, Sambalpur Papers, Acc. No. 1161S, Minutes of the Meeting, 14 December, 1947.

100. *Ibid.*

101. Mahtab-Orissa, Souvenir published in honour of Dr. Mahtab, 1979, pp. 68-69, and Anant Mishra, *op. cit.*, pp. 61-62.

102. *Proceedings of Orissa History Congress*, XV Session, 1989, p. 244.

103. All India Congress Committee Records, File No. S-P-1, 1945-48, (NMML)

without merging into Orissa province and thus could independently develop its own economic resources. There was division among the leaders of the *Prajamandal* in this issue. Some thought and alleged that Pabitra Mohan Pradhan was doing all these for his own personal interest, to acquire a key post in Talcher State in case it did not merge while others took him to be won over by the manipulations of the *Raja* of Talcher.

Even the thinking of Pabitra Mohan Pradhan was reflected by a number of *Prajamandal* leaders of the State. Copies of Oriya leaflets were circulated throughout Orissa which appealed all the feudatory chiefs to surrender unconditionally the State's administration to the *Prajamandals* to bring unity among all the States economically and culturally, to keep separate identity of the States in the field of economy and culture. The signatories of this vernacular pamphlet called 'Last appeal to the *Rajas*' were Bipin Behari Patnaik, Madhusudan Patnaik and Paramananda Patnaik of Tigiria; Achyutananda Das of Athgarh; Pratap Chandra Patanaik of Baramba; Udayanath Sahoo of Pallahara; Kashinath Mishra, Daitariji and Kunjabehari Panda of Dhenkanal.*

The *Prajamandal* of Narsinghpur, by this time entered into an agreement with its ruler.[104] H.K. Mahtab, the Prime Minister of Orissa tried his best to suppress the anti-merger activities. On the night of 13 December, he met Pabitra Mohan Pradhan and could persuade him in favour of the merger plan.[105] Sarangdhar Das, the Chairman of Regional Council, also made extensive tours to different feudatory States to mobilise the leaders and people of the *Prajamandals* to go in favour of the amalgamation.

Sardar Patel and Merger

Sardar Vallabhbhai Patel, the Home Minister of India visited Orissa on 13 December 1947 along with his officials of the States ministry. The merger of the feudatory States of Orissa to the Indian Union was discussed between H.K. Mahtab and his Council of Ministers and Sardar Patel. According to their discussions the rulers of the feudatory States were summoned to join the meeting at Cuttack on 14 December 1947. The morning session of the Conference was held under the Presidentship of Sardar Patel where twelve out of fifteen rulers of 'B'

---

* See Appendix V.

104. *All India Congress Committee Records, op. cit.*

105. H.K. Mahtab, *Sadhanar Pathe,* p. 334.

and 'C' Class States attended. They were the rulers of Ranpur, Kharswan, Khandapara, Baramba, Narsinghpur, Hindol, Athgarh, Pallahara, Talcher, Rairakhol, Nilgiri and Daspalla. Talcher was represented by its ruler Hruday Chandra Dev Birabar Harichandan.[106] Sardar Patel advised them to merge with the province for the benefit of the rulers as well as the people and assured their privilege, honour and dignity on behalf of the Government of India. When the rulers raised the question of joining Eastern States Union and moved against amalgamation Sardar Patel warned them and stated : "If you do not accept our proposal, I do not take responsibility for law and order in your State. You take care of yourself."[107] After a good deal of discussion and hesitation, all the twelve rulers signed and executed the agreement of merger on 15 December 1947[108] It was decided that the rulers of Bonai, Athmallik and Tigiria, who were unable to be present, would be asked to sign the agreement later.[109]

All the rulers of eleven 'A' Class States met the conference which was held on 14 December 1947 in the afternoon under Sardar Patel on the Chair. Since the merger process was difficult one, Sardar Patel had to take resort to threats and warning to get things done. Outside the conference hall military forces was kept ready to meet any challenge and to operate a bigger *coup d'etat*, if necessary.[110] In his speech Sardar Patel advised the rulers to take part in the building of a wealthy united Orissa. He observed that Orissa States were like ulcers on the body of the province and they must either be cured or eliminated. He further continued them if they listened to his advice they could be cured, otherwise they might find themselves uprooted by the people.[111] Such bold policy proclamation of Sardar Patel created panic among the feudal chiefs. They knew petty well that it would be foolish on their part to stick to their old position of allowing them independent States. In the absence of the British support they had no body to bank upon. Moreover, they were afraid of the mass fury, which was about to sweep them from power and position. They thought it better to accept the proposal of Sardar Patel as a face-saving as well as honourable

106. Orissa Records, Sambalpur Papers, Acc. No. 1161S, Minutes of the Meeting, 14 December, 1947. (OSA)

107. Durga Das, *India from Curzon to Nehru and After*, New Delhi, 1974, p. 282.

108. Orissa Records, Sambalpur Papers, *op. cit.*

109. *Ibid.*

110. H.K. Mahtab, *Beginning of the End*, p. 29.

111. Orissa Records, Sambalpur Papers, *op. cit.*

settlement. Any dilly-dalling would ultimately harm their own cause. After a good deal of pressure and persuasion the rulers except Mayurbhanj signed the merger on the next day morning.[112] The administration of these States was handed over to the Government of Orissa on 1 January 1948.[113] This was the day when Orissa got its own existence and the Orissan Government declared Oriya to be its court language in civil and criminal courts of Orissa.[114] As the ruler of Mayurbhanj had already transferred power to the hands of the people's representatives, he wanted to consult his ministry. Later the State of Mayurbhanj signed the merger on 17 October 1948 and the State was merged with Orissa on 1 January 1949.[115]

The States of Sareikala and Kharaswan were merged with Bihar province in 18 May 1948 due to its popular agitation.[116] Thus, twenty-four out of twenty-six Orissan States merged with Orissa and subsequently integrated with the province. The merger of the smaller States in Orissa spread from there to other princely States in India.[117]

After the agreement was signed by the ruler of Talcher of handing over the administration of State to the Government of India, a period intervened between the signing of the agreement by the ruler and taking over the administration by the Orissa Government which was chaotic and it was alleged that the *Prajamandal* workers were primarily responsible for the collapse of law and order in the State during the period when they, in a spirit of revenge, on the people who were shown favours by the previous administration, apparently at the cost of the *Prajamandal* workers, began recking vengeance on their rivals.[118] Lawlessness prevailed in the State. The Government of Orissa immediately thought of appointing an able administrator in Talcher who would take over the charge of Dominion Government on 1 January 1948.[119] After taking over the charge by the Government of Orissa, the

112. Orissa Records, Sambalpur Papers, *op. cit.*
113. White Paper on Indian States, p. 40 (OSA)
114. Orissa Records, Talcher Papers, S.V. Sohani, Additional Secretary to Government of Orissa to the Administrator of Talcher, Letter No. 472-A-Home Department, 10 January 1948, File No. 1 of 1948. (SRT)
115. V.P. Menon, *op. cit.*, p. 166.
116. *Ibid.*, p. 165.
117. Durga Das, *op. cit.*, p. 281.
118. Orissa Records, Talcher Papers, D.P. Tripathy, Administrator, Talcher to the District Magistrate, Dhenkanal, Letter No. 5393, Talcher 8 December 1948. (SRT)
119. Orissa Records, Talcher Papers, N. Senapati, Revenue Commissioner, Orissa to Dewan of Talcher State, D.O. No. 6848 (49) G Cuttack 24 December 1947. (SRT)

ruling dynasty in Talcher came to an end. Democracy occupied the seat in place of autocracy. In view of the changed administration of Talcher with effect from 1 January 1948 the designation of the officers were also changed as Senior State Officer in place of *Dewan*, State Officer in charge of Development in place of Development member and so on.[120] A new era thus began in the history of Talcher.

Thus the State people's Movement in Talcher that started on its own demand and grievances against the ruler and his style of government came a big way through various stages and developments to attract the attention of not only provincial political leaders but also of national level, to embark on a final phase leading to the successful merger of their States with the province of Orissa. The developments in post-war years in national level made their task easier when the Congress took up the task of merger of the feudatory States to be its own and moved in that line. The role of Sardar Patel, the iron man of Indian politics and his firm determination in this regard sealed the fate of the ruler of Talcher along with hundreds of his class. The struggle of the people of Talcher ended with success on 1 January 1948. By sweat and blood, they achieved the success for which they waited for years. Nothing succeeds like success and in the final analysis the long drawn struggle manifested the strength of the unity of the people and their selfless, determined struggle which only brought the end of feudal autocracy in Talcher.

◆

120. *Ibid.*, *op. cit.*, Administrator, Talcher in his Office Order No. 1, File No. I-1 of 1948, Talcher 4 January 1948. (SRT)

Conclusion

British imperialism had divided India into two unequal segments — British India and the so-called 'Indian States'. The former was ruled by the direct authority of the Viceroy who also exercised his indirect control over the latter through the princes. These princely States, referred to by the British as 'Native States' were as many as 563 in numbers covering an area of more than seven lakhs square miles with a population of more than eighty millions. The largest State was Hyderabad as large as Italy and the smallest one was Lawa with an area of nineteen square miles. The common feature of these States, big or small, was their recognition of the Paramountcy of the British Government, but in internal administration the native subjects were treated as India's step-children.

The uprising of 1857, the last attempt of Indian people to liberate their country under the feudal framework, though failed, provided an unforgettable lesson to the foreign rulers. The old policy of using any opportunity to add new territories to their domain at the cost of native rulers was discarded in favour of a more reactionary policy of foreign alliance with them as subsidiary powers which was termed by constitutional experts as subordinate cooperation, protected sovereignties, subordinates allies etc. The Indian princes got solace in the so-called 'breakwater policy' of the British Government and came closer to the British suzerain for their own safety and security of their internal administration. The Royal Proclamation of 1858 reassured the Indian feudal lords of the new policy of the British Government. The British preserved the Indian princes as its loyal instrument without having any political power and in return guaranteed the princes any threat, both internal and external to their autocratic power. Most of the feudal States were run as unmitigated autocracies, with the absolute power concentrated in the hands of the rulers, or their favourites, resulting in a type of administration which could be compared to Nazi Germany or Fascist Italy.

Under the condition of an unholy nexus of imperialism and feudalism, the condition of the common people deteriorated rapidly.

The welfare of the native subjects was never looked into. The so-called paternalistic feudal rule became a matter to be found in ancient Indian texts as a myth. The tenants had to pay heavier land revenue than his nearby British Indian counterparts. They were also overburdened with other types of obnoxious taxes and cesses like *bethi, begar* etc. Maladministration, exploitation, feudal despotism had no answer even from the paramount power. Without any democratic rule, people became fatalistic and bore the agony in silence. When the oppression and exploitation reached its climax, with no solution in sight, it burst out in the shape of spontaneous, unorganised mass uprisings in various parts of Orissa taking various shapes. The second half of 19th century witnessed this type of popular upheavals in the States of Ranpur, Nayagarh, Daspalla, Boudh, Kalahandi, and Keonjhar. Unfortunately, these were easily crushed down by their respective *Durbars* with the help of the British, ever willing to assist any spark of popular uprising lest it should affect its empire.

The crystallisation of nationalism and the birth and growth of Indian National Congress brought to the forefront the question of future of the British rule in India. The friendship and the support of the Indian native rulers, feudal elements and others was more and more necessitated in the early part of the twenties, when the national movement was leaving the path of mendicancy in favour of a militant one. The civil rights and democratic aspirations of the people were crushed everywhere. The princely States tried their best to insulate their territories from the mainstream of the national movement in British India. The Orissan States, numbering 26, took all precautionary measures to suppress any voice of protest in their territories. People who raised their voice of protest were imprisoned and severely punished. The entry of newspapers, detrimental to British and feudal interest were banned from entering their territories. Thus, the feudal lords were able to contain the national movement in their territories for a considerable time in their domains. The anti-feudal agitation in Talcher in 1911, 1922 and 1932 were suppressed. The causes would include the absence of proper, dynamic leadership, well-organised people's organisation and above all the complete apathy of the Indian National Congress to come out in open support of these movements and allowing its branches to be openly established and operative in these territories. The Congress policy of non-interference in the internal matters of these States was, to a greater extent responsible, though not fully, for the temporary setback to the anti-feudal uprisings in these small islands of feudal reaction in India.

Though the Indian National Congress in its Nagpur Session in 1920 called on the princes to grant at once full responsible government in their States, yet its policy of non-interference in their internal matters, not allowing the local people to establish Congress branches in their States, the over optimistic pious desire for the State people to start and continue their own struggle through their independent local organisations only delayed any coordinated effort to forge a common struggle in feudal India. The recommendation of the Butler Committee in 1927 for the establishment of better relationship between the States and Central Government, prompted some leaders of the Indian States to convene a meeting at all India level to examine the possibility of forming a central organisation of their own. The efforts yielded the result when on 17 December 1927 the All India States' Peoples' Conference (AISPC) was formed which demanded popular governments in the States and played a great role in linking the struggle inside the native States with the broad stream of national movement in the country in general.

As usual, Gandhiji and the Congress tried to stick to the old policy of non-intervention in matters of native States, but the younger, radical new generation of Congress leaders sought a more vigorous persuance of Congress policies and movement there. As a compromise, the resolution for the first time was passed in February 1938 at the Haripura Session pledging Congress close involvement with the ongoing movements in the native States. Gandhiji indicated a few months later that he would be satisfied if the princes granted a measure of civil liberties and independent courts. Besides Gandhiji, a number of prominent leaders of Congress pledged their full support to the struggle inside the States. Among them were Jawaharlal Nehru, Sardar Vallabbhai Patel, Jamnalal Bajaj, B. Pattabhi Sitaramayya, Satyamurti etc. When at Lahore, in 1929, Congress decided that the ultimate aim of freedom struggle was complete freedom, it made it clear that this freedom was both for the people of British India as well as the native States. To underline the common aspiration of all the people of India and Congress Party's support for the native struggle, the AISPC elected Jawaharlal Nehru as its President in its Ludhiana Session of February 1939. Gandhiji, also, decided to try out his technique of controlled mass struggle, for the first time, in the native State of Rajkot. The Congress and its leaders extended their support for the cause of these native subjects upto their merger with Indian Union after India's independence.

The struggle of the people in the native Orissan States began much before Orissa's emergence as a separate provincial entity. The State People's Conference in Orissa was formed in June 1931 under the impact of the formation of AISPC at the national level. But it was almost defunct till March 1937 when Sarangadhar Das took its leadership. By that time, the British had strengthened the powers of the princes by granting them new *Sanads* in 1937. The Second Session of the Orissa State People's Conference met at Cuttack in June 1937 where a prominent Congress leader Pattabhi Sitaramayaya presided and thus linked their struggle with the struggle led by Congress all over the country. A prominent Congress leader of Orissa, H.K. Mahtab presided over an 'Enquiry Committee' to examine the irregularities committed in the native States. The establishment of a popular Congress ministry in Orissa in 1937 only gave a further fillip to the struggle. Now the movements in various native States under their own *Prajamandals* were linked in a common chain of all Orissa body and the commitment and active involvement of Congress, Congress-socialist and Communist leaders in the struggle brought the movement from its narrow local sphere to join with the greater struggle going on throughout the country.

Talcher was a centre of popular revolt from the closing years of 19th century. The first recorded anti-feudal uprising in Talcher was in 1898 but failed to achieve anything. There were a number of popular risings against the feudal oppression in the 20th century till 1932 and all failed to achieve their charter of demands *in toto*, but gave a great nightmare to the feudal lord and contributed in its own way to rouse popular consciousness in organising larger and larger number of the deaf and dumb native subjects of Talcher in the next round of struggle. Every rising was an improvement upon the previous one, both in quantitative increase of the number of participants and the qualitative development of the charter of demands, organisation and leadership. There was a remarkable continuity of uprisings in Talcher in quick succession which became a training ground for a final assault in the forties. In 1908 and 1909, there were uprisings against the royal imposition of new cess and forced labour, when the spirit of Swadeshi movement in Bengal still engulfed popular imagination. They went for secret organisation to continue their struggles which was a forerunner of the future *Prajamandal*. In 1911, the *Durbar* imposed new taxes and there was again a popular outburst against the State administration.

The lull during the war years was broken in 1922 when the people rose in revolt against the royal extractions for *Pattayat's* sacred thread ceremony. Again in 1932 there was a popular upheaval of bigger magnitude. 1922 and 1932, the landmark years in our national movement, and those were the years when the people raised their banner of revolt against the royal oppression. When in the national scene, the Congress led movement was withdrawn or suspended as was the case after Chauri Chaura or Gandhi-Irwin Pact and Gandhiji's attending Second Round Table Conference, thus bringing halt to the movement, the King of Talcher took it a golden chance to impose some new tax or cess. But the people of Talcher stood firm in their protest and were suppressed ruthlessly.

The reorganisation of the Orissa States' Peoples' Conference under Sarangadhar Das and the formation of the first Congress ministry in 1937 gave a great boost to the movement in Talcher. That was the time when the workers in the coal mines of Talcher were organised for the first time to fight against the tyranny of the King along with their own economic demands. Because of these coal mines, which was greatly needed by the colonial authorities for locomotives, power generation etc., a strict vigil was kept on Talcher developments. That, also, helped the ruler to get a blank cheque from the British to suppress any movement that would pose immediate danger to British interest in Talcher.

That was the period when the Congress and its message became popular with the people of Talcher. In 1938, thousands of people left Talcher and came to Angul. This *Hizrat* was a unique character of the State People's Movement of Talcher. Earlier during the First World War, thousands of Muslims left India and went on *hizrat* to fight in favour of Turkey against Britain and her allies. They left India and went to Afghanistan, few to Turkey and some to Soviet Russia. Those patriot Muslims inspired with anti-British and Pan Islamic religious feelings adorned the pages of Indian history and the some comparison could be done about the Talcher exodus and the great patriotic fighting spirit that they exhibited at that time. Their charter of demand at Angul Camp again portrays their great sagacity to include the class and caste demands of various sectional interest to forge a common united anti-feudal and anti-British front. Their determined struggle brought the ruler to issue various proclamations giving more and more concessions and drew attention of all India leaders and even from abroad. Gandhiji used to take continuous interest in Talcher matters and wrote about it in *Harijan* and sent several guidelines to various national and provincial leaders on the matter. All these could bring the British Government to sign Hannessey-Mahtab Pact, a moral victory for Talcher people's struggle and their *Prajamandal*.

The World War II and the consequent royal effort to scrap all the concessions earlier given to the people again resulted in mass struggle. During the war years and especially Quit-India days, the *Prajamandal* actually propagated Congress policy and programme except the commitment to non-violence. As in any other part of India, there were two groups in its leadership, following the traditional Congressmen and Congress socialists. Barring few old heads, most of the others adopted the technique of Congress-Socialists at that time. Violent course was adopted by the people as was the case in other parts of India. The entire State administration collapsed for few days during that time. There was the establishment of a parallel independent government in Talcher which was again a novel experiment at that time. It recruited its own militia and formed its own medical group. Talcher came to occupy a unique place among all the native States of Orissa, so far as the Quit India Movement was concerned. It became more so, because unlike Dhenkanal another nearby native State, no outside leader was greatly involved in organising the people but the local leaders of middle classes origin were at the forefront of the movement. Perhaps, it can explain the widespread, deep rooted popular base of the movement; the success of the secret organisation of the *Prajamandal*, and its ability to paralyse the State administration everywhere and replacing it with its own *Panchayat* administration for some time. The sheer number of agitators was so alarming that the British Government had to fire from aeroplane on the people. Talcher is one among five places in India where people were machine-gunned from air. But it is a golden chapter in the history of Talcher *Prajamandal* and its struggle in all India standing. Here, also, the King tried to divide the people by setting lower, so-called the untouchable castes against the higher castes and, thus, to create a social tension to his advantage, but he failed in the long run.

In Talcher, the collapse of the most militant phase of struggle, the 'Quit India' period, gave birth to a short lived organisation of armed squads who took recourse to guerilla warfare, remaining in forest, against the British force employed by the State against the villagers. This short lived experiment, in the line of Indian revolutionaries, created another glorious chapter in the struggle of Talcher. The *Raja's* getting the title *Raj Bahadur* due to his role in supporting the British

Government in quelling the popular revolt only was deceptive as the ground had started to slip under his feet by the end of World War II. The hollow title failed to allure the common people any more. So far the popular demand was for the representative institution in the State, but the bitter experience of 'August Revolution' made the *Prajamandal* to revise its stand and towards the end of the war, the issue of merger of Talcher with British India was at the top of the agenda of that time. The popularity of such a demand alarmed the ruler. But the *Praja Parishad* that he formed and the purpose and the constitution of the body did not make it acceptable to the *Prajamandal* leaders and sealed its fate. So the only alternative was merger and giving the rein of administration to Prajamandal leaders, which he did not want. But how long one can stand to stop the flow of a stream? The King realised that his days were numbered.

But another curious feature of the last days before merger was the controversy over the merger question. A group of *Prajamandal* leaders of Talcher, as was the case in some other *Garjats*, believed that Talcher would gain little if it would merge with the province of Orissa. Its mineral and forest resources would be taken over by the provincial government and her own backward people would gain little from the merger. On the other hand, if it would remain as an independent province, it had got all the potentialities to develop the area on its own. So, on this question there were differences among the leaders. Motives could be ascribed to some leaders, who might have thought in terms of their own political gains in future. Independent status of Talcher would have provided few of them to gain political position and administrative powers, but, in general, the people of Talcher wanted, aspired and welcomed the merger of the State with the Orissa province and prepared to make their own contribution as well as sacrifice for building a bright and prosperous Orissa, for which they fought, as a part of broad Indian national struggle for liberation.

The popular wreath of the people of feudatory States swept away the feudal order that once dominated over a third of India's people and their days became as distant as those of the Mughals. Their palaces became museums, schools, hotels or crumbling shins. They had vanished from the popular memory as for the new generation their oppression is gradually becoming matters to be found in books or stories. But, still, in the native States, their deeds or rather misdeeds continue to remain in the minds of the older generation of that era which the new generation can physically see or realise as the royal oppression left some mark or the other on every family in their domains. Under the conditions of a double oppression, one of feudalism directly and imperialism indirectly, these popular struggles became a Saga of national movement, an important component, as the other contributing streams of Indian freedom struggle. Their struggle, sacrifice and sufferings which was much more than their counterparts in British India found little place in the pens of the historians as their chief pre-occupation still remains the Congress-led national struggle primarily carried on in the British India. Yet, the States' Peoples' Movement in Talcher in particular and other native States in general contributed its own share in mobilising the backward, ignorant millions in those dark, secluded, unapproachable areas in the great struggle of national liberation of India and made it a struggle of great magnitude, truly a struggle of entire India and Indian people, the success in which the people's revolt certainly occupies a unique place.

◆

Appendices

APPENDIX A*

List of the Orissa Feudatory States with their Area, Population, Income and Tributes

Sl. No.	Name	Area in Sq. miles	Population on 1931 Census	Income in Rs. 1933	Tribute paid to British Government
1.	Athgarh	168	50,184	1,48,000	2,800-0-0
2.	Athmallik	730	64.276	2,17,000	480-0-0
3.	Baramba	142	46,689	97,000	1,397-15-5
4.	Bamra	1,988	1,51,259	4,24,000	7,500-0-0
5.	Boud	1,264	1,35,248	3,21,000	800-0-0
6.	Bonai	1,296	80,144	1,76,000	2,700-0-0
7.	Daspalla	568	42,650	1,20,000	661-7-11
8.	Dhenkanal	1,463	2,84,328	5,31,000	5,009-0-9
9.	Gangpur	2,492	3,56,388	5,08,000	10,000-0-0
10.	Hindol	312	48,897	1,26,000	551-3-11
11.	Kalahandi	3,745	5,13,675	6,25,000	1,600-0-0
12.	Keonjhar	3,096	4,60,647	9,79,000	1,710-1-3
13.	Kharswan	153	47,451	—	—
14.	Khandapara	244	77,930	1,48,000	4,211-8-8
15.	Mayurbhunj	4,243	8,86,745	29,41,000	1,067-11-9
16.	Narasinghpur	199	40,882	1,11,000	1,455-8-3
17.	Nayagarh	590	1,42,399	3,96,000	5,525-4-1
18.	Nilgiri	284	68,598	1,73,000	3,900-7-8
19.	Pallahara	452	27,975	79,000	266-10-8
20.	Patna	2,399	5,66,943	9,07,000	13,000-0-0
21.	Rairakhol	833	35,715	87,000	2,000-0-0
22.	Ranpur	203	47,713	71,000	1,400-13-2
23.	Sonepur	906	2,37,945	4,92,000	12,000-0-0
24.	Saraikala	499	1,38,671	3,34,000	—
25.	Talcher	399	69,702	2,94,000	1,039-10-5
26.	Tigiria	47	24,680	45,000	882-0-0

* General Review of Administration of the Feudatory States of Orissa for the Year 1930-31, p. 29.

APPENDIX B

Baji Rout*

Baji Rout, a boy of twelve, belonged to the village Nilakanthapur in Bhuban Police Station of Kamakhyanagar Sub-Division who succumbed to firing by Dhenkanal State Police on 11 October 1938.

About twenty armed policemen came to Bhuban for suppressing the popular agitation against the Dhenkanal Chief. They perpetrated a lot of torture on the people at Bhuban. While they were going back, large number of people chased them. When they reached the ferry at Nilakanthapur, the people chasing them had already drawn nearer and were about to attack them. The policemen commanded the boatman to ferry them at once. But the boatman refused to obey the order. The mob had almost reached the spot. In the face of imminent danger of attack from the mob, they opened fire killing Baji Rout who held the rope of the boat. So gallantly he laid his life that he has now been classed as one of the martyrs in the freedom struggle.

Balaram Mohapatra**

Balaram Mohapatra was born in the Village Kandhal of Talcher Sub-Division. He was working in the Intelligence Department under Talcher *Durbar*. But during the People's Movement in Talcher he was communicating all the secret news of the *Durbar* to the *Prajamandal* leaders. There was a conspiracy on the life of Pabitra Mohan Pradhan by the *Durbar* as he was uniting the people of Talcher against the Chief's administration. This was made known to him only through Balaram Mohapatra for which the life of Sri Pradhan was being saved several times. Afterwards, the activities of Sri Mohapatra could be known to the *Raja* who dismissed him from his service and he was expelled from Talcher. He was the Vice-President of Talcher *Prajamandal* for sometime. He resided at Dhenkanal after leaving Talcher.

Bankanidhi Bhakta Ballav***

Bankanidhi was a man of village Poipal of Talcher. He was a wood merchant who happened to be a related uncle of Pabitra Mohan Pradhan. He was a man of high principles and a nationalist too. He

---

* *The Samaj*, 11 October 1985.

** Collected Information by the Author from the Villagers of Kandhal.

*** P.M. Pradhan, *op. cit.*, pp. 83-84.

used to read the *Gita*, the *Bhagabat* and the *Ramayan* with great devotion. His manners were very pleasant and enduring who had followed the Gandhian principles in life. In April 1937, he attended the *Garajat Praja Sammilani* and narrated the tyrannical rule and maladministration then prevailing in Talcher State. The People's Movement of Talcher in 1930-32 continued under the able guidance of Bankanidhi Bhakta Ballav.

Dibakar Parida*

Dibakar Parida was born on 30 November 1911 in the village Garhbanikillo, four kilometres away from Ranpur. His father Harihar Parida was working under the *Raja* of Ranpur, who was very independent minded and did not support the practice of corruption. Like his father Dibakar wanted to build-up his career. During his school life at Khurdha his father died. So he gave up school studies and entered into a job in the Narendra Press of Ranpur State. In the year 1933 he joined his hands for the people's cause against the Chief's tyrannical rule. He went to the village temple, Arteswar Mahadev, prayed Lord Shiva and started his political career. He had written a book titled '*Sri Asteswar Dev Janana*' in Oriya.

Dharani Dhar Nayak**

Dharani Dhar Nayak was born on 5 May 1864 in Kusumita village of Keonjhar in a tribal *bhuyan* family. After his primary education he went to Cuttack for higher study with the financial assistance of *Raja* Dhanurjay Narayan Bhanjdeo of Keonjhar. After his technical education he was appointed as a sub-overseer under the Keonjhar State. The Assistant Manager of the State Bichitra Nanda Das made a false allegation against Dharani Dhar before the *Raja* that he (Dharani) was involved in organising a *meli* of the *Bhuyans* against the State authority. With the advice of the Assistant Manager the *Raja* forced the *bhuyans* to do *bethi* for the State which was not tolerated by Dharani. He gave up his job and organised the *Bhuyan meli* against the State administration. He was imprisoned from 1891 to 1897 at Cuttack jail. After his release he did not return to Keonjhar. In 1912 he *built* a *matha* at Ali of Cuttack and spent the rest of his life there as a *Sanyas*. He died in 1914.

---

* J.N. Patnaik, *Odisa Itihasare Ketoti Romanchokar Kahani*, pp. 163-69.

** *Utkal Prasanga*, January 1992, pp. 19-21.

Harekrishna Mahtab*

H.K. Mahtab, the son of Jagannath Mahtab of Agarpara in Balasore was born on 21 November 1899. He was educated in the Ravenshaw College, Cuttack. From the very childhood he was a free thinker who joined the Non-Cooperation Movement in 1921. During the national struggle in India he was imprisoned several times in 1930, 1932 and 1941. He was the Chairman of Balwantrai Mehta Committee. Besides Talcher agitation, he was advising other States' agitations in Orissa. He acted as Gandhiji's political representative who communicated Gandhiji's messages to Talcher *Prajamandal* and instructed them to agitate constitutionally against the ruling Chief and Political Agent for the redress of their grievances. He became the Prime Minister of Orissa during 1946-50, a Cabinet Minister at the Centre in 1950, nominated as Governor of Bombay in 1954-56 and became the Chief Minister of Orissa on 19 October 1956. He was the President of Orissa State Congress Committee. He died on 2 January 1987 at the age of 88.

Maheswar Subahu Singh**

Maheswar was born in 1878 in the village Sarang, on the bank of the Brahmani in Dhenkanal district. After his matriculation he joined in the Police Department under Dhenkanal State. By the advice of *Raja* Surapratap he was appointed as *Sarbarakar* of *Garh* Parjang. In 1922 after the land settlement at Dhenkanal, heavy taxation was imposed on the people and condition of the people became worse due to financial burden. Subahu Singh organised the people against the administrative authority and demanded the withdrawal of taxation for which he was sent to jail. After his release he organised the youths in the State of Dhenkanal to fight against the tyrannical *Durbar* by hiding himself inside the forest. With his active participation and with the full support of his friends like Purna Chandra Mohapatra, Narottam Das, Braj Kishore Dhal, Baishnab Patnaik etc. the *Prajamandal* movement in Dhenkanal took a leading role among other feudatory States of Orissa to achieve power from the hands of the chief. Subahu Singh died on 1 August 1959.

---

* Collected from *Mahtab*, a Souvenir published in honour of Mahtab's 88th Birth Day, 1986.

** *The Samaj*, 30 July 1973.

Pabitra Mohan Pradhan*

Pabitra Mohan Pradhan was born on 8 February 1908 in the village Poipal of Talcher. After his graduation from Ravenshaw College, Cuttack he took a D. Ed training. Then, he joined as an assistant teacher in Jubraj High School, Talcher and became a private tutor of the royal family for sometime. During his service tenure he engaged himself organising the people of Talcher against the misrule and tyranny of the *Raja* of Talcher. In July 1938, he gave up his job and left Talcher for Angul, the British territory where he organised the People's Movement in Talcher quite actively. He became the President of Talcher *Prajamandal* and under his leadership the movement in Talcher took a different shape. He was imprisoned but escaped from Talcher jail under mysterious circumstances. After the merger, he was appointed a member of the Orissa Executive Council. By dint of his popularity, he became a member of the Orissa Legislative Assembly for a long period of twenty-three years. He was in the Cabinet for a long time and went up to the rank of Deputy Chief Minister of Orissa. Being a bachelor, he led a very simple life following the Gandhian principles upto his death on 13 June 1988.

Radhanath Rath**

Radhanath Rath, a man of ninety-seven was born at Athgarh, an ex-state of Orissa. He was educated at Satyabadibana Vidyalaya where he could come into contact with Gopabandhu, Nilakanta and Godabarish. He has established various institutions at Chakradharpur for the Oriyas. He had participated in the Non-Cooperation Movement and for that he went to jail several times. After independence, he was elected as an M.L.A. to the Orissa Legislative Council a number of times. He could manage as an able Minister of Education and Finance in the State. He is the Vice-President of Loksevak Mandal. Since long he has been the editor of '*The Samaj*' and for his effort only this Oriya daily is earning a good name in Orissa. He is very amiable and helps the poor people of Orissa during famine and flood.

Raghunath Mohanty***

Raghunath was born on 18 July 1910 in the village Badabhuin near Ranpur. Under the guidance of the father Natabar Mohanty and

* *Gadajat*, Special Issue 1989, pp. 17-20.

** Personal Interview with Sri R.N. Rath at his Cuttack Residence in 1981.

*** *The Samaj*, Weekly Issue, 2 September 1992, p. 17.

with the affection of the mother Labanya Devi, Raghunath was brought up under a routine life. Dibakar Parida was his childhood friend and both of them studied upto matriculation at Buxi Jagabandhu High School. Both of them had left the school studies and joined the *Prajamandal* activities at Ranpur to put forth their grievances against the misrule of the Ranpur Chief. Raghunath was quite brave and took a leading role in the people's agitation of the State. For some time he was serving in '*The Samaj* Office' at Cuttack. He wrote a book in Oriya entitled as '*Sabarbala*'.

Sarangadhar Das*

Sarangadhar was born in October 1887 in the village Harekrishnapur of Dhenkanal. After his school education he went to Japan in 1907 for learning technical education. After two years, he went to America where he got higher degree in Chemistry and Agricultural Science from California University. He married to Freeda, an American girl there. He served as Chief Chemist and Manager in and outside India in several Companies. With the hope of establishing a Sugar Factory, he came back to Dhenkanal State. But for some unknown reason the *Raja* of Dhenkanal did not help him, misunderstanding started and he had to leave for Cuttack. From 1933 onwards Sarangdhar engaged himself in the People's Movements of feudatory States of Orissa. He was the Secretary of Orissa *Garajat Praja Sammilani*. Due to his efforts, an Enquiry Committee for collecting detailed information about the States of Orissa was set up. He was also the Secretary of Balwantrai Mehta Committee and the Regional Council for the States' People of the AISPC. He was elected as an M.L.A. to the State Legislature in Orissa on Congress ticket. He joined in the socialist group and went to Lok Sabha in 1951. He died on 18 September 1956 after giving a will of his properties.

---

* B. Mohapatra, *Odia Andolanara Itihas*, Cuttack, 1976, pp. 233-34.

DHENKANAL

APPENDIX C

STATE GAZETTE

EXTRAORDINARY

PUBLISHED BY AUTHORITY

DHENKANAL, 12TH SEPTEMBER 1938

ORDER OF THE DURBAR IN COUNCIL

Whereas it appears from the report of the District Magistrate dated the 3rd September 1938 that a state of emergency has arisen in this State which calls for drastic action under provisions of extraordinary laws with a view to check the revolutionary and anti-Government movements and mischievous activities of unlawful associations, it is hereby ordered that with effect from the 12th September 1938, the provisions of the Criminal Law Amendment Acts, *i.e.* XIV of 1908 and Act., XXIII of 1932 shall be introduced and brought into force in the whole of the State in their entirety.

This is given under the seal and signature of the Executive Council of the State.

By Order
Sd/-
D.N. Das, (Dewan Bahadur)
Vice-President,
Executive Council,
Dhenkanal State,
D.11. 9. 1938

ORDER

Whereas the *Durbar* is of opinion that the association called the Dhenkanal *Praja Mandal* and its subsidiary associations working under its control and guidance since formed or to be formed within the State, unlawfully interfere, and have for their object unlawful interference with the administration of law and the maintenance of law and order and this constitutes or will constitute a danger to the public peace, these associations are hereby declared as unlawful with effect from the 15th September 1938, under the provisions of section 16 of the Criminal Law Amendment Act, No. XIV of 1908, and that all acts committed by members of such unlawful associations in furtherance of their common object shall be dealt with under the provisions of the Criminal Law Amendment Act No. XIV of 1908 and Act No. XXIII of 1932. So the public are hereby warned not to join such Associations and those who are already members of these Associations are hereby given the opportunity to withdraw from them before the date mentioned above.

Sd/-
D.N. Das, (Dewan Bahadur)
Vice-President of Executive Council
Dhenkanal State
D/11/9/1938

ORDER OF THE DURBAR IN COUNCIL

Whereas it appears from the report of the District Magistrate dated the 3rd September 1938, that a state of emergency has arisen in the State which necessitates the control of gun, sword and other arms licences in order to secure the safety of the State officials and other law-abiding citizens and the maintenance of peace; it is hereby ordered that all persons to be selected by the District Magistrate must deposit their guns and other weapons such as swords, spears, rifles etc. at the Police Stations in which they reside on or before the 15th September 1938, on pain of criminal prosecution under the provisions of the Indian Arms Act of 1878.

By Order
Sd/-
D.N. Das, (Dewan Bahadur)
Vice-President, Executive Council
Dhenkanal State
D/11/9/1938

APPENDIX D*

To

The Ruling Chief,
Ranpur

Dated, the 11th October 1938

Respected Sir,

I, the undersigned have been authorised by the people of Ranpur in general to lay the following matters for your kind consideration and favourable disposal.

1. People in Ranpur do not enjoy at present the ordinary rights of holding meetings and forming associations for lawful purposes. It is for this reason, the *Durbar* is not in a position to ascertain the popular opinion and feeling regarding matters of administration. Therefore the administration however much it may be desired, by the *Durbar* to be so cannot become popular. In all civilized countries public opinion is wholesome check on the administrations and for that reason all facilities are given to ventilate public opinion through meetings, associations and the Press. In Ranpur in the interest of the *Durbar* as well as of the people it is necessary that the civil liberties of press, platform and association may be grànted immediately.

2. Secondly the system of *Bethi* has been condemned as a form of slavery throughout the world. The British Gòvernment whom the Ranpur

* R. Ram, *op. cit.*, pp. 113-16.

Durbar have the privilege of owning allegiance to are opposed to the system of '*Bethi*'. But most unfortunately this uncivilized system is still prevalent in Ranpur.

3. Thirdly (A) the rate of rent prevailing in Ranpur is abnormally high in comparison with the rate in the adjoining British territories. This high rate of rent coupled with the general economic depression has hit hard the peasantry and therefore the prayer is that the rate of rent may be substantially reduced.

(B) The *Durbar* may not have known that the 'Sarbarkars' collect some cesses over and above the legal rent thus adding to the misery of the people. Immediate steps may be taken to abolish these illegal cesses.

(C) The procedure relating to the realisation of rent and other State and private dues through court may kindly be adopted in line with that followed in the adjoining British territory.

(D) Fees levied on adoption cases may be abolished.

4. The system of '*Magan*' levied as a cess should be abolished.

5. The forest laws should be so amended as will really benefit the subjects.

6. Free trade of agriculture produces may be allowed for the benefit of the agriculturists.

7. Monopoly on betel and special cess in kind levied on sugarcane cultivation may be abolished.

8. The cess levied on the dealers of fuel, the tax levied on the *Harijans* making baskets etc. of bamboos and the cess levie on the '*Hadis*' dealing in hides may be abolished.

9. People may be permitted to irrigate their lands from the waters of the tanks and *bundhs* in drought season.

10. The right of catching fish from dry tanks and other water sources may be granted to the people.

11. The fees levied for using torches, palanquins, drums etc. during marriage ceremonies should be abolished. It is superfluous to mention here that the system is not approved by civilization.

12. There should be no restriction on using double door-shutters and constructing platforms in front of houses.

13. Proper arrangements should be made for the conducting and inspecting schools in the State.

14. Preference should be given to qualified subjects of the State irrespective of castes and creeds in the State services.

15. The Public Health Department should be improved and qualified men should be put in charge of dispensaries.

16. The right to dig tanks and wells and construct temples and choutaras on their own land should be conceded.

17. The system of purchasing paddy at a lower price by making advance payments should be abolished.

18. The '*Jagiri*' in *mauza* Kandhanayagarh which has been leased by the Jagirdars (who has subsequently relinquished the land in favour of the State) and which is in possession of the leases for the last many years should be settled with them at the normal rate of rent.

19. Right over the fruits and timbers of trees should be conceded.

20. The rights to kill wild animals damaging crops should be conceded.

21. Sufficient postures should be supplied for the grazing of cattles, specially buffalloes.

22. The right to use the stones should be conceded.

I, therefore, pray that Your Highness should be graciously pleased to consider the legitimate demands of the subjects of Ranpur and conceded them immediately for which I shall remain ever grateful.

Yours most obedient servant,
Banamali Ram
President, Ranpur Prajamandal.

Ranpur Garh,
11.10.38

APPENDIX E*

Population Chart of Talcher (1991 Census)

Sl. No.	Name	Male	Female	Total Population	Literate male	Literate Female	Total Literate
1.	F.C.I. Township	4993	4360	9353	3891	2914	6805
2.	Dera Township	7382	5712	13094	5566	3270	8836
3.	Ghantapada Township	5552	4427	9979	3810	1956	5766
4.	TTPS Township	3970	3177	7147	3248	2169	5417
5.	Rengali Township	6438	4418	10856	4711	2300	7011
6.	Talcher P.S.	22253	20609	42862	13367	7230	20597
7.	Vikrampur P.S.	6526	5979	12505	3728	1960	5688
8.	Colliery P.S.	13145	12134	25279	8012	3908	11920
9.	Rengali P.S.	12120	11841	23961	6449	2612	9061
10.	Kaniha P.S.	26441	24396	50837	15034	6147	21181
11.	Samal P.S.	14707	13790	28497	8620	4155	12775
		1,23,527	1,10,843	2,34,370	76,436	38,621	1,15,057

APPENDIX F**

In the village of Gopal Prasad, about 14 miles to the South-West of Talcher States, there is found the site of Goddess who is worshipped under the name of Hingula. The site of the worship extends over the area of the coal-fields which extend for some two or three miles in the neighbourhood of the village; the actual manifestation consists of a jet of gas issuing from the coal, which is either lighted by the priest or itself ignites as contact with the air. The worship of the goddess takes place on the fourteenth day of full moon in the month of *Chaitra* (March-April). The Goddess Hingula is alleged to appear some days before this in a dream to her *Sebait* (priest), and indicates to him the exact spot of her coming revelation. The *Sebait* then proceeds to the spot indicated, and finding the natural fire burning keeps the flame burning by adding coal till the appointed hour of worship arrives, when a large crowd of worshippers attend from all quarters and make offerings of ghee, sugar, plantains, curd goats, hens, etc. Besides this annual worship, Hingula is also worshipped as an idol throughout the

* Orissa Records, Talcher Papers, Census File No. VIII-1/91, Office of the Tahsildar, Talcher.

** L.E.B. Cobden-Ramsay, *op. cit.*, pp. 330-31.

year in a secluded and solitary spot in the forest near the village. The Sebait sends forth emissaries throughout the States and the neighbouring districts. To spread the worship of Hingula with threats of secretly firing their houses these emissaries extract contributions from the people and from time to time put into execution their threats.

APPENDIX G*

Rules for the Administration of the Tributary Mahals formulated by A.J.M. Mills in 1840

Rule 1 declares the *Rajas* cannot exercise the power of life and death.

Rule 2 abolishes the practice of Suttee and human sacrifice, and declares all persons convicted of aiding and abetting in such practices; guilty of culpable homicide.

Rule 3 prohibits *Rajas* from engaging in hostilities with their neighbours.

Rule 4 empowers Superintendent to take cognizance of charges of murder, homicide, torture, robbery, and other crimes of enormity, by whomsoever committed, and to try any criminal whom the *Rajas* may commit to him for trial.

Rule 5 restricts the interference of the Superintendent, in other matters of criminal justice, to the suppression of feuds and animosities between *Rajas*, between members of their families, or between *Rajas* and their subjects, to the correction of systematic oppression, to the cognizance of any violation of their duties of allegiance and subordination, and generally to important points, which, if not attended to, might lead to general outrage or confusion, or to contempt of the authority of Government.

Rule 6 gives the *Raja* control over their subjects, with authority to Superintendent to interfere in extreme cases.

Rule 7 vests the Superintendent with the cognizance of all criminal offences in attached *Killahs*, as well as all offences committed by the inhabitants of any *Garjat Mahal* within the boundaries of another *Garjat Mahal*, and by all persons not inhabitants of the *Garjat*.

Rule 8 declares *Rajas* to be liable to such punishment as the Government may deem adequate, extending to death and confiscation

* Orissa Records, Board's Proceedings (Rev.), Acc. No. 97, A.J.M. Mills to the Secretary to the Government of Bengal 17 September 1840. (OSA)

of their country in cases of murder, and other cases to such punishment in person or property as may seen fitting.

Rule 9 holds the *Rajas* answerable for all property stolen within their territories under certain circumstances.

Rule 10 provides for the conduct of trial in the form and manner prescribed by the regulation.

Rule 11 gives the power to Superintendent to sentence offenders, not *Rajas*, to imprisonment for 7 years; any severe punishment, which it is proposed to inflict, to be reported for, confirmation.

Rule 12 provides for sentences to be carried into execution under the provisions of Section 3, Regn IX of 1822 (Note: They are to be reported half yearly for formal confirmation).

Rule 13 provides for the trial of any British subject for an offence committed in the *Garjat*, before any of the established courts of justice, if deemed advisable.

Rule 14 authorises the Superintendent to call on the *Raja* to appear before him in person, or by *Mukhtyar*, to answer any change which may be preferred against him, and provides for the trial of the case according to the spirit of the regulation.

Rule 15 interdicts the Superintendent from enforcing the personal attendance of the *Raja* without the permission of Government.

Rule 16 requires *Rajas* to deliver up to the Superintendent any fugitives charged with heinous offences, who may conceal themselves in their Estates.

Rule 17 permits the Superintendent to exercise discretionary interference and authority in cases not provided for in the Rules.

APPENDIX H
SANAD

To

Ram Chandra Dev Beerbar Haree Chandan,
Talcher.

In recognition of your position, I hereby confer upon you the title of *Raja* as a hereditary distinction, to be assumed by your successors in formal recognition of their succession.

Dated for William, the 21st May, 1874.

Sd/- Northbrook
Viceroy and
Governor-General of India.

APPENDIX I

SANAD

To

Raja Kishor Chandra Birbar Harichandan,
Raja of Talcher.

Whereas it appears to the British Government that the time has come when the existing restrictions on the judicial and administrative powers of the State of Talcher may be modified. His Excellency the Viceroy is pleased to grant to you, Raja Kishor Chandra Birbar Harichandan, this sanad with a view to assuring you that, so long as you remain loyal to the Crown, the British Government will continue to maintain you in the position and privileges which you have heretofore enjoyed and to permit you to govern your own territory, subject to the conditions hereinafter prescribed. In like manner your heirs and successors will become entitled to your privileges and liable to your obligations.

1. That you shall pay to the British Government regularly rupees one thousand and thirty-nine, annas ten and pies five per annum.

2. That you shall exercise full civil and criminal jurisdiction except that sentences of death, transportation and imprisonment for life shall be referred for confirmation to the Agent to the Governor-General, Eastern States, or such other Political Officer as may be vested with authority in this behalf by His Excellency the Viceroy.

3. That you shall do your utmost to suppress crime of all kinds in your State.

4. That you shall administer justice fairly and impartially to all alike.

5. That you shall recognise and maintain the rights of all your people and on no account oppress them or suffer them to be in any way oppressed and that in particular you shall charge yourself personally with the welfare of the aboriginal population of your State.

6. That you shall act in accordance with such advice as may be given to you by the Agent to the Governor-General, Eastern States, or such other Political Officer as may be vested with authority in this behalf by His Excellency the Viceroy.

New Delhi,
The 26th, Feb. 1937

Sd/- Illegible
Viceroy and Governor
General of India

APPENDIX J*

Statistics of Education in Talcher

Sl. No. Name	1928-29 (51006 population)	1934-35 (69,702 population)	1935-36 (69,702 population)	1940-41 (86,432 population)
1. High English School	1	1	1	1
2. Sanskrit Vidyalaya	1	1	1	1
3. Boys U.P. School	9	10	10	8
4. Girls U.P. School	1	1	1	1
5. Lower Primary School	56	57	55	34
6. Private U.P. School with State aid.	—	9	8	—
7. Muktab	—	1	1	1
8. Harijan School	—	1	1	2
9. Guru Training	—	1	1	—
10. Karmakanda School at Kaniha	—	—	—	1
Total number of Schools	68	82	79	49
Total number of students in all Schools	2792	3115	3195	1973
Total number of boys in all Schools.	2421	2859	2926	1806
Total number of girls in all Schools.	371	256	269	167
Percentage of Boy Students	86.71	62.12	62.12	91.53
Percentage of Girl Students	13.28	6.06	6.06	8.46

APPENDIX 'K'

ORISSA STATES' 'PEOPLE' CONFERENCE.

An Appeal

Sir,

You all know that as the Indians are growing more nationally minded and demand for democratic form of Government, the kings in the estates become more powerful with unbridled power. As a result the political condition of the people is getting worse day by day.

---

* Collected from the Administrative Reports of Talcher from 1928 to 1941.

A new form of administration will run from April next. A confederation will be formed taking the kings of all States as its members. A lot of discussion was made and some new laws were adopted for this kind of new administration keeping in view the interests of the people intact. The subjects in the estates seen to have no parents and their interests are being sacrificed at every step. They don't have the freedom to express their views freely and none seems to have any concern for them.

Under such circumstances, only the kings can find out some ways and means by which the conditions of the people will improve. We do find no benevolent kings in these days, where lies the guarantee that the ancestors of the few benevolent kings that we have will provide good and fair administration. Most of the kings are busy expanding their empire and power. They do abuse their power. There is acute exploitation and torture of the people. We do find maladministration almost everywhere. The political agents seen to be quite indifferent to all these. There is no end to the exploitation of the people.

The only way to fight legally against the maladministration is to create the public awareness. Some leaders from the west of the country are trying constantly to solve the problems of the tortured people by convening meetings. A permanent Institution by the name "All India States' 'Peoples' Conference" has been set up at Bombay. In Orissa, we should convene meetings of the Garhjat people and we can get all sorts of help from Bombay.

It is high time that the people should discuss their problems in the frequently called for meetings. Sarangadhar Das of Dhenkanal was appointed as the Secretary and Treasurer of the Reception Committee. The man who is well conversed with the problems of the Garhjat people will act as the President of the Committee. The conditions of the Mughulbandi people is in no way better than us. And we do hope to get full cooperation from them in this regard.

It is my sincere request that a good number of representatives from different parts of our States should attend the meeting and make it a great success. People in particular from Garhjat area should come forward in large numbers and attend the meeting. The date and venue of the meeting will be intimated to you in due course. There will be no discussion about the activities of any particular king. We have proposed to discuss the problems of the people of the Garhjat in particular. There is no need to be scared about it. We do hope that people should contribute funds as per their capability. Please do circulate this appeal among the people.

Sincerely yours,
Sri Sarangadhar Das,
Secretary

Address :
At:- Dagarpara,
P.O. Chandinichwok,
Cuttack.

20.3.1937

APPENDIX 'L'

ORISSA STATES' PEOPLES' CONFERENCE

A Second Appeal

Dear Sir,

The following discussions were taken unanimously in the meeting on 23 April, 1937. It was attended by many representatives from different Garhjat areas. Sri Harekrishna Mahatab, Sri Bhubanananda Das, M.L.A. and Sri Laxminarayan Sahoo also graced the occasion.

(i) Resolved that the next meeting will be held on 19th and 20th June of next month in the Town Hall of Cuttack.

(ii) Dr. Pattai Sitaramaya, an eminent leader and President of 'All India States' Peoples' Conference' will preside over the meeting.

(iii) Sj. Balunkeswar Acharya, a prominent Kaviraj of Orissa was appointed as the President of the Reception Committee.

(iv) A committee was formed to make necessary arrangements of the accommodation of the representatives members.

(v) It was decided to collect one rupee per head as membership fee. Four to five people can send one representative with a fee of one rupee. Those who can't contribute are allowed to attend the meeting as spectators.

The incentives we are getting from different quarters imply that people do extend their full support understanding the very purpose of the meeting. You are all cordially invited to attend the meeting in large numbers without fail. The future course of action of the Sammelani will be taken up in the meeting. Let us come forward to make the Sammelani a strong one. If you intimate us earlier, we will make all arrangements for your hospitality.

Dagar Para, Cuttack
27-4-1937

Sincerely yours,
Sri Sarangadhar Das,
Secretary

APPENDIX 'M'

(DEMANDS OF TALCHER PRAJAMANDAL)

1. Freedom to citizens

(a) Rights to hold all sorts of meetings openly and go out in processions.

(b) Rights to form organisations and Samitis and to collect fees from the members.

(c) Rights to publish and read all sorts of newspapers and leaflets.

2. Rasad and Magana

(a) During the tour of the State Officers, people should not be forced to supply essential commodities even if paid.

(b) No labour without wages.

(c) Tradition of presenting gifts on such occasions as Dassehera be stopped.

(d) People should not be forced to supply wood for chariot, straw and rice grains for the elephants of the king free of cost.

3. (a) People should have legal possession over their lands.

(b) *Dakhal kharaj* fees and penalty be waived out at the time of transfer of land.

(c) *Dakhal kharaj* fees be not collected from the legal heirs.

(d) The State should adopt the rules and regulations from the Mughalbandi areas regarding the collection of revenue.

(e) The provision of taking farming equipments and utensils be stopped.

(f) Lands of the people who have not paid their revenue may not be taken into the custody of the kings. The lands may be auctioned and after taking the revenues, the rest amount be returned to the defaulters. Action should be made in a fair way and steps should be taken not to hand over the land to the employees of the king.

(g) Because the cost of land at Talcher and its vicinity is more than that of Angul, so an extra amount of fifty paise for a revenue of Re. 1 may be collected from the people.

(h) Since the price of agricultural products have been less and land revenue has been more, most of the people have lost their lands because they could not manage to pay the heavy revenue. These lands may be returned to the people concerned. A committee may be formed to review whether the lands of the defaulters that have been sold away are done properly.

(i) The fallow lands that are used by the common people for tending of cattle may not be given to influential people on a nominal price.

4. Forest Laws :

(a) Rights to kill wild animals (that are damaging the crops) without paying fees.

(b) The farming equipments of a farmer may be made available free of *masul* (charge).

(c) Permission may be accorded to collect necessary logs of wood from the forest free of charge for the people whose houses have been destroyed in the natural calamities like flood and fire.

(d) People having no houses may be permitted to collect logs of wood and bamboos from the forest free of cost.

(e) People of the State may collect woods for fuel from the forest free of cost.

(f) Cattle tenders may be exempted from paying revenues for the purpose of tending their cattle in the pasteur land.

(g) Cutting of logs of wood from the jungle be stopped.

(h) Penalty for chewing sugarcane be eliminated.

(i) Permission may be given to the people to chop trees from their own land and for their personal use.

(d) The price of bamboos and usuable wood from the jungles of Talcher may be sold at par with that of Angul.

(e) The forest guards may not use the power to search the houses of the people arbitrarily for smuggled wood.

5. Ban on forest labour

(a) People should not be forced to labour with or without wages.

(b) Forced tax of five annas per Re. 1 be not collected. There is no provision for forced labour. But the people are forced to do so. People of Talcher have been putting forth this demand for a pretty long period.

(c) (Cancellation of trade-monopoly) — No restriction should be imposed on export and import of agricultural products and other commodities.

7. Social

(a) Fees collected per marriage, remarriage, cowslaughter be stopped.

(b) Court of Justice be not allowed to function.

(c) All disputes relating to caste be settled in the caste committee.

8. Lakharaj

(a) Extra land of Lakhraj area be treated as Lakhraj.

(b) Lakhraj be continued as same during transfer.

(c) Scholarship to the students continuing in Sanskrit Tol.

9. (a) Police Paikas be given a monthly salary of Re. 1. They should not be forced to work against their will.

(b) Rayat Paikas be not forced to give the beat without wages. Those who want to do so be given due wages.

10. Coal-Mines

(a) Provisions should be made to recruit 85% of the people of Talcher in coal mines. In case sufficient number of Talcher people are not available for the purpose, other people of Orissa State be given the opportunity.

(b) If the employees of the coal mines desire to form trade-union or go on a strike, the State should not oppose them.

(d) Unskilled employees in the coal mines be given opportunity to gain knowledge about machinery.

(e) There should not be any discrepancy in salary in respect of caste, creed and colour.

(f) Company can't retrench any employee arbitrarily.

(g) The Mining Act of the Government of India be introduced.

11. Children coming under scheduled caste category be given compulsory primary education. Meritorious students be given scholarships to continue their study. They should be recruited suitably as per their qualification.

12. Fees collected from the bahanias be fixed to 1/3rd.

13. Tax collected from oilmen, washermen and such other people be stopped.

14. People having family links with the royal family be not permitted to carry on their trade and business inside the State.

15. Five hundred acres of Taila land of Kaniha mouza have been encroached by the State to construct a helipad. The Government should give the cost of the mango trees that have been cut down for the purpose.

16. (a) More funds be allotted on the heads of education, health, irrigation, roads etc.

(b) The representatives of the people be allowed to verify the accounts of the funds collected from the school children.

17. **Representative form of Government** — People will have the rights to elect their representatives who will take an active part in the administration made by the king. They are to aid and advise the king. Even in the formulation of new laws, they should be duly consulted.

Yours sincerely,
Talcher Prajamandal

Paniola,
P.O. Angul, Angul

APPENDIX 'N'

MUKTI-PATHA — No. 5, Dated 30.9.38

Dear Brothers,

The doors of freedom was closed for us till date because we did not know how to get to it. Now the path is clear and the door of freedom is wide open for us. Our dearest brother Bika Naik of Chandravil village has opened our eyes. He sacrificed his life for the sake of the country's freedom. The Raj Government tortured him a lot and shot him dead. His death has made us fearless. The obstacles on the path to freedom have been cleared. His selfless service has made him immortal. He was forced to meet the king in person. He strongly denied to do so and was shot dead. Some of his friends named Magata Maharana, Rathi Behera and others have been badly injured by the bullets of the Kings' man. Dear brother, please be inspired to walk fearlessly on the path of non-violence. Have patience. Don't lose your heart. Learn to fight against injustice and maladministration of the king. Get ready to face the bullet, so that we can get freedom. The soul of Bika Bhai will never find peace in heaven, if we become timid and fearful. Let us pledge not to do *Sadak Bethi.*

Non-violence is our strength.

Yours sincerely,
Talcher Prajamandal

Dear Brothers of Garhtal,

A meeting on behalf of Prajamandal will be held at Paniola camp, Angul. Please do attend the meeting in large numbers and make it a success.

Yours sincerely,
Talcher Prajamandal

Dated 30-9-1938

APPENDIX OI (OI)

MUKTI-PATH

No. 2

Dear Brothers,

Again for the second time you defeated the king of Talcher keeping to the paths of non-violence. The Talcher administration tried to choke the voice of the people by torturing the innocent people. This is probably the reason for which the higher authority gave them orders to do away with it. Henceforth, the Government will try to get their works done by flattering the people. You are requested not to be swayed away by the sweet words of the Government. Don't be fear stricken. Your have already suffered a lot to get your due rights. A number of people have sacrificed their lives for this noble cause. People have lost practically every thing. It is high time to stick to the following duties and responsibilities.

(i) Don't labour for free of cost.

(ii) Don't be swayed away by sweet words.

(iii) Don't make an attempt to gather at one place.

(iv) Don't follow the arrested persons in groups.

(v) Don't trust others except the trusted ones.

(vi) Make it a point to follow the path of non-violence and peace.

Talcher Prajamandal

APPENDIX OII

MUKTI-PATH-No. 6, Dated 4-10-1938

Dear Friends,

Bika Naik of village Chandrabila was shot dead by king's men in the night of 21st of last month. Five of his freinds have been injured badly. Moreover, the king's men let loose in the nearby villages and looted them. Even the womenfolk were abused and their ornaments were snatched away. We never heard of such nuisances. Many people left their hearth and home in protest against the atrocities made by the king and they have not yet returned to the State. Prajamandal has aprised the king of the grievances of the people. But our king does not pay any heed to it. Under such circumstances, people should be determined to give a hard fight against the indifferent attitude of the king. There is a saying that united effort never fails. The people should wage a peaceful war against the king in a combined way. We will have to fulfil our pledges and in no circumstances we should be cowed down.

(1) No *Bethi* without wages.

(2) We should not give unnessary *Bethi* charhge of five annas.

(3) We should not give *magana* or *rasada.*

(4) Don't hesitate to kill wild animals to protect crops.

(5) To cut timbers for construction of houses.

(6) No one should pay revenue unless the demands of Prajamandal are fulfilled.

(7) To make use of articles made available at a lower cost.

(8) Nobody should go to weekly market.

(9) We should settle the disputes without going to court.

(10) People opposing Prajamandal be ostracised.

Yours sincerely,
Sri Prbitra Mahan Pradhan
President
Talcher Prajamandal

APPENDIX 'P'

Seventh Issue of 'Mukti-Path, Dated 6-10-1938

DIRECTIVES OF PRAJAMANDAL

Dear Friends,

The king turned apathetic despite the fact that we suffered a lot. Prajamandal has decided to stage a demonstration with effect from tomorrow as a token of protest. Nearly twenty volunteers have been jailed yesterday. They had gone for campaigning and picketting. While going singing in praise of Mahatma Gandhi and Prajamandal *en route* Jagannathpur, Bantol, Kukudula, Baghuabol and the town, they were arrested by the police. They were caned ten times each and were sent to jail. They went to jail with a smiling face. To-day, twenty more volunteers have come forward to carry on their half finished mission.

The Government is of the view that they will suppress our peaceful movement by torturing us. Don't be swayed away by the sweet words of the Government. Dear brothers and sisters — let us be united together and take a decision to go to jail in large number. No Government had the guts to accommodate so many revolutionaries in the jail and feed them.

It is an earnest appeal of the Prajamandal to send atleast twenty volunteers from each village for necessary talk at our end.

Yours sincerely,
Sri Pabitra Mahan Pradhan
President
Talcher Prajamandal

APPENDIX 'Q'

Declaration of Talcher Durbar of 1 May, 1939

(1) **Illegal and useless revenue** — The king is ever ready to find a proper solution to the genuine grievances of the people. People of the State have been benefitted a lot by the king. Some revolutionaries have been creating problems in the State in the name of peace and non-violence. People in the State have been paying the worthless revenue as a part of land revenue without any grumble for the last twenty-eight years. Now they are being instigated not to pay them by some people with vested interest. The revenue collected from different heads is in no way more than that of the nearby States. I deem it fit to discuss about the matter with Resident of the Eastern States before taking a decision to lower down the worthless revenue. Having examined the matter closely, if the Resident Orders to lower down the same, then I will have no objection to carry out his order.

(2) Ceilings on pan, gurakhu, salt, dhuanpatra, kerosene, coconut, biri, soda and soaps have already been waived out. Only ceilings on items such as opium, ganja-bhanga, leather, horns, country and foreign liquor have been fixed.

(3) **Religion related fees** — Fees relating to religion are no more being collected. If any such controversy relating to religion arises, people, if they so desire, can put forth the matter in the Dharma court, Panchayat or Civil Court. The decision taken by the Panchayat or Civil Court will be valid in the Dharma Court. Any appeal against the Dharma court may be filled with King. It is quite obvious that people may opt for Civil Court if they do not want to go to Dharma court.

(4) **Exemption of bethi (free labour)** — Labour without wages is not more in practice. There is provision for giving nominal wages for any work done for the royal family.

Repair of roads — Collection of road revenue by the British Government is under active consideration of the State in lieu of repair of roads.

Hunting Spree — Normally people do like to consume the meat of hunted animals. They considered it as their legal due. It has been decided to give wages to the hunters at par with the hunters of Angul.

(5) **Pole-tax** — The trader class in the State have not been taxed with any special revenue. The tax collected from the traders in respect of the materials collected from the reserve forest is no extra tax. There is no change in it.

(6) **No punishment for people in exile** — If the people in exile want to come back to the State no punishment will be given to them. They will be pardoned for the crime committed by them. (Dusehhera declaration dated 21.9.38, 2.12.38, 25.1.39, 8.2.39 and 3.3.39 be consulted).

Those who have been issued with extradition warrant will be excused and released, if they do agree to give in writing to the State about their good conduct. No restrictions will be imposed on them and the warrant will be declared null and void. Declaration given by them will be cancelled.

(7) **Administrative Reforms** — There have been reforms in administration by setting up of Provisional Councils. This system will enable the representative of the people to take an active part in the State administration.

(8) **Freedom to speech** — No restriction will be imposed on any meeting provided it should not flare up the public opinion. The meetings should not go against royal administration.

(9) **Preservation of crops** — People have the right to kill wild animals to protect their crops. Arbitrary hunting in the name of preservation of crops will be seriously dealt with. They are required to pay either in the form of money or the meat of hunted animals.

APPENDIX R*

"Confusion Worse Confounded"

In September 1938, the people of Talcher submitted a representation to the Talcher *Durbar* for the redress of several grievances, and they also demanded some form of responsible government in the State under the aegis of the Ruler. A copy of this representation couched in most respectful words was also sent to the Political Department of the Government of India. As soon as this representation was submitted, the *Prajamandal* was declared unlawful and a reign of repression followed. Services of British troups were requisitioned. There was firing and two persons were shot dead. The form of the civil disobedience started there was to refuse to do *bethi* for the repair of the roads. Those who were sent to jail were severely beaten inside the jail and many were branded on the buttocks. When the situation thus became intolerable there was an exodus from the Talcher State to the neighbouring British territory Angul. As soon as this exodus began the Political Department showed an act concern and the Resident and the Political Agent discussed the matter with the Orissa Government several times, but for various reasons nothing could come out.

This matter was represented to the Viceroy by the Orissa Government and also by the Prime Minister of Orissa when the Viceroy was passing through Orissa on his way to Madras.

On the 9th and the 10th March 1939, Major Hannessey, the Assistant Political Agent of Orissa States (North), went to the camps of the refugees and introduced himself as the representative of the paramount power and assured certain concessions to the people and on that assurance asked the people to go back. But the leaders of the people took time to consider the matter and wanted to have the assurance in writing. The concessions assured by Major Hannessey were published

* Harijan, 20 May 1939. (OSA)

in the Press. At that time Major Hannessey was staying at Talcher. As soon as the news appeared in the press some hope was created in all circles and it was thought that the end of the misery of the people was in sight. In order to regularise the assurance and create confidence of the people in those assurance meeting was organised at Angul between Sri Harekrishna Mahtab and all those who are interested in the affairs of the refugees on the one hand and Major Hannessey on the other, with Mr. Ansorge, the Revenue Commissioner of Orissa, deputed by the Orissa Government as an observer. Major Hannessey came well prepared to the Conference with all the papers from Talcher, and in that meeting an agreement was arrived at between Major Hannessey and Sri Mahtab that the former would recommend certain concessions to the Ruler, and that the latter, when the concessions were granted, would see that the refugees went back. Major Hannessey was absolutely sure that the concessions that he would recommend to the Ruler would be granted, but he doubted whether Sri Mahtab would be able to send the refugees back. In order to remove this doubt Major Hannessey secured signature from the leaders of the refugees asserting to the above agreement, and everyone felt assured that the concessions which Major Hannessey undertook to recommend to the Ruler would be granted. Major Hannessey went back to Talcher. At that time it was thought by everybody that the declaration containing the concession promised by Major Hannessey would come in a few days, and those who knew the terms of the *Sanads* granted to the Rulers and the relations of the Political Department with the Rulers were absolutely sure that the concessions would come. But gradually it was known that the Ruler was not prepared to grant the concession relating to the reduction of cess though he was quite prepared to grant the other concessions.

On 29th April after more than a month from the date of Major Hannessey's assurance and agreement, it was given out by the resident that out of the nine concessions assured by Major Hannessey he would like to examine only one concession regarding the reduction of cess and the Ruler was ready to concede the remaining eight points, tearing the point relating to reduction of cess for the Resident's arbitration and also to cancel the extradition warrants, requiring only those who would want to go into the State to furnish a small security for a limited period. This was the definite understanding that the Resident and his Secretary gave to Sri Mahtab and Miss Agatha Harrison on the 29th April last. This was considered to be acceptable under the circumstances, and at the instance of the Resident, Sri Mahtab went to Talcher to attend the declaration of the above concessions on the 1st May last. Most surprisingly the declaration made did not contain the above concession and moreover it contained things which the Political Department had long ago declared abolished, *e.g. bethi.* The Political Agent was all long present in Talcher and with his full knowledge the declaration had been made. The Governor of Orissa was also under the impression that the declaration would be like what the Resident had given Sri Mahtab to understand.

APPENDIX 'S'

Signatories of Various States Prajamandal Leaders.

1. Sri Chandrasekhar Dalua — Dasapalla, Puri.
2. Sri Sridhar Das, Nayagarh, Puri.
3. Sri Bidyadhar Nayak, Narsinghapur, Cuttack.
4. Sri Loknath Panda,
5. Sri Gouri Shankar Royguru, Sonepur.
6. Sri Sadhu Prasad Bidyadhar Mahapatra, Nilgiri.
7. Sri Dasarath Pradhan, Boudh.
8. Sri Bhagaban Behera, Athamallik.
9. Sri Govinda Chandra Mishra, Dasapalla.
10. Sri Chintamani Rath, Patna.
11. Sri Dwitiya Rout, Athamallik.
12. Sri Gatikrishna Bhanja, Dhenkanal.
13. Sri Bidyadhar Tripathi, Baudh.
14. Sri Gandhip Bhai, Kalahandi.
15. Sri Jayasingh Nag, Kalahandi.
16. Sri Aputu Sahu, Kalahandi.
17. Sri Gouri Shankar Pradhan, Talcher.
18. Sd. Illegible, Nilgiri
19. Sri Radhamadhab Panda, Nilgiri.
20. Sri Prahallad Bhoi, Patna.

21. Sri Madan Mohan Pradhan, Talcher.
22. Sri Radhanath Rath, Athagarh.
23. Sri Maguni Chandra Pradhan, Talcher.
24. Sri Dasarathi Mishra, Kochinda, Bananda.
25. Sri Dayanidhi Sahoo, Palahara.
26. Sri Pabitra Mohan Pradhan, Talcher.
27. Sri Kapileswar Prasad Nanda, Bolangir.
28. Sri Judhistir Mishra, Patna, Bolangir.
29. Sri Dakhya Prajapati Pradhan, Rairakhol.
30. Sri Laxmana Satapathy, Sonepur.
31. Sri Binod Behari Karna, Rairakhol
32. Sri Dinabandhu Acharya, Hindol.
33. Sri Brajakishore Dhal, Dhenkanal.
34. Sri Mahesh Chandra Pradhan, Dhenkanal.
35. Sri Muralidhar Das, Ranpur.
36. Sri Narottam Das, Dhenkanal.
37. Sri Fakir Mohan Pradhan, Palahara.
38. Sri Bipini Behari Patnaik, Tigiria.
39. Sri Banamali Panda, Badamba.
40. Sri Shashibhusan Pradhan, Rairakhol.
41. Sri Natabar Panda, Gangpur.
42. Sri Anup Sankar Singh, Gangpur.
43. Sri Antaryami Sahoo, Khandapara.
44. Sri Musa Mallik, Dhenkanal.
45. Sri Joginath Naik, Talcher.
46. Sri Ghanashyam Mishra, Dhenkanal.
47. Sri Hiralal Patnaik, Kharsuan.
48. Sri Srikant Routh, Dhenkanal.
49. Sri Laxmana Majhi, Sareikala.

APPENDIX 'T'

(CONGRATULATION APPEAL BY THE RULER OF ATHGARH ON DECEMBER 9, 1947 TO THE NEW POPULAR MINISTRY)

Honourable Ministers,

I welcome you all with a deep sense of pride and happiness. I have been able to fulfil the long cherished hope of the people of the State by transfering the reins of administration to you.

I know that the path before you is too hard to tread on various internal problems alongwith the merger problems will, no doubt, serious threat for you. I earnestly request the Government to provide some extra privileges to the people of Garhjat. At last I do request you to deal with the people of my State in a dignified and impartial manner.

Sd/-
Swami Vidyananda Saraswati,
Ruler, Athgarh. 9-12-1947

APPENDIX 'U'

(A VERNACULAR LEAFLET GREETING TO THE NEWLY FORMED PEOPLE'S MINISTRY BY THE PEOPLE OF ATHGARH)

Honourable Members of the newly formed Ministry of Athgarh,

The new Ministry formed by the elected representatives of the people is welcomed. Athgarh is one of the smallest States in India. Yet the illiterate people of this insignificant State have exhibited their calibres being guided by your efficient leadership. Even after being liberated from the bondage of 150 years of British rule, the people were made to suffer under the despotic rule of the kings. You have been able to establish democracy in Athgarh in the most peaceful and non-violent way by encouraging the people against the autocratic way of the kings.

During the short stay of your ministry, many low paid employees have been benefited a lot. A number of landless people have been pleased by acquiring lands. Many meritorious students have received aids for higher study. You have been kind enough to dedicate yourselves for the welfare of the people and State as well. No doubt, you would have done much more for the poor and illiterate people of Athgarh if time allowed to continue for some more time. Your few days in office amply signify it.

It is because of your sincere effort that Athgarh State could have a successful merge with that of Orissa. People of this State have high regards for you. They want that there should be tremendous development in the State under your efficient leadership. We do pray God that you should earn good name and fame in the political arena of the country.

People of Athgarh will never forget you because you have enlightened them. At this moment of your departure what more should we give you except our heart felt love and gratitude. The people of Athgarh have their strong supports behind your dynamic leadership.

With regards,

Yours sincerely,
People of Athgarh.

APPENDIX 'V'

(AN ANTI-MERGER APPEAL TO THE ORISSAN STATES RULERS BY SOME PRAJAMANDAL LEADERS)

Honourable Kings,

At the outset, we may kindly be excused for telling some open facts. We are not going to tell anything out of malice and hatredness. We do only present the views of the general public.

When we analyse the cultures of Orissa State and its Garhjats, we do find out the deep distinction between the advantages of the foreign rule and country rule. This humiliating scene is the product of your continuing misuse of power and reactionary attitude. People of Garhjats have been showing their loyalty to throne for years together. But all of your efforts have been directed to exploit their sincere loyalty to achieve your desired selfish ends. You have been considering their loyalty cowardice. You have been trying your best to keep the people in dark by not allowing them to be literate and well-off. And you have been trying to suppress their spontaneous flow of raising their voices.

The leaders of the Mughalbandi areas can't but tolerate this type of unbearable behaviour of your towards their fellow *bretherns* of the neighbouring Garhjats areas with whom they are closely associated in terms of social, financial and linguistic basis. So they have been trying to merge the Garhjats with the Orissa State.

Consequent upon this merger, the Garhjat people may obtain their political freedom. But their financial and culture deterioration will linger for some more time.

At first the people of Garhjats do want to keep themselves aloof from the despots. Secondly, their financial and cultural developments need to be alleviated. Thirdly, they need to have close affinity and co-operation with their moghulbandi bretherns.

As administrators, if you do really desire to know what your subjects expect from you, then you surrender your sovereignty to the people immediately. As a taken of gratitude the people of your States also sincerely wish you to get your due position in the society. The attitude to free themselves from the despotic rule will certainly bring all the Garhjat people came close together and help them to form a prosperous Garhjat State. Steps should be taken to set up, combined councils and administrative departments in both the States with a view to strengthening the relationship between the Garhjat and moghulbandi areas. As a result the Oriya people will get their due place in the national level.

Simultaneous struggle of the people against the despotic rule of the kings and the full merger of their States with Orissa will certainly put them into trouble. Now the opportunity has come, when you should hand over your power to the ordinary common mass, if you really want to secure the good will of your people, that you are gradually losing. You should also declare that you are having no ulterior motive. You are also requested to declare in public that you don't want to keep the territory of your State intact. We do extend our sincerest thanks to the kings of Athgarh, Tigiria, Ranapur and Khandapara, who have come forward for the merger of their States ungrudgingly. You are also requested to follow their foot prints. Otherwise the future will be dark for all.

It is now a common fact that the provincial kings of our country are giving a serious thought to the problem of the smaller and fragmented Garhjat States. It is very much on the cards that the matters will be taken up in the meetings during the visit of Sardar Patel to Orissa in the mid-December. Your combined effort will help to wipe out the despotic rule from the Garhjat areas.

1. Sd/- Bipini Behari Patnaik, President, Tigiria Prajamandal
2. Sd/- Madhusudan Patnaik, Ex-Minister, Tigiria State
3. Sd/- Paramananda Patnaik, Tigiria
4. Sd/- Achyutananda Dash, E.C. Member, Athgarh Prajamandal
5. Sd/- Pratap Chandra Patnaik, Secretary, Barmba Prajamandal
6. Sd/- Udayanath Sahoo, Ex-Prime Minister, Tigiria State
7. Sd/- Dr. Daitari Ji, Dhenkanal
8. Sd/- Kasinath Mishra, Dhenkanal
9. Sd/- Kunjabehari Panda, Advocate, Dhenkanal.

◆

Glossary

Abwab	—	Miscellaneous Cesses levied by Chief.
Adalat	—	A Court of Justice.
Adivasi	—	Tribal People.
Amin	—	Collector of Revenue in the State.
Amla	—	A Native Officer of Judicial or Revenue Court.
Andhari Kutchery	—	Night Court
Anna	—	The Sixteen Part of a Rupee.
Asar	—	The Oriya month corresponding to June-July.
Ashram	—	Asylum for Recluses
Baboo	—	A title of respect attached to a name.
Bakshi or Buxi	—	Commander-in-Chief of the Raja
Bazar	—	Marketing Complex
Bebarta	—	Chief Officer of an Estate
Bethi	—	Forced Labour
Begari	—	Forced labour without payment for public service.
Behera	—	A domestic servant, Circulator of Raja's Order, news, letters by hand to hand.
Behera Pradhan	—	Chief of Beheras
Bhang	—	An intoxicating preparation hemp.
Bheti	—	A sort of tribute collected by Raja from the ryots on Suniya.
Bhuyan	—	A class of tribal people.
Bidi	—	A sort of cigar
Biri	—	Black gram

Biswa	—	A village measurement worth about 75 grams.
Bisoi	—	Tribal head
Brahmin	—	The highest caste of Hindu Society entrusted with religious affairs.
Bundh	—	Tank
Bungalow	—	Rest-house for travellers built by the Government.
Bustee	—	Residential area of low class people.
Charkha	—	Spinning Wheel
Chasa	—	Cultivator
Cheyt	—	An Oriya month corresponding to March-April.
Choukidar	—	A village watchman
Circar	—	An administrative unit.
Cooli	—	Labourer of inferior rank
Cowree	—	A small shell used as money, which is one-sixth of an anna.
Cutchery or Kutchery	—	A Court, an Office.
Dak	—	Letter-post
Dakua	—	Night watchman in royal service
Dalbehera	—	An officer in the command of the Paiks in the State.
Dandapat	—	An administrative division or unit in the State composing a number of Villages.
Darogah	—	A customs, excise or police officer.
Dasi	—	Concubine
Debottar	—	Lands assigned for the worship of an idol.
Dharma Adalat	—	Religious Court
Dharma Sabha	—	An association of influential Hindus to uphold their religion.
Dharmasala	—	Inn

Dhobi	—	Washerman
Diwan	—	Chief Executive Officer in the State.
Diwani Adalat	—	Civil Court
Dom	—	A lower caste Hindu
Durbar	—	A Royal Court
Dushera	—	A religious festival of Hindus for worshipping Durga.
Faujdar	—	An Officer enjoying both civil and military power over one division.
Gadi	—	Throne; the seat of Royalty
Gajapati	—	The name by which the King of Puri is generally known.
Ganda	—	A low caste Hindu
Ganja	—	A kind of intoxicating drug prepared from the hemp.
Garh	—	A hill fort
Garjat	—	The lands constituted of mountains fortresses.
Garnaik	—	A Military Commander in charge of a fort; a village head.
Gaud	—	Milkman
Ghat	—	A landing place near river bank for loading and unloading of goods from the boats.
Gherao	—	Encircling and not allowing the Officer to go without yielding to the agitator's demand.
Gountia	—	A village headman in Sambalpur State.
Gunda	—	Hooligan
Guru	—	A religious preceptor among the Hindus.
Hadi	—	A low caste Hindu
Harijan	—	Scheduled Caste group
Hartal	—	Strike
Hat	—	Market

Hatikheda	—	A special ditch for trapping wild elephants.
Hizrat	—	To move *en mass* from one place to other due to excessive oppression.
Hingula	—	A popular Hindu Goddess
Jagir	—	Revenue free land held on condition of rendering service to the Chief.
Jagirdar	—	The holder of Jagir
Jatra or Yatra	—	A religious festival
Jema	—	Princess
Jeyt	—	The name of an Oriya month, corresponding to May-June.
Juanga	—	A hill tribe
Jubaraj or Yuvaraj	—	Crown Prince
Jungle	—	A forest
Kabuliyat	—	A wirtten agreement
Kabya tirtha	—	An honorary degree for writting epic.
Kahan	—	A measure equal to 1280 cowries.
Kali	—	A popular Hindu Goddess.
Kara	—	Tax
Kazi	—	A Muslim Magistrate
Khadi	—	Home-spun coarse cotton cloth
Khaki	—	Inferior quality cloth resembling in colour the groundnuts.
Khalsa	—	Lands comprised of revenue paying estate.
Khamar	—	Grain store; a land granted to relatives of royal family for their maintenance.
Khandual	—	Watcher of weapon house
Khansama	—	Royal Cook
Khas	—	An estate managed by Government
Kheda	—	An enclosure to capture elephant.

Khilat	—	A dress of honour, presented by the Raja or superior authority to a subordinate as a mark of distinction.
Khond or Kondhs	—	A class of wild tribe
Killah	—	Fortress under jurisdiction of Tributary Raja.
Kol	—	Tribal people
Krushak or Krishak	—	Farmer
Kulta	—	A word used in western Orissa meaning farmer.
Kumar	—	The son of a King next to the eldest son.
Lakhiraj	—	Rent free land for some particular reason.
Lathi	—	A bamboo stick used by Police Constable as weapon.
Magan	—	Fees exacted by the Raja from the tenants mostly on social rituals.
Mahal	—	An estate, a revenue paying unit.
Mahant	—	The abbot of a monastery.
Maharaja	—	Emperor
Makkaddam or Mukkaddum	—	A village proprietor who pays through a superior.
Mali	—	Gardener
Malikana	—	Proprietorship
Mana	—	A village measurement equivalent to half a kilogram.
Mandal	—	Peasant body
Matha	—	Monastery
Mauza	—	A village or a group of villages.
Meli	—	Rebellion
Meriah	—	Human sacrifice performed by tribals like Kandhs.
Mofussil	—	Village area.

Mughalbandi	—	The cultivated-coastal belt of Orissa (Cuttack, Puri and Balasore Districts) under direct administration of British from which the Mughal Emperors derived their revenues.
Mukdab or Makdab	—	Primary School of Muslims.
Mukhtyar or Muktair	—	An authorised agent; Junior Pleader.
Mung	—	Green gram
Naib	—	A deputy
Naik	—	The head of a small body of the Paiks generally in charge of a village.
Nawab	—	A Muslim ruler
Nazarana	—	Gift from an inferior to a superior.
Nimak-haram	—	Betrayer
Niskar	—	Lands exempted from tax.
Nizamat Adalat	—	The Supreme Court of Criminal Justice.
Nuzzer or Nazar	—	An Officer
Paik	—	Foot soldier of Raja holding lands on tenure of military service.
Pan	—	The betel leaf.
Pana	—	A low caste employee.
Pania	—	Water carrier
Panchayat	—	A native court of arbitration
Panda	—	A priest of a Hindu temple.
Pandit	—	A learned Brahmin with the knowledge of Sanskrit study.
Pargana	—	A Sub-division of a district.
Parishad	—	Council
Parwana or Purwana	—	An order or a letter under royal seal.
Pattah	—	Guaranteed deed
Pattayat	—	The scion of the king who does not have a claim on the gadi.
Peshcus	—	A tribute

Pradhan	—	Village headman
Praja Parishad	—	People's Council
Qanungo or Kanungo	—	Revenue Officer
Qubulnamah	—	Acknowledgement of rights.
Rabi	—	The spring harvest
Raiyat or Ryot	—	Cultivator
Raj	—	Crown
Raja	—	King
Raj Purohit	—	Royal priest
Rani	—	Hindu Queen
Rajbati	—	Royal Palace
Rasad or Russud	—	Supply of necessities to the officers to their camping ground.
Ratha	—	Car
Ressums	—	Ration
Sraban	—	The Oriya month corresponding to September-October.
Sadak	—	Road
Sahara	—	A Scheduled Tribe
Sahib or Saheb	—	Englishman
Samant	—	Nobles
Sammilani	—	Conference
Salami	—	A complementary present
Sanad	—	A document conferring privileges under the seal of the ruling authority.
Sangha	—	Association
Sarbarakar	—	A title given to the village headman in the States.
Sardar	—	A chief or commander.
Sati or Suttee	—	The rite of widow burning alive with the husband's funeral pyre.
Satyagraha	—	Protest demonstration in peaceful manner.

Satyagrahi	—	One who participates in Satyagraha.
Sawar	—	A Scheduled Caste group.
Sena	—	Soldier.
Ser or Seer	—	A measure of weight.
Sepoy	—	A soldier of India dressed in European style.
Shikar	—	Sport in the sense of hunting.
Sonia or Suniya	—	The Oriya New Year's Day.
Subah or Soobah	—	A large division or province of the Mughal Empire.
Swaraj	—	Self-Government.
Tahsildar	—	The Chief Native Revenue Officer.
Taluk	—	An estate smaller than a Zamindari.
Tamakhu	—	Tobacco.
Thana	—	A Police Station.
Tol	—	Indigenous School.
Tola	—	A measure of weight.
Umlee	—	Year commencing between 27 August and 26 September.
Vaidya	—	A traditional village doctor using herbal medicine.
Zamindar	—	A landlord; a proprietor directly responsible to the State for the revenue of the land he possess.
Zamindari	—	The tract of land consisting the possession of Zamidnar.
Zenana	—	A secluded house for women members of the family.
Zilla	—	A division or district.

◆

Bibliography

PRIMARY SOURCES

A. Manuscript Record

a. National Archieves of India, New Delhi

1. Foreign Department, Political Proceedings including original consultation and foreign correspondence, 1868-1948.
2. Foreign Department, Judicial Proceedings, 1912-1936.
3. Home Department, Political Judicial, Revenue and Public Branch, 1908-1942.
4. Relevant records on feudatory States of Orissa, 1907-1948.

b. Nehru Memorial Museum and Library, New Delhi.

1. Files on All India Congress Committee.
2. Relevant files on Prajamandal Movement in Orissa, 1922-1945.
3. Files on All India States' Peoples' Conference.

c. Orissa States Archieves, Bhubaneswar.

1. Revenue Records, 1803-1895.
2. Judicial Proceedings, 1852-1908
3. Secretariat Records, 1935-1950.
4. Cuttack Revenue Records, 1840-1910
5. Bolangir Records, 1872-1947
6. Dhenkanal Records, 1912-1950
7. Dasapalla Records, 1872-1919
8. Kalahandi Records, 1900-1948
9. Keonjhar Records, 1882-1947
10. Mayurbhanj Records, 1870-1947
11. Sambalpur Records, 1862-1947

12. Sundargarh Records, 1890-1947
13. Balasore District Records, 1850-1905
14. Private Records (relevant) Collected from some individuals.

d. Sub-divisional Record Room, Talcher

1. Records on Political (Home) and Judicial administration of Talcher, 1901-1950.
2. Records on Prajamandal Movement in Talcher, 1911-1948.
3. Records on the correspondence of the Raja with British Government, 1910 onwards.

e. Talcher Palace Record Room

1. Some Records on Talcher People's Movement, 1905 onwards.
2. Raja's correspondence with the British, 1918-1945.
3. Raja's declaration, proclamation and correspondence with his officials regarding Talcher Movement, 1920-1948.

f. Office of the Sub-Collector, Talcher and Office of the Tahsildar, Talcher.

Records on the Census of Talcher, 1991.

g. Office of the General Manager, M.C.L., Talcher.

Records on the Coalfield of Talcher.

B. Printed Report

Annual Administrative Report of Athgarh State for 1935-36 and 1945-46, Athgarh, 1936-1947.

Annual Administrative Report of Athmallik State for 1933-34, 1942-43 and 1945-46, Authority of Athmallik State, 1934-1947.

Annual Administrative Report of Bamra State for 1943-44 and 1945-46, Authority of Bamra State, 1944-46.

Annual Administrative Report of Dhenkanal State for 1922-23, 1934, 1936, 1942-43, Authority of Dhenkanal State, 1923-43.

A Report on the Budget of Dhenkanal State for the year 1941-42, Dhenkanal, 1942.

Annual Administrative Report of Hindol State for 1934-35 Authority of Hindol, 1935.

Annual Administrative Report of Khandapara State for 1944-45, Authority of Khandapara, 1945.

Annual Administrative Report of Kalahandi State for 1945-46, Authority of Patna, 1946.

Annual Administrative Report of Mayurbhanj State for 1929-30, 1937-38, 1940-41 to 1944-45, Authority, Baripada, 1930-1946.

Annual Administrative Report of Nayagarh State for 1939-40 to 1945-46, Authority of Nayagarh State, 1940-1947.

A Report on the Revision Settlement of Nayagarh State, 1906-18.

Annual Administrative Report of Nilgiri State for 1942-43, Authority of Nilgiri, 1944.

Annual Administrative Report of Pallahara State for 1946-47, Authority of Pallahara, 1947.

Final Report of the Original Survey and Settlement Operation of Ranpur, Ex-State Area of Puri District, 1943-1952.

Annual Administrative Report of Tigiria State for 1943-44, Authority of Tigiria, 1944.

Annual Administrative Report of Talcher State for 1928-29 to 1945-46, Authority of Talcher 1929-1946.

Annual Report of Talcher Prajamandal for 1940-41, Secretary, Talcher Prajamandal, Angul, 23 September, 1941.

Annual Report of Talcher Municipality for 1941-42, Chairman, Talcher, 16 April, 1942.

A Report of the District Officer on Settlement, Talcher, 10 October, 1893.

Compilation Report of Talcher State Revision Settlement, 1928-29.

A Report of the Land Revenue Settlement of Talcher State, 1911-12.

A Report of the Survey and Existence of Coalmines in Talcher, 1927.

Secret Report on the Second Session of Orissa States' Peoples' Conference, Talcher Police Department.

General Review of the Administration of Feudatory States of Orissa and Chhotnagpur for the year 1922-23, Patna, 1923.

Report of Land Tenure and Revenue System of Orissa and Chhatisgarh States, Vols. I, II and III, R.K. Ramdhyani, Berhampur, 1940-1944.

Report on the Administration of Bengal for 1879-80, Bengal Secretariat, Calcutta, 1880.

Bengal Administrative Report, 1878-79, Calcutta, 1879.

Report on the Administration of Bihar and Orissa, 1913-14.

Report on the progress of Education, Orissa Tributary Mahals, 1891-92, Radhanath Rai, Joint Inspector of Schools of Orissa Division.

Report on the Administration of the Feudatory States of Central Provinces for the year 1899-1900, Nagpur, 1901.

Report on the Administration of the Feudatory States of Orissa for the year 1910-11, Calcutta, 1911.

Report of the Famine Commission, 1866, Vol.I, Calcutta, 1867.

Report of the Indian Constitutional Reforms, 1919.

Report of the Agricultural Statistics of India, 1916-17, Vol.I, Governor General in Council, Calcutta, 1919.

Report of the Indian Statutory Commission, Vols. I to IV, 1930.

Report of the Orissa Boundary Committee, O'Donnel, 1932.

Annual Report of Board of Revenue, Cuttack, 1936-1948.

Report of the Orissa States' Enquiry Committee, Cuttack, 1939.

Report of the Chief Intelligence Officer on Political Situation in India, 1942.

Annual Report on the Progress of Education in Orissa, 1936 to 1948.

Report on the work of the Constituent Assembly, Jawaharlal Nehru, Bhopal, 2 May, 1947.

Report on the Census of Orissa, 1991, Directorate of Census, Government of Orissa.

C. Proceedings

Proceedings of the Board of Revenue, 1891-92.

Proceedings of the Indian Legislative Council, 1915-1920.

Proceedings of the Agency Utkal Conference, Jeypore, May 1935.

Resolutions of Utkal Union Conference, Cuttack, November, 1935.

Proceedings of Bihar and Orissa Legislative Council Debates, 1912-1936.

Proceedings of Indian Legislative Assembly, 1921-36.

Proceedings of the Standing Committee of Chamber of Princes, Delhi, March 1932.

Proceedings of the Chamber of Princes, 11-12 March, 1940.

Proceedings of the Standing Committee of the Ministers of Indian States, Bombay, 17-18 August, 1936.

Proceedings of Indian States Committee, Montague House, London, 27 November, 1928.

Proceedings of the First Legislative Assembly of Orissa, Vols. I to X, 1937-1944.

Proceedings of the Second Legislative Assembly of Orissa, Vols. I to IV, 1946-1947.

Proceedings of the meeting of the Rulers of Eastern States at Raj Kumar College, Raipur, 17-23 December, 1946.

Proceedings of the meet of Council of Rulers, Eastern States, Jamshedpur, 18-20 April, 1947.

Proceedings of the meet of the Council of Rulers, Eastern States, Puri, 12-14 May, 1947.

Minutes of the meeting of Prajamandal leaders of Orissan States, Cuttack, 25 April, 1947.

Proceedings of the Indian History Congress :
Bhubaneswar Session, 1977.

Proceedings of Orissa History Congress :
Berhampur Session, 1977
Jyoti Vihar Session, 1978
Mayurbhanj Session, 1982
Ravenshaw College Session, 1987
B.J.B. College Session, 1988
Rajdhani College Session, 1989.

D. State Manuals and Gazettes

Governor General, Calcutta, The Angul Laws and Regulations, 1913, SRT

Authority of Talcher State, Talcher State Manual, Part I, Oriya, 1916, TPRR.

———, Talcher Forest Manual, 1928, TPRR.

———,Talcher State Manual, 1937, TPRR.

———, Talcher State Gazette, 22 September, 1938, SUA.

———, Talcher State Gazette, 1 May, 1939, TPRR.

———, Dushera Declaration in Oriya, 1 May, 1939, TPRR.

———, Talcher State Gazette, 7 May ,1939, TPRR.

———, Talcher State Gazette, 18 September ,1939, TPRR.

———, Talcher State Gazette, Supplementary, 29 August ,1942, TPRR.

———, Talcher State Gazette, Extraordinary, 18 August, 1945, SRT.

Authority of Dhenkanal State, Dhenkanal State Gazette, 30 July, 1938, SRT.

———, Bulletin in Oriya, 8 August, 1938, SRT.

———, Dhenkanal State Gazette, 29, August, 1938, SRT.

———, Dhenkanal State Gazette, 9 September, 1938, SRT.

———, Dhenkanal State Gazette, Extra ordianry, 12 September, 1938, SRT.

———, Dhenkanal State Gazette, 20 September, 1938, SRT.

———, Dhenkanal State Gazette, 24 September, 1938, SRT.

———, Declaration in Oriya, 24 September, 1938, SRT.

———, Dhenkanal State Gazette, 20 November, 1938, SRT.

———, Dhenkanal State Gazette, 3 September, 1942, SRT

———, Dhenkanal State Gazette, 4 September, 1942, SRT.

President, Eastern States Agency, The Eastern State Gazette, Nagpur, 15 November, 1947, SRT.

E. Gazetteers

Angul District Gazetteers Statistics, 1900-1911, Patna, 1915.

Bengal District Gazetteers of Cuttack, L.S.S. O'Malley, Calcutta, 1906.

Bengal District Gazetteers of Angul, L.S.S. O'Malley, Calcutta, 1908.

Bengal District Gazetteers, Singhbhum, Sareikala and Kharswan, Calcutta, 1910.

Bengal Gazetteers, Feudatory States of Orissa, L.E.B. Cobdon Ramsay, Calcutta, 1982.

Bihar and Orissa District Gazetteer, Cuttack, P.T. Mansfield, Patna, 1933.

Central Province District Gazetteers, A.E. Nelson, Raipur.

Chhatishgarh Feudatory States Gazetteer, 1909.

Cuttack District Gazetteer Statistics, 1900-1901 to 1910-11, Patna 1915.

Imperial Gazetteer of India, Vols. IV, XI and XXVIII, Oxford, 1906-1908.

Orissa Tributary States Gazetteers Statistics, 1901-02, Calcutta, 1905.

Orissa District Gazetteers, Mayurbhanj, Government of Orissa, 1967.

Orissa District Gazetteers, Dhenkanal, Government of Orissa, 1972.

Orissa District Gazetteers, Sundargarh, Government of Orissa, 1975.

Puri District Gazetteers Statistics, 1900-1901 to 1910-1911, Patna, 1915.

F. Memorandum, Correspondence and Leaflets

Memorandum for the Indian Statutory Commission on the working of the Reforms in Bihar and Orissa, Patna, 1930, OSA.

Memorandum to the O'Donell Committee by the Utkal Union Committee, 1931, OSA.

Memorandum on Native States in India, Calcutta, 1911, TPRR.

Memorandum on Treaties, position and status of the Feudatory States of Orissa submitted to the Indian States Committee, year unknown, TPRR.

Memorandum to the Chief Administrator of Talcher by President, Talcher Prajamandal, 9 January, 1948, SRT.

Memorandum on personal rights, dignities and privileges of Rulers with constitutional position of Indian States including the Eastern States as examined by Sir Tej Bahadur Sapru, A.K. Roy, P.R.Das etc. issued by Maharaja of Patna, Calcutta, 1948, TPRR.

Memorandum on Talcher Coalfield area given to the Chairman-*cum*-Managing Director, Coal India Limited during his visit to Talcher, 8 October, 1988, OGMMCL.

Memorandum on Jagannath Coalfield area at a glance given to P.A. Sangama, State Minister of Coal, Government of India, during his visit to Talcher, 4 February, 1992, OGMMCL.

The Indian Annual Register, 1921-1942, OSA

White Paper on Indian States, Ministry of States of Government of India, New Delhi, 1950, OSA.

Bengal and Madras Papers, Vols. II and III, 1688-1757 and 1757-1975, G. Forrest, OSA.

Leaflets

Odisa Gadajat Praja Sammilani Nibedan, Oriya, Cuttack, 20 March, 1937, Circulated by Sarangdhar Das, SRT.

Odisa Gadajat Praja Sammilani Nibedan, Oriya, Cuttack, 27 April, 1937, Circulated by Sarangdhar Das, SRT.

Muktipath, Oriya, 30 September, 1938, Circulated by Talcher Prajamandal, SRT.

Muktipath, Oriya, Second Issue, Date unknown, Circulated by Talcher Prajamandal, SRT.

Muktipath, Oriya, Sixth Issue, 4 October 1938, Circulated by Talcher Prajamandal, SRT.

Muktipath, Oriya, 6 October 1938, Circulated by Talcher Prajamandal, SRT.

Talcher Prajamandal ra dabi, Oriya, 10 October 1938, Circulated by Talcher Prajamanddal, Paniola Refugee Camp, Angul, SRT.

Odisa Gadajat Raja nku Sesa Nibedan, Oriya, December, 1947, Circulated combinely by some Prajamandal leaders of Tigiria, Athgarh, Baramba, Pallahara and Dhenkanal, Self custody.

Nutan Lokapratinidhi Mantri Mandalanku Raja Sahebnka Swagata Bhasan, Oriya, Athgarh State, 9 December, 1947, Circulated by Raja of Athgarh, Self Custody.

Athgarh Manyabar Janapriya Mantrimandala nku, Oriya, Circulated by people of Athgarh, Self Custody.

G. Treaties, Engagements and Sanads

Aitchison, C.U., *A Collection of Treaties, Engagements and Sanads, Relating to India and Neighbouring Countries,* Vol. I, Calcutta, 1909.

———, *A Collection of Treaties, Engagements and Sanads, Relating to India and Neighbouring Countries,* Vol. II, Calcutta, 1930.

Qubulnama of 1803, Given to Raja Bhagirathi Birabr Hari Chandan of Talcher by English East India Company, 22 November, 1803, TPRR.

Sanad of 1874, Given to Raja Ramachandra Birabar Harichandan of Talcher by Viceroy and Governor General of India on 21 May, 1874, OSA.

Sanad of 1908, Given to Raja Kishore Chandra Dev Birabar Harichandan of Talcher by Viceroy and Governor General of India on 12 October, 1908, OSA.

Sanad of 1915, Given to Raja K.C. Dev of Talcher by Viceroy and Governor General of India on 15 May, 1915, OSA.

Sanad of 1937, Given to Raja K.C. Dev of Talcher by Viceroy and Governor General, India on 26 February, 1937, OSA.

H. Compilations

De, S.C. and N.K. Sahu, *Who's Who of Freedom Workers in Orissa, Dhenkanal District,* Cuttack, 1970, OSA.

———, *Who's Who of Freedom Workers Orissa, Cuttack and Puri Districts,* Cuttack, 1970, OSA.

Talcher Prajamandal Itihas Committee, *Talcher Prajamandal (Congress) Itihas,* Cuttack, 1950, Self Custody.

I. Memoirs

Baliarsingh, S., *Ranpur Bidroha,* Oriya, Cuttack, 1985.

Dhal, B.K., *Bhulibu Nahi,* Oriya, Cuttack, 1980.

Dwivedi, S.N., *Mo Jibanara Eka Adhyaya : Agasta Biplaba,* Oriya, Cuttack, 1972.

———, *Sradhanjali*, Oriya, Rourkela, 1984.

Lal, J.M., *Odia Bijay,* Oriya, Cuttack, 1876.

Mahtab, H.K., *Sadhanar Pathe,* Oriya, Cuttack, 1972.

———, *The Beginning of the End,* Cuttack, 1972.

Mishra Anant, *Talcher Andolana,* Oriya, Cuttack, 1948.

Mishra Akuli, *Radhanath Granthabali,* Oriya, Cuttack, 1957.

Mishra Ghanashyam, *Talcher Bhugola,* Oriya, Talcher, 1916.

———, *Talcher Itihas,* Oriya, Talcher, 1934.

Mishra Godavarish, *Ardha Satabdira Odisa O Thanhire mo Sthana,* Oriya, Cuttack, 1921.

Mishra, K.M., *Kendujhar,* Oriya, Cuttack, 1938.

Nanda, R.C., *Dhenkanal Itihas,* Oriya, Dhenkanal, 1929.

Patnaik, S.N., *Odisare Swadhinata Andolana,* Oriya, Cuttack, 1972.

Patnaik, H.M., *Dhenkanal Andolana,* Oriya, Dhenkanal, 1983.

Pradhan, P.M., *Muktipathe Sainika*, Oriya, 3 Vols., Cuttack, 1973-1979.

Ram, R.C., *Sangrami,* Oriya, Cuttack, 1986.

Rath, T.C., *Ghumsar Itihas,* Oriya, Cuttack, 1913.

Routroy, N., *Smruti O Anubhuti,* Oriya, Cuttack, 1986.

Roy, S.B., *Adhunik Talcher,* Talcher, 1940.

Singh Samant, R.N., *Khandapada Prajamandalara Sankhipta Itihas,* Cuttack, 1950.

J. Unpublished Dissertation

Samal, A.K., "The Political Turmoil in Orissa : An Attempt for the revival of Hindu Rule in the 18th Century (Ph.D. Thesis, Benaras Hindu University, 1989).

K. Interviews

1. Dev Sauhagya Chandra, Raja of Talcher
2. Mahtab Harekrishna
3. Patnaik Baishnab
4. Patnaik Sura
5. Patnaik Harmohan
6. Pradhan Pabitra Mohan
7. Pradhan Bichhanda
8. Rath Radhanath
9. Rath Biswanath
10. Sahu Udayanath

L. Newspapers, Periodicals and Journals

Amrit Bazar Patrika, Daily, 1922-1947.

Anand Bazar Patrika, Daily, 1938-1942.

Asha, Oriya, 1927.

Deshakatha, Oriya Daily, 1930-1940.

Gadajat, Oriya Periodical, 1986-1989

Gadajat Basini, Oriya Weekly, 1930-1935.

Harijan, English Daily, 1938-1946.

Imprint, Monthly, Vol. IX, 8 November, 1969.

Journal of Kalinga Historical Research Society, Vol. I, No. 4, March 1947.

Journal of Orissa History Congress, Vol. IV, 1982, Vol. VIII, 1988, Vol. IX, 1989, Vol. X, 1990.

Krushak, Oriya Weekly, 1937-1940.

Mahtab-Odisa, Oriya Periodical, 1979, 1986.

Nabeen Oriya, Weekly, 1930-1948.

Orissa Historical Journal, Vol. II, 1953, Vol. IV, Nos. 1 and 2, 1955, Vol. V, No. 1 and 2, 1956, Vol. VIII, Nos. 3, 1959, Vol. VIII, No. 4, 1960, Vol. XI, No. 3, 1962, Vol. XXVIII, Nos. 1 and 2, 1982.

Orissa Government Tourism Department, Tourism Diary, 1982.

Orissa Review, August 1972, January 1981, August 1981

Orissa Review, July-August 1982, January 1983, January 1989, August 1989, August 1990, January 1991, April 1991, January 1992, June 1992, September 1992, October 1992.

Prajatantra, Oriya Daily, 1931-1948.

———, Oriya Weekly, 1991-1992.

Samaj, Oriya Daily, 1920 onwards

———, English Special Issue, 1 April, 1987.

———, Oriya Weekly, October 1992 onwards.

Statesman, Daily, 1938-1950.

Satya Samachar, Oriya Daily, 1930-1939.

Sahakar, Oriya Weekly, 1931-1941.

Sambad, Oriya Daily, 1985 onwards.

Star of Utkal, Vol. II, No. 5, 10 February, 1906.

Sambalpur Hitaisini, 1889-1923.

The Vaitarini, Vol. IV, No. 8, April 1932.

The Observer, English Weekly, 1935-1942.

Utkal Dipika, Oriya Monthly, 1869-1933.

Utkal Prasanga, August 1972, January 1981, August 1983, August 1991, November 1991, January 1992, September 1992.

SECONDARY SOURCES

Books

Abhayankar, G.A., *Problems of Indian States,* Poona, 1928.

Acharya, P.M., *Odisa Itihas,* Cuttack, 1925.

Auber, P., *Rise and Progress of the British Power in India,* 2 Vols., London, 1837.

Azad, M.A.K., *India Wins Freedom,* New York, 1960.

Bagal, J.C., *Peasant Through Ages,* Bombay, 1959.

Baily, F.G., *Politics and Social Changes — Orissa in 1959,* California, 1963.

Banerjee, R.D., *History of Orissa,* 2 Vols., Calcutta, 1930.

Barton Sir, W., *The Princes of India,* Vol. 26, Delhi, 1987.

Beames, John., *Memoirs of a Bengal Civilian,* London, 1961.

Bhatacharya, S.C., *Indian Nationalist Movement,* Allahabad, 1958.

Bhatia, B.M., *Famine in India, 1850-1945,* Bombay, 1963.

Bipan Chandra, *India's Struggle for Independence,* Delhi, 1988.

———, *Peasant Movements in 1930s and 40s,* Delhi, 1988.

Bose, S.N., *Indian National Movement : An Outline,* Calcutta, 1982.

Buckland, C.E., *Bengal under the Lieutenant Governors,* Vols. I and II, Calcutta, 1901.

Charukabi, Raghunath, *Odia Gadajat Itihas,* Oriya, Vol. I, Digapahandi, 1922.

Chaudhuri, S.B., *Civil Disturbances during the British Rule in India,* 1765-1857, Calcutta, 1955.

Chopra, P.N., *India's Struggle for Freedom : Role of Associated Movements,* Vols. I to V, Delhi, 1985.

Chudgar, P.L., *The Indian Princes under British Protection,* London, 1929.

Colond G.B., Malleson, *An Historical Sketch of the Native States of India,* London, 1875.

Dalton, E.T., *The Tribal History of Eastern India,* New Delhi, 1973.

Das, C.R., *Gandhi and Modern Times,* Cuttack, 1985.

Das, Durga, *India from Curzon to Nehru and After,* New Delhi, 1981.

———, *Sardar Patel's Correspondence,* 9 Vols; Ahmedabad, 1971-77.

Das, Ghanshyam (ed.), *History of Freedom Movement in Orissa,* Vol. IV, Cuttack, 1957.

Das, M.N. (ed.), *Sidelights on History and Culture of Orissa,* Cuttack, 1977.

———, *Economic and Social Development of Modern India,* Calcutta, 1959.

———, *Indian National Congress* Versus *The British,* Vol. I, 1885-1918, Delhi, 1978.

Das, N.K., *Autobiography*, Oriya, Cuttack, 1963.

Das, S.N., *Desaprana Madhusudan,* Oriya, Cuttack, 1971.

Das, Surya Narayan, *Odisa Swadhinata Sangramar Itihas,* Oriya, Puri, 1957.

Das, Sribastcha, *Badamba Itihas,* Oriya, Baramba, 1940.

De, S.C. (ed.), *Trend of Political Events in Orissa, 1882-1936,* Cuttack, 1966.

———, *Diary of Political Events in Orissa, 1936-1947,* Cuttack, 1964.

———, *History of Freedom Movement in Orissa*, Vol. I, Cuttack, 1957.

———, *Guide to Orissan Records,* Vols. I to V, Cuttack, 1961.

Desai, A.R., *Indian Feudal States and National Liberation Struggle,* Bombay, 1969.

———, *Social Background of Indian Nationalism*, Bombay, 1986.

Dhangare, D.N., *Peasant Movements in India : 1920-1950,* Delhi, 1983.

Dutta, R. Palme., *A Guide to the Problem of India,* London, 1942.

———, *India To-day,* Calcutta, 1979.

Dutt, R.C., *The Economic History of India,* London, 1906.

Elwin, V., *The Religion of an Indian Tribe,* London, 1955.

Fraser, Sir Adrew H.L., *Among Indian Rajas and Ryots*, London, 1912.

Gandhi, Devadas, (ed.), *India Unreconciled,* New Delhi, 1944.

Gandhi, M.K., *To the Princes and People,* Karachi, 1942.

Ghose, L.N., *The Modern History of the Indian Chiefs, Rajas, Zamindars etc.,* Part-I, Calcutta, 1879.

Ghose, Sunit, *Orissa in Turmoil,* Calcutta, 1978.

Handa, R.L., *History of Freedom Struggle in Princely States,* New Delhi, 1969.

Hans Raj, *History of Modern India,* Delhi, 1987.

Hunter, W.W., *History of Orissa,* 2 Vols., London, 1872.

———, *Indian Empire,* London, 1872.

———, *A History of British India,* London, 1899.

Iyre Ranga, *India Peace or War*? London, 1930.

Jeffrey, Robin, *People, Princes and Paramount Power, Society and Politics in the Indian Princely States,* Delhi, 1978.

Jena, K.C., *The Ascendancy of the British Raj in Orissa,* Calcutta, 1982.

Jena, P.K., *Orissa, A New Province,* Calcutta, 1988.

Jha, M.R., *Role of Legislature in the Freedom Struggle,* New Delhi, 1972.

Jit, N.K., *The Agrarian Life and Economy of Orissa — A Survey 1833-97,* Calcutta, 1984.

Kaya, J.W., *The Administration of the East India Company,* Delhi, 1966.

Kulkarni, V.V., *Future of Indian States,* Bombay, 1944.

Kulkarni, V.B., *Princely India and Lapse of British Paramountcy,* Bombay, 1985.

Larry Collins and D. Lapierre; *Freedom at Midnight,* New Delhi, 1989.

Low, Sir Sidney, *Indian States and Ruling Princes,* London, 1921.

Mahanty, B., *Swadhinata Sangram O Odisa,* Oriya, Cuttack, 1973.

———, *Odisara Rajanaitika Itihas,* Oriya, Cuttack, 1979.

Mahanty, N., *Oriya Nationalism, Quest for a United Orissa, 1866-1926,* New Delhi, 1982.

Mahanty, S., *Satabdira Surya,* Oriya, Cuttack, 1970.

Mahanty, S.N., *Chhatra Andolanara Itihas, Oriya*, Cuttack, 1986.

Mahapatra, B., *Odia Andolanara Itihas,* Oriya, Cuttack, 1976.

Mahapatra, Chakradhar; *Prajameli,* Cuttack, 1962.

Mahapatra, R.P., *Military History of Orissa,* Vol. 55, New Delhi, 1987.

Mahtab, H.K., (ed.), *History of Freedom Movement of Orissa,* 4 Vols., Cuttack, 1957.

———, *History of Orissa,* 2 Vols., Cuttack 1959 and 1960.

———, *Dasabarsara Odisa,* Oriya, Calcutta, 1977.

———, *Gandhiji O Odisa,* Oriya, Cuttack, 1972.

———, *Odisa Itihas,* Oriya, Cuttack, 1958.

Majumdar, B.C., *Orissa in the Making,* Calcutta, 1926.

Majumdar, R.C., *History of Freedom Movement in India,* Vol. III, Calcutta, 1963.

Majumdar, R.C., *Struggle for Freedom*, Vols. IX & X, Mumbai, 1978.

Mansingh, M., *Odia Sahityara Itihas,* Oriya, Cuttack, 1985.

Martin, M., *The Despatches, Minutes and Correspondence of Marguis Wellesley during his Administration in India,* 5 Vols., London, 1840.

Menon, V.P., *The Story of the Integration of Indian States,* Calcutta, 1956.

———, *The Transfer of Power in India,* Calcutta, 1957.

Mishra, B.B., *The Administrative History of India,* 1834-1947, Mumbai, 1970.

Mishra, K., *Utkal Itihas,* Oriya, Cuttack, 1933.

———, *Barabati Durga,* Oriya, Cuttack, 1964.

Mishra, P.K., *Political Unrest in Orissa in the 19th Century,* Calcutta, 1983.

Mishra, S., *Swadhinatara Jayajatra,* Oriya, Cuttack, 1984.

Mittal, A.C., *An Early History of Orissa,* Benaras, 1962.

Mosley, Leonard, *The Last Days of the British Raj*, London, 1961.

Mukherjee Hiren, *India's Struggle for Freedom*, Calcutta, 1962.

Mukherjee, P.K. (ed.), *History of Freedom Movement in Orissa,* Vol. II, Cuttack, 1957.

———, *History of Orissa,* Vol. VI, Utkal University, Cuttack, 1964.

Nair, Pyarelal, *States of Indian Princes,* Ahmedabad, 1941.

Nanda, Dasarathi, *Sahid Laxman Nayak,* Oriya, Berhampur, 1977.

Nehru, J.N., *An Autobiography,* Delhi, 1980.

———, *The Discovery of India,* Delhi, 1989.

Padhi, S.C., *British Relation with the Chiefs and Rajas of Orissa, 1803-1858,* Calcutta, 1986.

Panda, B.N., *Concise History of the Indian National Congress,* 1885-1947, Delhi, 1987.

Panigrahi, K.C., *History of Orissa,* Cuttack, 1981.

Pannikar, K.M., *British Policy towards Indian States, 1774-1858,* Calcutta, 1929.

Patnaik, J.N., *Feudatory States of Orissa,* 1803-57, 2 Vols., Allahabad, 1988.

———, *Odisa Itihasare Ketoti Ramanchakar Kahani,* Oriya, Cuttack, 1990.

Patnaik, K.M., *Indian States,* Mysore, 1942.

Patnaik, L.M., *Resurrected Orissa,* Cuttack, 1939.

Patnaik, P.K., *A Forgotten Chapter in Orissan History,* Calcutta, 1979.

Patnaik, Sudhakar (ed.), *Sambada Patraru Odisara Katha,* Oriya Cuttack, 1972.

Patra, A.C., *The Administration of Justice under the East India Company in Bengal, Bihar and Orissa,* Mumbai, 1962.

Patra, K.M., *Orissa under the East India Company,* New Delhi, 1971.

———, *Orissa State Legislature and Freedom Struggle, 1912-47,* ICHR, New Delhi, 1979.

Patra, S.C., *The Formation of the Province of Orissa,* Calcutta, 1979.

Pochhammer, W.V., *India's Road to Nationalism,* Delhi, 1981.

Pradhan, S., *Agrarian and Political Movements in the States of Orissa: 1931-49,* Delhi, 1985.

Rath, R.N., *History of Freedom Movement in Orissa,* Cuttack, 1964.

Ray, B.C., *Orissa Under Marathas,* Allahabad, 1960.

———, *Foundation of British Orissa,* Cuttack, 1960.

Rayguru, G., *Angul Itihas,* Oriya, Cuttack, 1986.

Roberts, P.E., *History of British Indian under the Company and the Crown,* London, 1970.

Rout, Bansidhar, *Ranpur Itihasara Ajnyata Adhyaya, Oriya,* Khurda, 1984.

Rowlinson, H.S., *British Achievement in India,* London, 1948.

Roy, M.K., *Princely States and the Paramount Power,* New Delhi, 1981.

Sahu, L.N., *Orissa Garjat,* Cuttack, 1931.

Sahu, N.K. (ed.) *Orissa from the Earliest Times to the Present Day,* Calcutta, 1956.

Samal, J.K., *Orissa Under the British Crown,* New Delhi, 1977.

Sarma, S.P., *Three Years in Orissa,* Cuttack, 1982.

Sarma, J.S., *India's Struggle for Freedom,* Vol. II, New Delhi, 1965.

Sarkar, J.N., *Bihar and Orissa during the Fall of the Mughal Empire,* Patna, 1932.

Sarkar, Sumit, *Modern India, 1885-1947,* Madras, 1985.

Samantrai, N., *History of Oriya Literature, 1803-1920,* Bhubaneswar, 1964.

Sastry, K.R.R., *Indian States,* Allahabad, 1941.

Sharma, Jagdish, *Encyclopaedia of India's Struggle for Freedom,* New Delhi, 1971.

Senapati, F.M., *Autobiography,* Oriya, Cuttack, 1901.

Shieve Kumar, *Peasantry and the Indian National Movement, 1919-33,* Meerut, 1980.

Singh Deo, N.N., *Singhbhum, Sareikala and Kharaswan-Through the Ages,* Calcutta, 1954.

Sitaramayya, B. Pattabhi, *History of the Indian National Congress,* Vols. I and II, Bombay, 1944, 1946.

Stirling, A., *An Account of Orissa Proper or Cuttack,* London, 1846.

Suri, P., and Zaidi, I., *Impact of British Rule on Indian Economy,* New Delhi, 1985.

Tara Chand, *History of Freedom Movement in India,* Vol. IV, New Delhi, 1983.

Thompson and Carret, *Rise and Fulfilment of British Rule in India,* London, 1934.

Thorn, W.K., *Memoir of the War in India,* London, 1818.

Tomlinson, B.R., *The Indian National Congress and the Raj, 1929-42,* London, 1976.

Toynbee, G., *A Sketch of History of Orissa, 1803-28,* Calcutta, 1873.

Two Bachelors of Arts, *The Oriya Movement,* Ganjam, 1919.

Vadivelu, A., *The Ruling Chiefs, Nobles and Zamindars of India,* Vol. I, Madras, 1915.

Warner, W.L., *The Protected Princes of India,* London, 1894.

———, *Native States of India,* London, 1910.

93